Where BSAs Dare.

BSA's 1952 ISDT Golds and Maudes Trophy

Norman E Vanhouse

With updates by

Graham Vanhouse C.Eng., F.I.Mech.E.

Panther Publishing

First published by Panther Publishing Ltd in 2015

Panther Publishing Ltd
10 Lime Avenue
High Wycombe
Buckinghamshire HP11 1DP, UK

www.panther-publishing.com
info@panther-publishing.com

Illustrations
Most of the photographs in this book were taken by BSA official photographers and are believed to have been the property of BSA, supplied to the Author, Norman E Vanhouse. The publisher is grateful to OEAMTC for permission to reproduce selected pages from the 1952 ISDT Programme and Auto Touring. Whilst the publisher has made every effort to trace the copyright owners of all the images reproduced in this book, this may not have always proven possible. If a copyright holder has inadvertently been offended, please contact the Publisher.

ISBN 978 1 909213 21 0

Contents

Foreword by Jeff Smith MBE   v

Preface by Graham Vanhouse   vi

Acknowledgments by Norman Vanhouse   vii

Introduction   1

Summer 1952   3

Across Europe   11

Behind the Iron Curtain   22

The International Six Days Trial   31

    The First Day   38

    The Second Day and Night   47

    The Third Day   57

    The Fourth Day   66

    The Fifth Day   74

    The Sixth Day   83

Up to Scandinavia   96

    End to End in Germany   96

    Into Scandinavia   102

The Speed Trial   107

Claiming the Maudes Trophy   114

    Report of the Examination of BSA Star Twin

    Engines after 1952 ACU Observed Test   124

What Happened Next   126

Part 2

Maudes Trophy History 1923-1994   133

    Observed Trials and the Start of the Maudes Trophy   133

    The Maudes Trophy: Attempts and Winners   136

Appendix 1 Results of the 1952 ISDT   182

Appendix 2 Official Programme of the 1952 ISDT   186

One of the most remarkable performances ever by British motorcycles.

> Mick Walker and Rob Carrick: *International Six-Days Trial, The Olympics of Motorcycling.*

To get a standard roadster machine through the ISDT without loss of marks seemed to be impossible. But three off-the peg models - it was beyond belief. The perfectly standard Star Twin was by no means an ideal ISDT mount, their faultless performance is one of the legends of the ISDT.

> C E 'Titch' Allen: *Motorcycle Sport*

One achievement of the Small Heath folk must never be forgotten.....the best Maudes of all.

> Bob Currie: *Motor Cycle Weekly*

Foreword

by

Jeff Smith, MBE

As you will read, BSA's Maudes Trophy attempt in 1952 was a spectacular success. It is hard to believe that a company of BSA's stature would have rolled the dice on the likelihood of three production motorcycles chosen at random completing 5,000 miles driving around Europe including a 1,500 miles ISDT.

Norman was a fine writer and for many years his clear and imaginative writing graced the Kings Norton Club magazine. Up to now his excellent *BSA Competition History* was his only foray into the book format, but here we have the second, a definitive discussion of perhaps the most meaningful Maudes Trophy win of all: because it represented a true measure of the quality and durability of the machines involved. It was not just an advertising gimmick.

I knew Norman for more than sixty years as a Kings Norton club member, a trials competitor and a friend. As I read the easy flowing story I can hear Norman's voice, so closely does he write to the way he spoke.

I must have first met Norman at a club night or a Midland Centre Group Trial about 1950. Me on my Bantam and he on his Ariel works machine. But by the next year I was offered the use of a 500 Dominator Norton for the ISDT in Italy. With less than a month to go to the Italian event it was decided that I should run the machine in the 'Birmingham 24', a 24 hour timed event which started at 7 pm and would finish at 7 pm, 24 hours later after looping through some wild areas of Wales.

During the night run my dynamo stopped working and the lights failed as the battery ran down. I latched on to the tail of the fastest passing competitor and, when dawn broke about 5.00 am, I found myself following Norman on his works Ariel. It was a brisk rainy morning in Wales and we rode alongside each other talking about the breakfast stop, when Norman noticed I had gone to sleep! Norman yelled and I woke with a start, he had me stop and lie down with my eyes closed for five minutes on the pavement. That shut-eye did the trick, but there was no breakfast at the breakfast stop - they thought the event was the next day! Norman and I were the only clean rides, and therefore the only two special golds given out. I won a gold medal in Italy but it might not have happened if Norman had not been so observant and prevented me from hitting Welsh granite.

This book brings back memories crowding in on all sides and it's a testament to not only the quality of those BSA twins but to the men who rode them. All of them were friends I remember with gratitude and respect, author Norman Vanhouse, Brian Martin, who became BSA Competition Manager for many successful years and Fred Rist, the undoubted leader of the pack. It is a book which needed to be written and has been penned by a craftsman.

Jeff Smith MBE,
June 2015

Preface

Graham Vanhouse

The author of this work, my father, Norman E Vanhouse (NEV) wrote this original draft manuscript in the early 1980s. At that time he was also writing for a number of publications including the monthly *The Classic Motorcycle*, *Classic Bike*, and *Motorcycle Sport* magazines, having spent a lifetime both competing and working in the motorcycle world. In 1985 he was asked to write the definitive account of BSA's competition history. His track record, namely his inside knowledge of BSA and the motorcycle industry, and particularly his BSA competition involvement, coupled with his already mentioned writing experience, must have been the ingredients the publishers sought. Thus *BSA Competition History* was published in 1986, and was re-printed again during 1998, and is generally held in high regard by BSA aficionados. I can only think that with the level of historical research required for the *BSA Competition History* work, that the draft for this book was put on one side to be completed to his satisfaction at a later time.

NEV was a member of the team of three riders who in 1952 completed one of the most arduous tests ever undertaken by a motorcycle manufacturer - in the full glare of the public eye. This is his personal story of that event, together with a history of Maudes Trophy winners starting in 1923. Winners that include many evocative names such as Norton, Ariel, Dunelt, Triumph, Phelon & Moore, BSA, Honda, BMW, Suzuki, and Yamaha.

NEV passed away in 2011, and amongst his papers I uncovered this manuscript in draft. I read the work and it was obvious that it was a unique and exciting story, containing also extensive factual motorcycling history that should be recorded. I have sought to publish this work in his memory. I am therefore greatly indebted to Rollo Turner of Panther Publishing for the opportunity, wisdom and experience he has given in realising this ambition.

BSA's 1952 Maudes Trophy project incorporating the ISDT, that year held in Austria, was truly an audacious and brave attempt with many potential pit-falls. That it was ultimately successful was a massive achievement. I'll do no more than cite the words of some highly regarded observers of the motorcycle world.

One of the most remarkable performances ever by British motorcycles. *Mick Walker and Rob Carrick, International Six-Days Trial, The Olympics of Motorcycling.*

To get a standard roadster machine through the ISDT without loss of marks seemed to be impossible. But three off-the peg models... it was beyond belief. The perfectly standard Star Twin was by no means an ideal ISDT mount. Their faultless performance is one of the legends of the ISDT. *C E 'Titch' Allen, Motorcycle Sport.*

Hence I have attempted to finish NEV's work, primarily updating details for today's reader and also writing the story of the last successful Maudes Trophy award, by Yamaha in 1994.

Opposite is his acknowledgments from the original draft manuscript

Graham Vanhouse,
February 2015

Acknowledgments

Norman E Vanhouse

As with most books involving a modicum of historical facts and figures related to a period of many years, this book is only made possible through the help of others; help given freely and generously without thought of personal gain. I am thus indebted to several such benefactors: in particular to Ken Shierson, Secretary General of the Auto-Cycle Union (ACU), and the enthusiastic staff who made me very welcome at ACU headquarters at Rugby and made available the official records of all past ACU official tests dating back to 1911, which facilitated most of the historical content of this book. In expressing my gratitude to the ACU, I only hope that reward will come their way by virtue of this book helping to restore the interest and prestige - and indeed glamour - which once made the Maudes Trophy unique and desirable.

The permanent staff of the Motor Cycle Association of Coventry likewise made me very welcome at their offices when I required access to past copies of the motorcycle press in order to prompt my flagging memory, and here I am indebted to both Alex Scobie and Steven Corsi. Birmingham Honda motorcycle dealer Peter Rose of Sherwood Garage kindly refreshed my memory by identifying the three Honda models used in the successful Honda test of 1962. And Bob Currie of *Motor Cycle Weekly* clarified a couple of points on which I was uncertain.

I am particularly grateful to Colin Wall for his personal story dealing with the discovery and restoration of BSA Star Twin MOL 303; an accomplishment which means that he has preserved for posterity one of those remarkable motorcycles which are featured in my story.

With charity beginning at home it is with pleasure that I acknowledge the help I had from near neighbour Reva Lincoln who helped me a great deal with translations from an Austrian publication dealing with the 1952 ISDT. And lastly, but by no means least, I must thank my wife Barbara for her help, forbearance and encouragement. It proved to be an almost full-time job correcting the spelling and grammatical errors which I find so easy to make.

The main purpose or objective in writing this book was one of personal pleasure and satisfaction. With the job completed, if the reading of it provides equal pleasure then it will have made the writing even more satisfying.

Norman E Vanhouse,
Birmingham, 1984

Norman Vanhouse's bike, BSA Star Twin MOL 303, now fully restored at the National Motorcycle Museum

Introduction

As a direct result of television coverage and sponsorship with commercial exploitation as the primary objective, today, at the highest levels of sport, great importance is attached to the entertainment and performance aspects rather than the 'doing' of that particular activity. This holds true too for motorcycle sport. Witness the average Moto Grand Prix today, where competitors circulate for typically forty-five minutes round a highly refined circuit, approximately three miles long. A great spectacle to all fans of the sport, but it was different in times gone by! In those far-off pioneering days, it took the giants of the era four hours of riding to complete seven - and on one occasion eight! - laps of the 37.73 mile Isle of Man TT course to finish a single race. Recall too the mind-boggling achievement of stocky and tough Ernie Nott, who as long ago as 1928, covered no less than 200 miles in two hours on a rigid-framed 500cc Rudge, with primitive girder forks, at the notoriously bumpy Brooklands circuit in Surrey, England.

Such was the standard in those far-off times, it seemed such things were not regarded as unusual. It was indeed normal, with hardly a trumpet in sight to herald accomplishment. Such feats of endurance were commonplace with pioneer manufacturers of motorcycles anxious to test and demonstrate the reliability – often sadly lacking – of their products, be they production models or specials. The long history of reliability and endurance events is as old as the industry itself, contributing in no small measure to the development of the product, and thus to the benefit of those who bought them for personal transport and recreation. The high standard of reliability enjoyed and taken for granted today has been reached by virtue of the early struggles of pioneers on two and three wheels, who performed prodigious feats of endurance long since forgotten. Indeed, such feats, both official and private, were in many cases never adequately documented, with the facts thus lost in the mists of time.

It was against this pioneering background that the Auto-Cycle Union (ACU) observed and certified test came into being: created with the object of establishing the credibility and truthful accuracy of such claims of endurance and reliability.

From then on claims without the ACU stamp of approval were worthless. During the period from the first such ACU test in 1911 until the last one (at the time of writing) in 1994, no less than 339 observed tests had been registered with the ACU, representing something like 170 actual tests undertaken (tests were frequently jointly registered by co-sponsors such as fuel companies and the like). Of the tests undertaken only 19 received the ultimate accolade of being awarded the Maudes Trophy: an award which during the inter-war years acquired a reputation within the motorcycle industry as sacred as that of the Senior TT trophy itself.

One of these successful ACU-observed tests was the first post-war challenge of BSA, then leaders of the industry. They undertook what many believed to be impossible, whereby three perfectly standard 500cc Star Twin production models were selected at random by the official ACU observer prior to them being ridden across Europe to Austria for participation in the International Six Days Trial (ISDT). This event had long since been acknowledged as one of the toughest motorcycle contests in the world, in which only specially prepared machines stood any chance of survival.

To enter three standard models in such an event without any individual selection or preparation seemed, by normal criteria, to be asking too much. But that wasn't all. Confidence in the BSAs at the time was such that apart from coping with the arduous conditions which were inevitable, it was considered that all three bikes would be more than fit enough to be ridden a further 2,000 miles to Oslo in Norway after the conclusion of the ISDT. It was boldness bordering on folly, and once the test objectives had been registered with the ACU and details published, there was no turning back.

During the three week period of the entire test, the Star Twins totalled a collective 15,000 miles; or just over 5,000 miles per machine from door to door, including almost 1,500 miles each during what proved to be one of the toughest ever ISDTs, through the mountainous alpine country of Austria. The event created havoc and had a high casualty rate amongst the British and Continental competitors. For the British National teams it proved to be a disaster, highlighting all the more the superb performance of those three BSA Star Twins.

What follows is that story.

Summer 1952

As one goes through life, luck does tend to play its part. It is a question, without predetermined planning, of being in the right place at the right time. Most people, no doubt, can look back and recognise situations when luck played a major part. That certainly was the case in the summer of 1952 when I first started work with BSA. For by June 1ˢᵗ, when I joined the sales department staff, Bert Perrigo and his staff must already have been working on the details of the plan. The outline scheme had clearly been agreed in principle months before, as the ambition to be the first to win the Maudes Trophy post-war must have been smouldering throughout those early post-war years when BSA competition activity was gilt-edged with success. The opposition in the Isle of Man TT Junior Clubman's series had been swamped by the Gold Star and confidence among the BSA management had obviously been stimulated by worldwide success.

The Maudes Trophy was a tempting peak to conquer. BSA had won this coveted trophy in the past, most recently in 1938, but in 1939 had been beaten by Triumph (see p133 for a brief history of the Trophy). But how to win it this time? The 1952 International Six Days Trial (ISDT - today called the International Six Days Enduro, ISDE) was to take place in Austria in 1952, and that provided the inspiration. "We will enter three standard models in the ISDT," said Bert Perrigo. "And to really prove the capability and quality of our production models, we will ride the bikes to the start of the trial, and furthermore to prove our confidence in them, we'll ride them back home when it's all over".

And so the scene was set.

I was not in on the meeting, and neither did I hear those words uttered. But that is the essence of what the management was prepared to undertake. Bold stuff by anyone's standard. We all knew that specials for events of the status of the ISDT were conveyed to the start point wrapped in cotton wool - never ridden there. At the conclusion of such an event many specials were the worse for wear. And confidence in the product on its own was not enough. Three riders would be needed. Three additional riders that is, for the factory would still be fielding the usual manufacturer's team on 'specials', and

The ISDT

The ISDT itself effectively came into existence in 1913 when the annual ACU Six Days Reliability Trial adopted FIM (*Fédération Internationale de Motocyclisme*) rules to become the International Touring Trial. The first event's competing nations were Britain and France. Riders were required to achieve set speed schedules on long, challenging routes, complete speed and flexibility tests, navigate the routes, and maintain their machines. By the 1920s the ISDT had become very much a team event. National teams competed to win the International Trophy – this was for teams competing on machines manufactured in their home country. The Silver Vase award was similarly for the best national team using motorcycles not originating from their homeland. The rules dictated the number of riders and the range of machines required to form each team, and evolved during the years – for example until 1947 a sidecar outfit was required in each nation's Trophy team. In addition to the National Trophy and Silver Vase teams, the event attracted many Manufacturers' teams, Club teams, and individual competitors, all seeking recognition and prestige. The event was hosted annually by various nations and was to become regarded as the Olympics of motorcycle sport.

By 1952 each nation's Trophy team comprised five solo riders and required the use of two different machine capacities within the team. Vase, Manufacturers' and Club Teams required teams of three riders but were not subject to the engine capacity variants ruling. The ISDT of that year was to cover almost 1500 miles of the Austrian alpine scenery. The loss of any single mark would forfeit the winning of that coveted ISDT Gold Medal.

with David Tye nominated for the British Vase 'B' team. One of the three additional riders to be needed was an obvious choice, and BSA was fortunate to have the services of such a fine rider as Fred Rist. His leadership of the team provided the back-bone and prestige required. He had been captain of the British Trophy team for several years past and had proved himself a superb and impeccable Six Days rider with a string of gold medals to his credit. He had decided to open his own retail motorcycle business in Neath, South Wales which would demand all of his time, but despite this, he agreed to stay on with BSA in order to do this last important job for them.

Bert Perrigo's second choice was none too difficult either. At the beginning of 1952 he had signed on a young Brian Martin as a BSA works trials rider, who had promptly gone out and won the Victory Trial. Prior to that, Brian had done a great deal of winning with a works 125cc Francis Barnett, in which capacity class he had proved virtually invincible. His ISDT experience was limited to the 1951 event in Italy in which he had won a silver medal. Bert Perrigo's shrewd judgment classed Brian as a rider of great potential, and in this he did not disappoint, in future years going on to win several gold medals while representing Great Britain in the Trophy Team of subsequent ISDTs.

Selection of the third rider required was less obvious or easy. Bert Perrigo had one or two names on a short list, which incidentally did not include my own, and he was still deliberating when he got news of my joining the company. As far as Bert was concerned, his quest for a suitable third rider had ended. At this stage I knew nothing until one day, when I was still feeling my way into the new job, Bert Perrigo sent for me. We were by no means strangers: I had got to know him quite well during my years with Ariel at Selly Oak, mostly at trials but also socially at the Motordrome headquarters of the Birmingham Motor Cycle Club.

"Sit down," said Bert, "I've got something to tell you". Whereupon he proceeded to outline the entire plan and its objectives, and finishing up by saying, "and I would like you to be one of the riders; to make up the team with Fred and Brian". There is no doubt I was taken aback. It was the last thing I had expected, for by then I had decided my riding days were over. Having ridden Ariels in trials and scrambles since 1946, including in the official works team, I had left Selly Oak late in 1950 to take up employment with Douglas at Bristol as a sales representative. This seemed a better prospect than continuing to don overalls, but it also meant, in my case, turning my back on competition riding. At least I had believed it did.

In my terms of reference there had been no mention of riding Douglas in competitions. Then one morning in early 1951, a few days before the Colmore Cup Trial, the traditional trade opener of the season, I had a phone call. "Come and get your bike: it's ready for the Colmore". So in the Colmore Cup that year I sat astride a rigid framed Douglas trials bike for the very first time.

It was, in my estimation, an unusual device. I had been spoiled, almost certainly, by the superb 500cc Ariel big single which had been a joy to handle, with the result that this medium capacity, horizontally-opposed, flat-twin was unfamiliar. By the time the Scottish Six Days Trial came round in May, I had come to terms with it, more or less. I did survive the week, and in so doing was the only Douglas finisher - the other three starters having retired during the week - and I collected a First Class award in the process.

A week later I managed a Second Class Award in the Mitchell Memorial Trial in Wales, and making allowance for the fact that only 10% of finishers were awarded First Class awards, that was not as lowly as it may sound. Then, as suddenly as they had lumbered me with the bike the previous January, Douglas took it away. It had been decided to withdraw from motorcycle competitions from that moment on. The Mitchell was the last trade-supported national trial with an official Douglas entry.

I still had my privately-owned 350cc Ariel in scrambles trim. With rigid frame and fairly low compression engine, it was no longer very competitive. There was a new generation of scrambles machines with McCandless rear suspension ridden by a new and younger generation of riders, and this combination had made it all rather evident that I was getting too old for such things and that discretion was now the better part of valour.

So there I was, with my riding days behind me, sitting in Bert Perrigo's office being asked to take part in what was clearly going to be a major factory-planned operation with an awful lot at stake. After Bert had finished talking and I had digested what he had said and all that it implied, I said simply, "Why have you asked me to ride Bert?" Without the slightest hesitation he replied, "Because I know you can do it. You won a Gold Medal in Wales in 1950 as a member of the Ariel works team plus a Manufacturers team prize, so a man with your experience is just what I need". That was it. If the great and shrewd Bert Perrigo thought I could do it, then do it I could. It was just as well at that moment I was not able to fully visualise just what it all involved. The prospect regarded as a whole is rather akin to the television camera taking in all those frightening jumps of the Grand National steeplechase with one sweep of the camera before the race starts. Tackled one at a time they must appear much more surmountable to the jockey.

Having agreed to ride, I had no further part to play until the operation started. It was all up to Bert Perrigo's staff, and even long before the machines destined to be selected by the ACU observer had come off the production line, weeks of planning and detailed preparations had to be done. This long and tedious process fell mainly on the shoulders of Ted Fithian the assistant competitions manager, Fred Rist and Bert Perrigo's long-serving secretary Mrs. May Harris.

There were Customs documents to be secured, plus passport visas and special permits required for the Russian sector of Austria. In those days special currency allowances for overseas travel had to be obtained from the bank for each member of the party. Insurance cover for all countries to be visited required arranging, and right at the beginning the proposed route planned with the RAC. When that had been finalised, all BSA European distributors or dealers to be involved required date and time details to enable them to organise press receptions and publicity.

All this involved visits to London, telephone calls by the score and reams of correspondence. In addition, new riding gear was obtained; Barbour suits, goggles, gloves, riding boots, crash helmets adorned with BSA logos, green berets, lightweight golfing jackets (the forerunner of today's team jackets) and even dubbin and eye lotion. And of course boat reservations. The list seemed endless and formidable.

Producing the motorcycles and the men to ride them was the simple part.

As the month of August drew to a close, with most of the planning jobs done, it was time for the ACU observer to visit the factory to select three machines at random from the floor stock. It had been decided to use the 500cc Star Twin for the test. Most British manufacturers of that period were concentrating on the vertical twin format and trying to reduce the lead Triumph had built up with the type since they had pioneered it pre-war. By the early 1950's a major part of BSA production was devoted to producing vertical twins, so it was in that direction promotional activity needed to be directed. With the ISDT in mind, the 500cc model was considered more suitable than the larger 650cc A10, and since all three machines would be required to maintain the same speed schedule during the route across Europe and Scandinavia, this dictated three machines of identical capacity.

On Saturday, August 30th we all gathered at the factory to meet John McNulty, the ACU official who had been appointed to observe the test throughout, and watched him select three Star Twins from about 50 of them from amongst the rows of new machines lined up in the finishing shop. All the models lined up that

Saturday 30th August 1952 - ACU Observer John McNulty selects one of the three BSA Star Twins from production at the Armoury Road factory.

Sunday 7ʰ September 1952. BSA Armoury Road factory - Ready to go! .
On the bikes from the left: Brian Martin, Norman Vanhouse and Fred Rist. Behind from the left: Sales Manager George
Savage, ACU Observer John McNulty, BSA Sales Director Stan Digby and BSA Works Manager, Tom Whittington. The
Austin A70, used to carry John McNulty with George Savage driving, is in the background.

morning were destined for world markets far and wide, including those picked by
the ACU official. It was like observing three innocent hostages picked out to face
the firing squad. No matter how confident and proud the management were of
production quality in those days, I for one could not help but wonder, privately, if
John McNulty had picked three good ones. They were genuinely-produced standard
models. But even today, results cannot be guaranteed, including even with one-off
specials. The vagaries of things mechanical respect neither type.

Once selected, mechanics had been laid on to do the jobs required. These
included changing the rear wheel, which had a solo 45-tooth sprocket, for a wheel
with the 49-tooth sidecar sprocket. Lower gearing would be vital in the ISDT.
This also meant changing the chain for a longer one, and also the bigger rear
wheel sprocket affected the speedometer gearing so the speedometer was changed.

Close up of one of the Star Twins ready to go - reversed ISDT number plate displays the ACU Certified Test details

This was originally positioned centrally on the top fork yoke, so in order to make provision for mounting an ex-war department aircraft-type clock, a flat plate was mounted on the fork top. The speedometer was then offset to the left on this plate and the clock offset to the right. The still standard spring saddle was replaced with a dualseat, together with pillion footrests, and the tank-top tool bag *cum* route card holder was fitted, as were the green, oval competition number plates with our ISDT numbers already painted on. At this stage the plates were reversed with the outer side bearing the message, 'Standard BSA Undergoing 4500 miles 7242 Kms ACU Certified Test'.

Two sets of holes were then drilled in the cylinder head, cylinder barrel and crankcase - one set for John McNulty's sealing wire and the other, with the same purpose, for the ISDT officials in Austria. With the whole trip being jointly sponsored by Esso, there remained the important job of draining the oil tank, gearbox and primary chaincase and refilling with Essolube 40. The petrol tank was also drained and refilled to the top with Esso fuel.

There only remained the completion of documentation, which accounted for this ritual taking place eight days in advance of the planned start date. All vehicles being taken abroad in those days required a carnet document which detailed particulars of the vehicle, such as frame and engine numbers. Those could not be provided until the ACU observer had selected the machines. So after the appropriate information had been secured and registration numbers affixed (the numbers having been obtained in advance) John McNulty proceeded to apply his special sealing paint to practically every part of the three Star Twins. Finally, with the models all prepared and ready for the off eight days later, it was a question of putting them under lock and key until then. A private lock-up garage away from the factory site had been dictated, where the three bikes were parked very close together, enabling them to be covered by a large groundsheet which in turn was roped down with cord passing through the spokes of each bike, and the whole thing sealed with wire and lead seal.

But that wasn't all. The garage doors were also given the lead seal treatment. It seemed that John McNulty had heard about the tricks motorcycle factory personnel had been capable of in the past. He meant to do the job properly right from the start, and it wasn't lost on us that his bottle of special sealing paint was kept in a tin which in turn was sealed with a lead seal. There was no doubting just where we stood.

Those three Star Twins thus spent eight days in solitary confinement as though serving a period of undeserved punishment; in a dark, ignominious lock-up garage in the back streets of Small Heath. Hardly the way to treat three motorcycles destined to achieve fame and glory.

Across Europe

Sunday 7th September dawned wet and cold. By the time we had all gathered at Armoury Road a weak sun had broken through the grey, watery sky throwing shadows behind each Star Twin as they were photographed complete with riders fitted out with pristine new riding gear, looking a bit like tailor's dummies. It was a low-key affair, with just three senior executives there to see us off – Sales Director Stan Digby, General Works Manager Tom Whittington and Advertising Manager Noel Brealey. Curiously, the one man mostly responsible for the whole thing, Bert Perrigo, was prevented from leading the party initially. He had been committed to a business trip to the United States which had to be honoured.

In his place as party leader and official car driver was Home Sales Manager George Savage – the very same George Savage who had taken part in the first ever BSA ACU-observed test when he and three companions had stormed the heights of Snowdon nearly 30 years before (see p137). George Savage would be driving the Austin A70 which in addition to conveying the important personage of John McNulty, would also carry the luggage of the whole party, seven people in all. It was going to be a

Norman Vanhouse on MOL 303 and Brian Martin on MOL 302 ready to go on Sunday 7th September

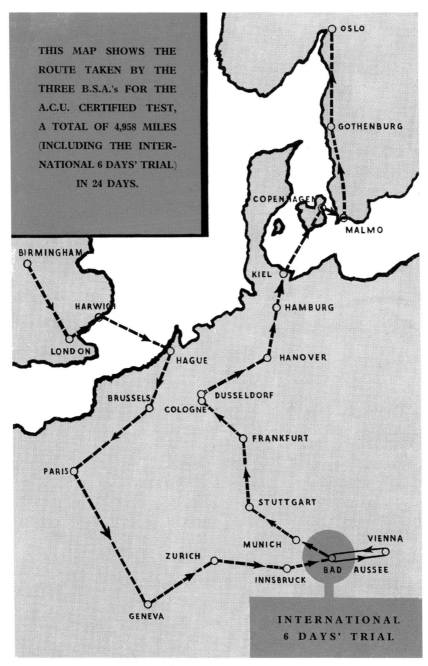

THIS MAP SHOWS THE ROUTE TAKEN BY THE THREE B.S.A.'s FOR THE A.C.U. CERTIFIED TEST, A TOTAL OF 4,958 MILES (INCLUDING THE INTERNATIONAL 6 DAYS' TRIAL) IN 24 DAYS.

INTERNATIONAL 6 DAYS' TRIAL

The route taken by the three Maudes riders from the BSA factory to Bad Aussee in Austria and then North to Oslo. The return trip from Oslo was by ferry to Newcastle-on-Tyne. The map was prepared by BSA's publicity department after the event and published in their brochure 'The Machines you might have bought'.

The refueling stop on the first day on the outskirts of London. The machines are all still very clearly factory fresh. John McNulty watches closely as Brian Martin's MOL 302 is replenished. Esso supported the BSA ISDT Maudes project. Fred Rist, MOL 301 and Norman Vanhouse at the rear.

test of the A70 as well as the Star Twins! The other two members of the party were the official photographer and his wife. They would be using a 650cc A10 Golden Flash with a single-seat sidecar. The idea behind the use of a combination was that it would provide both independent transport for the photographer, and during the course of the ISDT in Austria, superior access to the more remote parts of the course likely to be inaccessible to a car.

With the A70 car well loaded with luggage accommodated both in the car and on a roof rack, final departure photographs taken, it was into gear, down Armoury Road and onto the A34 for Oxford and London. Before setting out, John McNulty had stressed the importance of keeping ourselves under observation at all times, and that the responsibility for achieving this was ours as much as his. Cruising speed was kept at a modest level on this leg of the trip to give the engines every chance of settling down nicely, knowing full well that subsequent performance could depend much on their early treatment.

Sunday 7th September. The official welcome from the ACU. Standing on the left is George Savage, BSA Home Sales Manager, and John McNulty ACU Observer, on the bikes are Norman Vanhouse, Fred Rist and Brian Martin.

A somewhat less formal welcome as the ACU official offers the BSA trio a cigarette!.

At the ACU the BSA trio check the route to Harwich, bikes and riding gear still looking factory fresh. Left Norman Vanhouse, centre Fred Rist and on the right, Brian Martin.

Before making the first stop at ACU headquarters, Pall Mall, we had filled up with Esso fuel on the outskirts of London, by which time we had experienced the first of the rain which was to plague the trip throughout, all the way to Sweden. At Pall Mall we were welcomed by Norman Sharpe of the ACU who in later years joined the editorial staff of *Motor Cycling*, and in due course was appointed Editor of that now defunct but then highly-regarded weekly magazine. Our destination was Harwich and the night boat to the Hook of Holland, but long before we had reached Harwich the rain was pouring down. It was a reminder that the elements are no respecter of things or persons or such human endeavours as the one on which we were embarking; it was the unknown factor which could disrupt the best laid plans.

Nonetheless, we experienced a calm crossing of the North Sea, and when we landed on Monday morning Holland was basking in beautiful sunshine which made the short trip to The Hague very pleasant. We rode along dead flat roads bordered by what looked like disused and weed-covered canals on the one hand, and on the other, green pastures dotted with grazing cattle against a background of gaily-painted

Left. Monday morning on the 8th September. Arrival and quayside Customs checks at the Hook of Holland for Fred Rist, MOL 301.

Above, Mr. Flinterman, the principal of Hart Nibbrig & Greeve, the Dutch BSA importers, greets Norman Vanhouse.

windmills. Already we were in another world and for the moment a pleasant one at that. We had been met by Mr. Flinterman, the principal of Hart Nibbrig & Greeve, the Dutch importers of BSA, who then escorted us to the Hague where we were introduced to Peter Nortier, the president of the *Commission Sportive Internationale* of the *Fédération Internationale de Motocyclisme* (FIM), who would also be in Austria the following week as a member of the International Jury for the duration of the ISDT.

An extremely charming man, Peter Nortier made time to take us on a mini tour of the city pointing out the various prominent buildings and landmarks before returning and joining Mr. Flinterman and his wife for a rather splendid lunch. During it we heard all about their own son J.L. Flinterman who would also be riding in the ISDT in Austria as a member of the Dutch Vase 'B' team. With some reluctance we had to bid farewell to our new friends in The Hague and head south for Antwerp about 100 miles away and the next rendezvous, passing through on the way Rotterdam with its stone-sets (cobbles) road surface, and the reminder that it was the first city to be blitzed by the Nazis when they over-ran the Low Countries in May 1940.

At the Belgian frontier we were met by the English-speaking brothers who ran the Belgian BSA-importing business of Moorkens, who then proceeded to lead the way and guide us to Antwerp. But I'm not sure if 'guide' is the best description. I think 'pace-setter' would be more accurate. It was as though their reputation was

Monday 8ᵗʰ September, Holland. The BSA team meet a BSA combination mounted patrolman of the Wegenwacht Dutch roadside assistance organisation. Left to right, Brian Martin, Wegenwacht Patrolman, George Savage, John McNulty, Norman Vanhouse, Fred Rist.

at stake, such was the speed of our advance on Antwerp where rush-hour traffic was already piling up when we entered the fray. Our guide and mentor set about the city traffic with the skill and verve of a London taxi driver and in so doing seemed oblivious to the three solo bikes, one motor car and sidecar outfit behind, all striving to maintain contact and only just managing to do so.

Next morning, after pulling-down the cylinder head bolts and adjusting rear chains on all three machines, we headed for Brussels at the now expected breakneck speed in our own private Grand Prix practice session. Fortunately the Star Twins were freeing-off nicely and appeared quite happy to respond without complaint.

Haste, however, did appear to be justified, because our hosts had laid on a series of visits to BSA dealers in and around Brussels, each with an estimated time of arrival. Just how many calls we made that day is not clear all these years later, and I'm not sure if it was clear at the time because each dealer provided the customary hospitality.

During the early stages of the venture, the BSA importers in Belgium, Moorkens, arranged numerous publicity visits to BSA dealers in the Brussels region, each one supplying the customary hospitality! More time than was planned was spent fulfilling these engagements. From the left, a Belgium BSA Importer, Fred Rist, Norman Vanhouse,and Brian Martin raise their glasses to the ISDT ahead of them.

With each call came the growing desire to dally. We certainly entered into the spirit of the thing, and to prove it Brian Martin showed just how easy it was to produce sparks from the underside of the silencers when cornering. George Savage too had been infected by the cut-and-thrust tactics practiced with such perfection by our hosts in their native traffic, for in one city square with a single-decker tram bearing down fast from our left, it looked pretty certain that all vehicles in our convoy would not beat the tram to the point where our paths crossed. With George Savage and I bringing up the rear it seemed we would have to give way, but at the last split second I decided to follow Fred and Brian through. To my considerable surprise George Savage thought likewise. How he got the car through I shall never know.

Our destination that night was Paris, a distance of some 250 miles, and our programme in Brussels had cost us dearly in time. So from then on our guides led the way to the Belgian-Franco border, past the historic battlefield of Waterloo,

Each night the three BSA Star Twins were quarantined under lock and key by John McNulty. Here McNulty (second from right) starts his securing procedure in the warehouse of one of the importers.

with a genuine sense of urgency. We bade our Belgian friends farewell and headed southwest across the flat agricultural lands of northern France, dreary and inhospitable as the rain once again set in and grew steadily worse all the way to Paris. By then the effects of the mid-day imbibing had worn off and once again it was a cheerless world of stark reality. Fred Rist was out in front followed by Brian Martin with me bringing up the rear, our self-imposed order of riding, and the last time I had cocked an eye astern the car was just visible through the mist of rain and spray. On the outskirts of Compiègne we came to one of those road junctions, all too familiar in France, where one direction indicates the centre of the Ville and the other *Toutes Directions*. Which one to take? The car was not in sight. We waited a while, but with it raining at the time, we were impatient to press on. The route round the town seemed the obvious one, so off we went.

It was a foolish thing to do. By the time we hit the main road to Paris on the other side of town, we had realised that the car could have taken the shorter route through the town and might already be ahead of us. We had no means of knowing. We had lost the official observer. All we could do was to carry on to Paris and hope to find them there. Fifteen miles from Paris a large BSA banner strung from the dripping roadside trees indicated our rendezvous point, and to our dismay we realised we were the first there. There was no sign of the official car. It was another twenty minutes before the green A70 emerged from the misty distance, out from which stepped a long-faced John McNulty to rebuke us for our lapse. He again reminded us that keeping each other in sight at all times was a joint responsibility, and the incident meant that he would have to record that the Star Twins had not been under observation from 17:05 pm to 18:35 pm. He then meticulously checked the sealing paint on each component on all machines to his satisfaction, and as the situation defused, they told their story.

They had run out of petrol. With the tight schedule of mid-day calls in Brussels and the need to press on since then, George Savage had not had the opportunity to change traveller's cheques and, perhaps lulled into a sense of *sang-froid* by the mid-day routine, had decided Paris could be reached without the need for Francs. Suddenly they were in the middle of nowhere with a dry petrol tank. Then, whilst at the roadside discussing with the photographer the prospects of getting a cheque changed in the next town, bearing in mind that it was about 5 pm, along came a Good Samaritan in the shape of an American GI who rolled to a stop in his large brown US Army vehicle. In response to his query of "What's the trouble bud?" George Savage explained the predicament, whereupon the GI said "Guess you'd better have some of mine". "But I can't pay you, not unless you will accept a traveller's cheque," George pointed out. "That's OK bud" said the GI swinging down a four gallon jerry can from the back of his truck, "I guess the US Army can spare a splash of gas for a stranded Limey". With a further laconic "You're welcome bud" in response to profuse thanks he climbed aboard his truck and loped off down the road. I doubt if petrol ever smelled sweeter than it did at that moment.

We were wet and cold and dirty and somewhat dispirited, but once the party was reunited our spirits soared as we were escorted to the plush surroundings of the French Automobile Club in the very heart of Paris by the staff of the BSA French distributors Movea where, still attired in wet riding gear with grimey faces, we met their managing director Monsieur J. Rabuteau and other members of the Paris staff, who served champagne to commemorate the occasion and create an antidote to the traumas of the previous few hours of wet misery.

Then followed the nightly ritual, carried out with due circumspection by the erudite John McNulty, of securing the three Star Twins for the night under lock and

After a long wet ride from Brussels to Paris the BSA team are immediately welcomed to Paris by Monsieur J Rabuteau of the French BSA importers, Movea. Left to right, unknown Movea representative, Norman Vanhouse, Brian Martin and Fred Rist. The day's road grime is evident on the three riders' faces and much wet weather riding gear remains in evidence - clearly no time to lose to get to the Cheese and Wine reception party!

key which in turn was secured with his official lead seal, a procedure repeated every night of the test with the exceptions of the period of the ISDT when they came under the jurisdiction of FIM rules. After a hot bath and a change of clothes we were wined and dined at an exclusive restaurant where the food and the atmosphere created the social ambience for the evening in a happy and carefree way, and the delightful company included one member of the Movea staff who had moved to work for the Paris company after leaving BSA in Birmingham.

Our one night in Paris was but the first of many such memorable evenings we were to enjoy before and after the ordeal of the ISDT. They were the little perks that went with the job.

Behind the Iron Curtain

The following day, Wednesday, was one none of us would ever forget. With now over 500 miles on the speedometers of each machine, the day started with the mundane task of replacing the engine oil and a quick check of nuts and bolts to make sure none had worked loose. With that we headed south away from Paris, across the rain-soaked countryside, with Geneva our destination for the day, a distance of 350 miles. As we headed along the N5 towards Sens, the rain got steadily worse, semi-obliterating those great long sweeping stretches of *route nationale* with the bordering tall poplar trees creating a distant vanishing point which seemed perpetually out of reach.

At breakfast that morning it became known that the photographer was not well. Too much wine the night before maybe, and time would prove to be a good healer - it usually does. As we put the distance behind us the photographer seemed to crouch lower and lower over the handlebars of the A10 and sidecar in an attitude of grim determination to cope with the elements and the unpredictable cambers of those French highways as we kept the needles of the speedometers on the 60 mph mark. When we stopped for petrol there was no sign of any improvement in his condition. If anything, he was even worse.

It was as we slowed down and trickled into the small country town of Tonnerre that George Savage decided we needed a break, so having found a spot to park the car and bikes we ambled along to a nice looking cafe-restaurant and ordered some food and drink. All, that is, apart from the photographer. He curled up in the quietest corner of the restaurant he could find to suffer in peace and silence. By then George Savage knew it was more than a hang-over. But with everything closed-down for the customary two-hour mid-day break, nothing could be done until it had turned 2 pm. When the shops opened the chemist took a careful look, asked a couple of leading questions and with an air of authority said, "I think, monsieur, that you have appendicitis. The hospital is quite close. You must go quickly".

George Savage undoubtedly thought the chemist was being a little dramatic. After all, the suspect had been dicing a 650cc combination in dreadful conditions

Another day another country and another BSA Distributor to visit! This time an evening reception with the Directors of Fibag in Zurich, the BSA Distributor for the Austrian Tyrol, Baden, Wurttemberg and Bavaria in Germany and parts of Switzerland. R Fourmin (Fibag) talks with Norman Vanhouse (right).

a short time before. It could not be, surely. But it was so, and the hospital doctor who confirmed the chemist's opinion added, "Yes, but you are very lucky. The areas surgeon only visits us once a week and he is due here this very afternoon. We must get you into bed".

By 4:30 that afternoon when the rest of us had resumed our grim battle with the elements, the offending appendix had been removed. Not unnaturally, his wife elected to remain behind, so after unloading their personal luggage we bade them farewell at the entrance of that small hospital. Unbeknownst to us they had installed our unfortunate friend in a private ward. And to further enhance the French reputation for hospitality, they pushed another bed into the ward for the use of his wife.

And there she stayed until her husband was strong enough to return home to England. The dramatic timing of this incident and its effects were pretty good press copy in their own right and coupled with that lovely human touch of the French hospital medical staff, it was too good not to be used.

So weeks later, after the PR men at Small Heath had made the most of the main story, they put that one out to the local Birmingham press. Next morning, after the story had appeared in the paper, a certain outraged lady was on the phone. She claimed she had never been anywhere near that hospital in France; she hadn't even been to France. It was a pack of lies; and she would be seeing her solicitor and so on. There was surprise, shock, embarrassment and red faces at Small Heath that day. The attentive lady accompanying our fated friend with the camera had not been his wife at all. Not very provoking today, but sixty years ago the story could be told with some relish. The French would have enjoyed the story there and then had they known the facts!

No doubt the incident was a classic example also of the best laid plans of mice and men. It could have ruined the entire trip before it really got going. It could have been one of the riders or the ACU observer. What then?

But time waits for no man. We were by then hopelessly behind schedule as we headed for Dijon and beyond, in appalling weather, striving to maintain a high cruising speed on slippery, steeply-cambered and twisting roads, and as darkness came down we were faced with crossing the Jura mountains. The darkness and the rain made the use of goggles hazardous and to ride without them a painful business. It became bitterly cold as we climbed to higher altitudes and with it came the added hazard of floating banks of mist which at times almost obliterated the sharp downhill bends. If that wasn't enough, huge diesel commercial vehicles, climbing at a snail's pace, belched out great clouds of foul black exhaust smoke which lingered long in their wake, adding to the problems of overtaking. It had been a nightmare ride. It seemed that fate had been determined to throw everything at us in one go to test our resolve and determination and having found us unremitting, relented and let us go. Nothing ever seemed quite so bad after that. It was 10 pm before we made the Swiss frontier to find our host Mr. Van Leissen, the BSA distributor for the west side of Switzerland still waiting patiently to escort us to our hotel in Geneva. We had been three hours overdue, and after a good comfortable meal, it was straight to bed to sleep the sleep of the just.

The next day's destination was Zurich, 175 miles in a north-easterly direction. The route may not have been the most direct from Geneva to Austria, but the dictates of the itinerary was mileage, coupled with the need to call on BSA distributors. So having said goodbye to our friends in Geneva, the next port of call would be Fibag of Zurich who distributed BSA throughout the eastern side of the country.

With one more milestone behind us, still in relentless rain along the northern shore of Lake Leman to Lausanne, we headed for Yverdon and Lake Neuchatel, through Biel, Olten and down to Zurich, with the Alps on the right hand side shrouded in mist and rain clouds. A more uninviting prospect would have been hard to imagine. But more importantly, all three Star Twins were going beautifully. They were running sweetly and smoothly and by then we knew from the instinct which develops with experience that all three models would be more than up to what lay ahead. If that had been pure mileage without other imponderables, then their future prospects seemed infinite. But one of the imponderables which lay ahead was the ISDT, an event in which, as Fred Rist knew better than most, the machine's reliability and performance can be influenced by the way it is used - or abused. Throughout the long history of the ISDT, many of the machine problems experienced have been rider-induced.

It did seem that the factory had done a good job with the production of these Star Twins. And it also seemed that John McNulty had done just as well in his random selection. So even that early, we began to realise that the required success lay in the hands of the riders after all. The Star Twins were proving good enough. Would the riders? It was a train of thought best discouraged. The feeling of responsibility came into greater focus during the following days as we headed through Austria along their main roads, which we discovered to be extremely treacherous when wet – as they were most of the time. This should have come as no surprise as our distributors in Vienna had warned us by letter, and had suggested with a degree of sadistic humour that practice on a skidpan before we left would not go amiss.

Our friends in Vienna had not been joking. I had not experienced main roads like those in Austria in that time since my army days in Palestine during the last war. After many months of hot dry weather, a shower of rain would turn main roads into a skid pan where a bike would slip sideways down the camber on a flat road without provocation. Round many tight turns on that main road between Salzburg and Vienna I held my breath for fear of disturbing my balance. Even throughout the ISDT it was a relief to get off the tarmac surfaced roads and onto the un-surfaced tracks and forest paths. They seemed much safer.

The overnight stay in Zurich, with the evening spent in the company of the directors of Fibag, the BSA distributors, and some members of the staff, was the usual pleasantly social occasion and with several of them having an excellent command of English the conversation developed into a discussion of trade politics - a delicate situation in so far that we had no briefing from Export Department management prior to departure.

Before leaving Zurich next morning, about 40 minutes was spent on each Star Twin. This was a general check-up, and work done was no more than rear chain adjustment plus oiling and the application of a grease gun to various points. Nothing else required adjustment or attention. With the total mileage now exceeding the first thousand, this surely boded well for the future.

With those basic service tasks completed, we attired ourselves once more with our efficient Barbour suits which were proving more than a match for the conditions - extreme as they were - bade farewell to our Swiss hosts and set out on the next leg of the trip. With the rain still blotting out distant views, we headed through Liechtenstein to Feldkirch and the delightful country of Austria with its

The team are welcomed on their arrival to Innsbruck. From the left, Fred Rist, John McNulty, Maria Haidegger (secretary to Josef Schleicher), George Savage, Norman Vanhouse, Josef Schleicher (Secretary of the Automobile Touring Club of the Tyrol), and Brian Martin.

magnificent Alpine scenery, which at that time, like France and Switzerland on the previous days, was under siege by rain and cloud. Our route lay through Bludenz and on and up to the Arlberg Pass above the snow level, and the scene of a tragic avalanche earlier that year. It was also destined to be the scene of a road accident five years later which took the life of the legendary Joe Craig of Norton racing fame.

And so we progressed through Landeck, Imst and Telfs to Innsbruck on a road which criss-crossed the River Inn, a fast-flowing torrent fed by icy mountain water which passed through the bustling town. The rain by then had relented and given way to the sun which, as we dropped towards the town, shone with brilliant splendour on the snow-capped peaks that surround Innsbruck with lofty eminence. Situated in the heart of the Austrian Tyrol, that fairyland of mountain peaks and remote picturesque villages, Innsbruck is one of those rare places where the town is as attractive as the name itself, and the backdrop of mountains seem to rise sheer like a great wall just beyond the town, dwarfing the buildings into insignificance.

It had been an easy day with less than 200 miles covered since leaving Zurich. The Star Twins continued to run faultlessly. Even the rain had relented and allowed the sun to shine on a world which was transformed into one of warmth and pleasant prospects. The evening was equally relaxed and enjoyable when we were joined by two officials of the branch of the *Österreichische Automobil, Motorrad und Touring Club*, the chairman of the club and the charming lady secretary who took us along to their clubroom for drinks. Then back to the hotel and an early night.

Our friends of the night before saw us off next morning, when George Savage took the opportunity of presenting our lady host with a bouquet of flowers as a way of expressing our joint thanks for their kindness. Leaving Innsbruck behind we headed east towards Salzburg of music festival fame, through the small villages of Schwaz, Wörgl, and Lofer and thence to the little frontier village of Melleck, for this route to Salzburg passes through a thin strip of Germany which bulges into Austria like a parson's nose, involving Customs formalities for entering Germany and again within a few miles when re-entering Austria. It was at the former German Customs checkpoint that our gaze became fascinated by a short, stocky figure in smart breeches and jack boots who strutted towards us to examine our documents. This apparition, complete with rakish peaked cap, expressionless face and trim black toothbrush moustache, was surely Adolf Hitler himself. With Berchtesgaden a short distance from there, could it be that Hitler was earning his post-war keep in that remote quiet backwater of Germany? If it was not Adolf himself or his twin brother, then it was a local Customs official savouring, with obvious delight, the notoriety his image created.

So for us it was back into Austria again after these short few miles in Germany, with the fine city of Salzburg soon reached and left behind as we made for the small village of Altaussee where we were booked in for the night. Situated only a few miles from Bad Aussee, the town which would be the centre of the forthcoming ISDT, the Spanish national teams were also installed at this hotel for the event and had already been out on the course practicing. From our mutually limited ability to converse, it was nonetheless obvious that they regarded what they had seen of the course thus far, as pretty awful and demanding. We couldn't help but wonder what they would have thought of our prospects had we been able to convey to them that we would be tackling those 'awful' conditions with perfectly standard motorcycles - without prior practice into the bargain.

Although now in the area of Bad Aussee, on which would converge during the course of the next few days many competitors from all over Europe and Scandinavia to compete in the Olympics of the motorcycling world, our destination was Vienna. Until that had been reached, the observed test's first objective had not been achieved. So after breakfast on that Sunday morning, having once more loaded the car and climbed into our riding gear, we headed east for the unknowns of the Iron Curtain.

The visas and special permits with loaded instructions had made it all sound so ominous. The British Foreign Office had been quite emphatic. Our route to Vienna must be via the Semmering Pass. To deviate from this route 'might cause undue embarrassment' was the typical under-statement. Once inside the Russian Zone, the advice of the Foreign Office seemed to appear of paramount importance. We experienced no incidents to test this sage advice. But there was an atmosphere of menace and foreboding. Armed Russian soldiers seemed to be on every street corner, even in the smallest of villages. On one occasion on the return trip from Vienna, an armed Russian soldier un-slung his rifle, stepped into the road and waved us to stop. Before we had rolled to a standstill he had changed his mind and waved us on. We required no second bidding. Then there was the occasion, also on the trip back from Vienna, when George Savage decided he would like a souvenir photograph of a wayside building adorned with the red stars of the Russian army.

George got no further than raising his camera - and it is surprising he got it that far - when the door opened and out trooped a squad of armed soldiers, obviously bent on proving that such action involving cameras was not to their liking. Quickly realising that he was being imprudent, George slipped back into his car and cleared off. I think we had already done so!

But reverting to the point of where we were approaching the Semmering Pass on the run-in to Vienna, we came to the British control point first. It was manned by soldiers from the Royal Warwickshire regiment and we had barely opened our mouths with the first hint of our nationality - let alone that we were from Birmingham - before we were invited to share their morning brew-up. They were cheerful, easy-going, wise-cracking young soldiers, typical of the British army for generations. But in stark contrast, just down the road at the Russian checkpoint, we encountered the Soviet example. Frigid, poker-faced, authoritarian. They examined our documents closely and individually and when satisfied, waved us through with their guns. Now Fred Rist was a great extrovert. On this sort of trip he had a friendly word for everyone. A wave here and a wave there, his friendly style was unmistakable to all – except Russian soldiers. When they had cleared his papers and waved him through in order to deal with Brian and myself, Fred had intended to hang on and try to converse with them in his usual easy-going manner. They had cleared his papers and he was required to move on instantly and to make this quite clear these soldiers un-slung their rifles from their shoulders with a menacing wave in the direction we were required to go. Fred required no second bidding. Fraternisation of any sort was clearly out.

In a somewhat sober frame of mind, we motored gently towards Vienna, conscious of the austere atmosphere in the villages through which we passed. Property looked shabby and unpainted and the shop windows devoid of goods. There was no doubting it. The Russian controlled zone of Austria was a different world to the Austria of the West. It lacked signs of prosperity and development, in complete contrast to the rest of Western Europe we had seen in recent days.

As we entered the outskirts of Vienna on that pleasant Sunday afternoon, the atmosphere seemed to mellow; the air of hostility, real or imaginary, evaporated like mist. Well-dressed Viennese folk were out taking their customary Sunday stroll as though without a care in the world or a thought for foreign occupation forces. I think really, we were coming under the charm of one of the once-great cities of Europe with its immense cultural traditions, our initial impressions unspoiled by modern architecture.

Having made contact at the rendezvous set up by the BSA distributors, Maximillian Koniger, we were introduced to Vienna by a conducted tour of the city that contributed to a frame of mind which became increasingly conscious of an undefined atmosphere of magic. Undoubtedly in my case, more so than Brian Martin as a younger man, it was mostly in the mind. I had come to Vienna - the most romantic name in the world. A name immortalised by music and song, and Johan Strauss in particular, and by the great film makers of Hollywood who had glorified, in countless extravagant productions, the elegance and opulence of Vienna when it was the heart of the Austro-Hungarian empire in the days of its glory; when officers of the privileged Austrian army in stylish and colourful uniforms came from the aristocracy and, it seemed, had a part to play in the social whirl.

That evening the sense of unreality, if anything, was even stronger, with more echoes of days gone by. We were taken to an elegant restaurant set on high ground overlooking the city, spacious and traditional; complete with chandeliers and string orchestra which played soft Strauss-like music throughout the evening. And there we met the managing director of Maximillian Koniger, Dr. H. Alt, a tall, softly spoken man of culture and charm. Called-up twice to serve with the Wehrmacht during the war, he had lost a leg fighting the Russians, but with the aid of a tin leg and walking stick, the handicap was barely noticeable. In addition there was the Esso Petroleum Company's representative, an Austrian. Before the war he had married an English lady who then lived in Austria throughout the war years, whilst he was called up and forced to serve in the Wehrmacht. In parallel, his wife's brother in England had been called-up to serve in the British army - two members of two families related by marriage serving with opposing armies. Such is the stupidity of war!

With the main course of the dinner consisting of the ever-popular *Wiener Schnitzel*, it could not be described as ostentatious, but the atmosphere and the company - and indeed the occasion - made it one of the most memorable dinners ever. Furthermore, it marked a successful conclusion to the first phase of the operation, which had gone so well despite the rather dramatic delay when travelling down through France.

Knowing this was our first visit to Vienna, our hosts, sensing our mood, took us up to the flat roof of the restaurant to view the city by night. "You cannot leave Vienna without having a view of the Danube from this vantage point," they said. And there it was, a black shiny ribbon curving its way through the city, bordered on either side by twinkling lights, and spanned at intervals by bridges easily picked out by the glowing lights which topped the parapets.

Then, no doubt to remind us that Vienna, in reality, was just as modern and cosmopolitan as say London or Paris, our hosts whisked us off to a nightclub to while away the next hour or two in an atmosphere of brash furnishings and subdued lighting - but it was not enough to destroy my image of the real Vienna. When we went our separate ways at about 3 am, confirming arrangements to be at the premises of Maximillan Koniger in Stubenring by a certain time, Dr. Alt replied, "I shall be there; I am always at my desk by 7 am". A rather sobering thought, at least to us at 3 am in the morning.

Next morning, having removed the Star Twins from John McNulty's 'quarantine', with over 1,600 miles recorded on the speedometers, another oil change was made. No other work was done. We had checked the valve clearances before departure from Geneva although no adjustment had been necessary. All three models were running like watches, and almost as quietly, which inspired the utmost confidence for the days ahead. So with fond farewells to Dr. Alt and his staff we turned our backs on Vienna and headed for the Semmering Pass on the treacherously slippery roads, for once again it was raining, a reminder that, despite our few hours of respite in Vienna, there was still a man-sized job to be done.

Once again we passed through the Russian checkpoint, carefully and gently as though walking on thin ice; to relax and breathe again just down the road in the familiar and informal atmosphere created by men in British khaki uniforms. It was like getting back home. And so to Bad Aussee with the day's mileage of 183 bringing the total distance since we left Birmingham to 1,793. We booked in at the Hotel Post which was to be our home for the next nine days, but only after the Star Twins had been put under the usual lock and key, which was where they stayed until the bikes were admitted to the official *parc fermé* after weighing-in on the Thursday.

Other than oil changes and rear chain adjustment - and pulling-down the cylinder heads in Holland - nothing else had been done. Even thus far, the Star Twins were proving to be rather remarkable motorcycles.

The International Six
Days Trial

The bright warm sunshine which greeted us on Tuesday morning was more than welcome. It was not only in direct contrast to the miserable wet conditions to which we had become accustomed, but with a great deal of work to be done on all three Star Twins, it would make outdoor work throughout the day not only possible, but also enjoyable. So with shirt sleeves rolled-up, in rather idyllic surroundings adjacent to a swift-flowing mountain stream, we tackled jobs which were pure maintenance – such as adjusting contact-breaker points and cleaning out carburettors – plus work that would render the machines more suitable for the ISDT which lay ahead.

One of the most important of these jobs was the replacement of the standard Dunlop tyres with Dunlop Trials Universal tyres. Whilst doing this the rims were drilled to permit the use of security bolts. However, it is important to make it quite clear that whilst we were permitted to fit Trials Universals, we could not vary the standard catalogue sizes i.e. 19" x 3.25" front and 19" x 3.50" rear. A compressed air bottle and nail catcher were fitted to each machine, as was a crankcase shield. Tommy bars were also fitted to the wheel spindles, and padded covers to the headlamps to protect the glass.

None of these things altered in any way the standard specification of the Star Twin. Any privately entered competitor with a similar standard production motorcycle could, and would, do the self-same things; in fact, any such competitor would have been free to do more. For example, no private runner in his right mind would have entertained the ISDT with those wheel and tyre sizes. He would have replaced the front with a 21 inch wheel fitted with the 3 inch tyre normally used in those days to provide more stable steering and increased ground clearance. And the 3.50 inch rear tyre would have been replaced with the usual 4 inch to provide greater grip. A private entrant would also have replaced the dreadfully low-slung exhaust systems. The standard tyre sizes and exhaust systems would prove to be the two major handicaps imposed.

ÖSTERREICHISCHER

AUTOMOBIL-MOTORRAD-UND TOURING CLUB

WIEN. I.,SCHUBERTRING7

Sportabteilung

Mr.
Norman E. Vanhouse,

8o, Blenheim Road,
Birmingham 13
England

IHR ZEICHEN: UNSER ZEICHEN: Spa/Ing.K/Si   WIEN,   Vienna, 26th august
                                                                                1952

BETRIFFT:

Subject: XXVII International Six Days' Trial,
         from 18.9. to 23.9.1952,
         Bad Aussee.

Dear Sir ,

        We confirm receipt of your entry for the above contest
and kindly ask you to take note of the following :

1.) Starting number :
The starting number : .209. . . . . has been allocated to you.

2.) Preliminary examination :
        The weighing out of your engine will take place on
~~Tuesday,16.9.1952~~ Wednesday, 17.9.1952 at .14.00 . . . hrs.

        The weighing out will take place at the Parkplatz
(parking place) in the immediate neighbourhood of the railway
station Bad Aussee.
        For the preliminary examination, we wish to ask you to
take care that the engine is suitably drilled for the sealing as
prescribed in the code. We wish to point out that the front
competition number plate must be drilled in a similar manner
so that it may be sealed to any marked part of the vehicle. The
numberplates are to be furnished with the finish and the colour
as prescribed in the general conditions as well as with the
starting number.
        The wearing of crash helmets of a pattern approved
by the national FMNR is compulsory. The crash helmets are to be
shown for inspection at the preliminary examination.

                                                        ./.

TELEPHON: U 13-5-80 SERIE (INTERURBAN U 19-0-17)   TELEGRAMMADRESSE: AUTOTOURING WIEN   POSTSPARKASSENKONTO: WIEN 189.618
BANKVERBINDUNG: CREDITANSTALT-BANKVEREIN, WIEN, I, KONTO: kg 2500

Norman Vanhouse's letter of confirmation for the ISDT above and overleaf. Note, overleaf, the octane
level of the Austrian fuel!

3.) Insurance.

The necessary insurance against third party risks will be contracted by the organizers. According to the general conditions, all drivers have to insure themselves against the risk of a personal accident. Such an accident insurance may also contracted at the preliminary examination. The premia for such insurances are in Austria with an insurance value of

A.S. 15.000.- Death   )
  "   30.000.- Invalidity   )   A.S.   326.9o
  "   2.000.- medical Expenses   )

with an insurance value of

A.S. 30.000.- Death   )
  "   60.000.- Invalidity   )   A.S.   653.8o
  "   4.000.- medical Expenses   )

4.) Important Adresses in Bad Aussee :

a) Headquarters of the trial : Kurhaus, Bad Aussee,
                                Tel. Fahrtleitung, (Headquarters)
                                from 1o.9.1952, 8.00 hrs.

b) Lodging office :   Kurkommission Bad Aussee,
                                Tel. 69 and 23,
                                opposite the Hotel "Kaiser von
                                Österreich",
                                from 1o.9.1952, 8.00 hrs

                                up to the 1o.9.1952, Vienna I.,
                                Schubertring 7.

5.) Accommodation.

Your accommodation has been booked. We ask you to get in contact personally, producing this letter, with the lodgings office immediately after your arrival in Bad Aussee where you will receive the assignment of your lodgings and other directives. We want to draw your attention to the fact that your accommodation has been firmly booked by us and that an alteration can only be arragend with our lodgings office.

6.) Fuel.

If you wish the fuel to be supplied by the organizers, the necessary petrol coupons are at your disposal at the lodgings office.'
As the Austrian fuel firms must be informed, which mixture is used by the foreign two stroke engines, that is, if you wish that your fuel is supplied by the Austrian Mineral Oil Pool, we must ask you to provide us with the proportion of the petrol - oil mixture you will require.
At the same time, we wish to inform you that the fuel as supplied by the Austrian Mineral Oil pool is a petrol-benzol mixture of 7o % import petrol and 3o % benzol with a lead contents of not quite 0.01 , octane value 77. The cost is approximately A.S. 4.5o per liter.
Drivers and mates badges, route maps, timetables, starting cards will not be handed to you before the preliminary examination of your vehicle.

Yours faithfully

XXVII INTERNATIONAL SIX DAYS TRIAL
        Ö.A.M.T.C.
        Secretary

(Ing.A.Kubesch)

Whilst the wheels were out for tyre changing it was convenient to inspect the brake linings as a matter of routine, as was the checking of the gearbox oil level. One additional job which was tackled in a rather more surreptitious manner was the inspection of clutch and primary drive on Fred Rist's model. During the previous couple of days Fred had been aware of a curious noise from that direction, but this he had kept to himself. He thought it wise to keep it from John McNulty if at all possible. The job was thus excused as a one-off exercise to see how the primary transmission was behaving. It proved to be in faultless condition and was re-assembled. From then on the noise never re-appeared and it remained a mystery. Whilst all this work was happening, at a relatively leisurely pace in the warm sunshine, more and more trade people and riders were appearing on the scene. Trade banners were going up all over the place and the flags of the competing nations, in a long impressive line, were streaming in the breeze. A quiet Alpine town 2,000 feet above sea level nestling at the foot of the giant mountain peaks, Bad Aussee was rapidly acquiring that unique atmosphere so familiar with all top-level international contests and events.

During the day Bert Perrigo arrived, in another green coloured Austin A70 like that of George Savage. He had set out with his wife the moment he returned to the UK from his American trip and wasted no time crossing Europe. From then on Bert took over from George Savage as leader and team manager, but George stayed on long enough to see the start of the Six Days on the Thursday, before packing his bags and heading home. His return trip was rather more relaxed than the outward leg had been, and whilst crossing France he stopped at the little hospital in Tonnerre to see how our photographer was progressing after the operation.

Despite the incident of running out of petrol when heading for Paris, George had done a good job as party leader throughout the first leg which terminated at Bad Aussee. He was very good company and with his cultured, almost aristocratic manner, he was a great ambassador for BSA. Upon my return to England I was appointed to his Home Sales team, so from then on, our paths crossed frequently. In 1956 we even accompanied each other on a trip on two wheels when we rode down to Sunrising Hill on the Warwickshire / Oxfordshire border, to test the hill-climbing capability of the ill-fated BSA 'Beeza' scooter.

In addition to taking over the responsibility of the ACU-observed test from then on, Bert Perrigo was also in charge of the other three BSA factory riders. These consisted of regulars Tom Ellis and David Tye, but for this one event only, the team was made up with Dutchman Gerrit Brouwer. As well as his BSA factory team status, David Tye was also representing Great Britain in the Vase 'B' team. These three factory team men were using the very latest 500cc Gold Star models with the new swinging-fork rear suspension, as were the official British Army teams. Our standard Star Twins had the old-type frame with un-damped plunger rear springing, so it follows that Fred, Brian and I contemplated their updated models with not a little envy.

The two British army teams included Captain Eddie Dow. He had won a gold medal in the previous year's ISDT in Italy and went on to further successes in the years ahead including winning the Clubman's Senior TT on the Clypse circuit in the Isle of Man. In partnership with another rider, he also won the Nine Hour Race at Thruxton. Subsequently in business at Banbury, he was also well-known for his public address commentating at race meetings such as the British Grand Prix at Silverstone.

Eddie Dow and his army colleagues had been at Bad Aussee several days by the time we had arrived and by virtue of first-hand experience, they had gained a great deal of information regarding the daily routes to be used and knowledge of the conditions. Eddie seemed to have a photographic memory. As each day's route card was made available, he could sit down and visualise the terrain encountered between each check marked on the route card, and express his opinion on the route card grading. All ISDT mileage was graded as one, two, three or four which indicated very good, good, fair or bad conditions respectively. According to Eddie, the route plotter's opinion on grading was highly optimistic for the most part; indeed, there was no grade four mileage at all until the third day if the route card information was taken at face value.

From the Wednesday evening onwards, Eddie Dow came to our hotel room and briefed the three of us on the conditions to be faced on the following day. This enabled us to amend the route cards with realistic notes, and proved to be of immense value. There is no doubt in my mind that this contribution by Eddie Dow, given so freely, was a major factor in our ISDT success.

The British army riders were not alone in their early practice sessions. Apart from various foreign teams, British factory teams had put in an early appearance and with them came news of the first British casualty. On the Monday whilst we were travelling from Vienna to Bad Aussee, Jeff Smith, that year a member of the Norton works team, had been involved in a collision with a private civilian motorcyclist. Jeff sustained leg injuries which required hospital treatment and prevented him from taking part in the event.

With the official weigh-in and sealing not due until Wednesday - in my case with riding number 209 it would be at 14:00 precisely, with Fred and Brian a little before - we still had ample time in which to complete machine preparation during Wednesday morning, when such mundane tasks as topping-up batteries, re-setting spark plug gaps and oiling control levers and cables were carried out. In addition, two pilot bulbs and one rear light bulb were replaced.

Where such work had been very much a pleasure on the Tuesday, on the Wednesday it proved very irksome - at least for me. During the previous evening Brian Martin and I had rather foolishly gone to the Cafe Veska, a sort of unofficial trial headquarters frequented by all the 'trade barons'. And things had got rather out of hand. Before the night was out music was provided by the much lamented Dickie 'Dunlop' Davies, an accomplished pianist in his own right, with the intended music makers, the little Tyrolean band in leather breeches and leather braces, competing with the rest of the customers for dance floor space. It was all very spontaneous and infectious, and before the night was out, it was debateable who was the most drunk – the customers or the resident Tyrolean band!

Hotel Post, Bad Aussee, Austria. The BSA team's home for the ISDT. Dunlop Universal tyres now fitted and ISDT number plates in place, the trio take the BSAs for the ISDT weigh-in, temporarily swapping the ACU's John McNulty's supervision for the ISDT Officials' supervision and quarantine arrangements.

By the time Fred Rist, with riding number 193, was due to hand-over the Star Twin for official scrutineering, everything had been done. At least we hoped so. All adjustments required had been made and various things checked and in some cases double checked. He was followed soon after by Brian Martin, and at 2 o'clock my Star Twin went up the scrutineer's ramp, and out of my hands. That was it until 7:30 next morning when Fred, as the first of the three, would come under starter's orders. From then on it would be in the lap of the gods. We already knew that the Star Twins had proved to be capable thus far, but we also realised that during the six days of arduous conditions which lay ahead, much would depend on how they were treated. We did have the advantage of riding on the standard speed schedule unlike the national and manufacturers' teams who, in those days, had to adhere to a speed schedule of plus 10%. That gave riders on the standard schedule an extra six minutes every hour. For example, the first checkpoint on the first day was 32.6 miles from Bad Aussee. Whereas national and manufacturers' teams had 59 minutes in which to reach the check, we had 66 minutes.

With many checks about 30 miles apart, an additional time margin in our favour of three minutes may not sound very profound, but having run at the higher speed schedule in Wales in the 1950 ISDT, I know from experience that it did make a big difference. The mind had to be conditioned to riding that bit quicker all the time; to catching and overtaking slower riders more frequently which demands greater concentration. And the greater the speed, the greater the likelihood of encountering trouble. So running on the standard 500cc time schedule was an advantage. On the other hand, the advantage was counter-balanced by the standard specification of the Star Twins. Using standard tyre sizes and low-slung exhaust systems more than cancelled out any advantage. Having ridden 'specials' at the higher speed, I knew which combination I would have preferred if the option had been mine.

None the less, Fred, Brian and I faced the morrow with confidence. We were about to tackle something never before attempted by a British manufacturer. That evening, after the Eddie Dow briefing session, it was straight to bed. One night at Cafe Veska was quite enough. And in the morning we would be faced with the cold reality of the job which Bert Perrigo believed we could do.

The First Day
Over The Grossglockner Pass

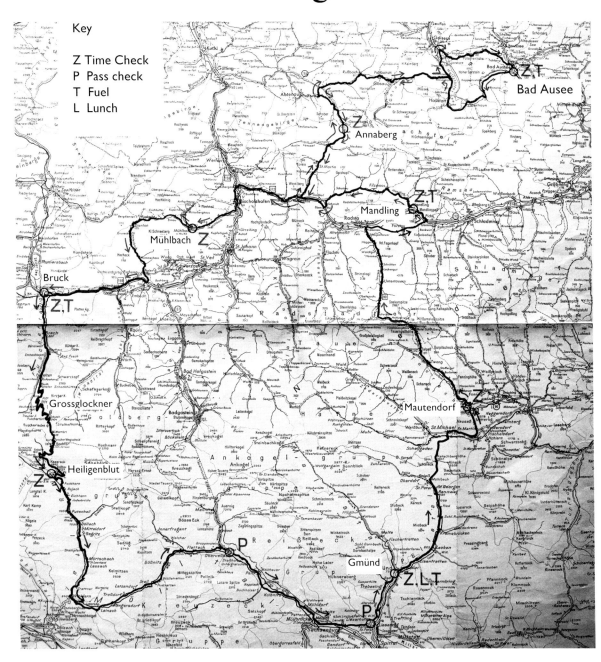

Key

Z Time Check
P Pass check
T Fuel
L Lunch

It had rained heavily during the night, and by 5 o'clock in the morning when officials, press men and early competitors began to make a move for the 6 am start, it was very wet and extremely cold. Protection for the bikes, since being handed over the day before and retained in the closed control, had not been much more than tented accommodation providing little barrier from the low temperatures usual at such an altitude and time of year. This was to be a big worry every morning throughout the week, right from the first morning. Would one's own model start in the time allowed? This was three minutes, and in that time, it was necessary to get the engine running by use of the kickstarter and cross a second line under power. Failure to do this incurred penalty points. So that very low temperature on the first morning created the first worry of the week.

At 5:45 am the first two competitors were admitted to the *parc fermé*, number one, Sante Camporese of Italy on a 73cc Alpino - one of the smallest machines in the event, and number two, E. Fischer of Germany with a 98cc o.h.v. NSU. At 6 am the starter's flag dropped. The little Alpino burst into life and the Italian screamed down the road in a proper racing start, determined to save every second from the word go, but the four-stroke engine of the NSU was less willing and required a fair amount of prodding by the rider. Nonetheless, he was away after the Italian within the three minutes allowance without penalty. Organised by the *Österreichische Automobil Motorrad und Touring Club*, the 27th International Six Days Trial was underway. It was the first time the Austrian body had attempted the massive organisational task of putting on the Olympics of the motorcycling world.

From then on, the riders were flagged away in pairs every minute. Some emulated the racing start of the Italian up front, some used a fair part of the three minutes allowance and others went beyond, thus losing a gold medal before even hitting the course. With all work done on the Star Twins on the previous day, on this first morning, having been admitted to the closed control 15 minutes in advance of the start time, there was nothing to do but to conceal one's feelings, maintain a calm frame of mind and ignore those with starting problems. The minutes ticked away. At 7:36 am Fred Rist came under starter's orders. The flag went down, Fred swung once, perhaps twice, the engine burbled into life and he was into gear and away. At 7:41 am it was Brian Martin's turn with the same easy result, and at 7:44 am the starter's flag dropped to signify my turn. Like Fred and Brian, I swung once, perhaps twice. The engine burst into life neat and clean on both cylinders without any hint of sluggishness and I was into gear, leaving behind my Swedish starting companion still cranking his stubborn BMW on the line.

Norman Vanhouse making progress on one of the fast, loose surfaced roads alongside the Halstatt See.

Heading west out of Bad Aussee for Hallstat and for a short distance along the west bank of the Hallstat See, it was clear that the organisers had decided it would be wise to give us time to warm-up to the task, to get the feel of things and accustomed to the type of terrain which would dominate the trial during the following days. This was done by locating the first check of the day and the trial some 32 miles away at Annaberg. A tight check over a short distance early in any day's route can be a bit demanding. It takes a little time to warm to the job of making haste with confidence and safety. This initial 32 miles to Annaberg in alternating rain and sunshine provided the breathing space I needed to feel my feet, and to some extent, gain the resolve required for the long days ahead.

Heading for the Gschütt Pass which climbs to over 3,000 feet, we were already on twisting metalled roads and on tracks, which in reality were a relief after the 'black ice' type surface of the tarmac roads which we had already learned to regard with caution and respect. Instead a new hazard was encountered. This consisted of rustic-type bridges made from peeled tree trunks, spanning the many mountain streams and rivers. These proved to be extremely slippery and it was surprising just how many times the track on the far side of the log bridge swung sharply to the left or right. This meant that the apex of the turn was more-or-less on the slippery logs and where the approach to the bridge was downhill, the whole thing was hazardous in the extreme. Many were the riders who fell foul of these hazards – including Brian Martin who bent the left footrest into the chaincase, causing a minor fracture of the alloy case which seeped oil slightly thereafter.

The rough tracks were badly potholed and frequently crossed with gullies and water courses which made great demands on the rear suspension, and none more so than on the un-damped plunger rear springing of the Star Twins. The slides topped and bottomed with great violence in tune with a mighty metallic clonk, and at times the rebound of the wheel was such that the rear of the bike seemed to be propelled upwards by some great force. Thus early on I feared for the frame. Surely it could not survive such unfair treatment for six whole days?

Although the 32 miles to the Annaberg checkpoint were graded number two roads on the card, the seven-mile descent from Lindenthal to the check should have been graded number three, meaning fair. Nonetheless, as I arrived at the check to be greeted by Bert Perrigo and George Rowley who was also out there in a helping capacity, Fred Rist had not left the control. That meant that I was over eight minutes in hand over my time allowance. It also meant that all three of us on the standard time schedule had been quick enough to maintain the higher, national team schedule. But had we been compelled to maintain the faster time schedule throughout the week, handicapped as we were with standard specification motorcycles, it could well have been another story.

The next check at Mühlbach, at an altitude of 2,700 feet, was only 24 miles distant on grade one roads according to the route card. But not according to Eddie Dow. He had warned that the first nine miles of this stretch was grade two in reality, but nevertheless, not bad enough to cause problems. It was a similar distance to the next check at Bruck, but immediately after leaving the Mühlbach check there were several miles of vicious going where the muddy and rutted track climbed to over 4,400 feet and certainly justified a grading of four as opposed to the official grading of three.

By this time of course, most of the later numbers on bigger capacity models had long been overtaking earlier-numbered riders on smaller capacity models as well as sidecar outfits. It is many years now since the ISDT included a class for sidecar combinations, and present day ISDT/E competitors have no idea of the problems posed by sidecar outfits in that type of event. Sometimes it was a major task for a solo to get by when coming up astern during a narrow, muddy forest section. We are not talking here about the present day concept of the lightweight sporting trials outfit with its ultra-narrow track. Those outfits, the German BMW specimens in particular, were massive things and wider, if anything, than standard road outfits. When encountered in tight forest sections, the sidecar driver and his crewman could be locked in mortal combat with the outfit and the world in general. Any thought for following solo riders was the furthest thing from their minds. You strove to overtake at your peril.

Also during that period from Bad Aussee up to about midday, I had been overhauled by those running on the higher speed schedule who had started out from Bad Aussee after me. Many of these riders were members of the British Trophy and Vase teams, such as Ted Usher, Hugh Viney, Jack Stocker and David Tye. When one caught the sound of an approaching machine, the drill was to take a quick look over the shoulder when conditions allowed and if it was a green number plate, indicating a British runner, you pulled over as soon as possible to facilitate their overtaking.

Between checkpoints it was possible to estimate one's progress all the time. This was done by resetting the speedometer trip mileage to zero at every check, with the route card mounted on top of the petrol tank and the inter-check mileage easily readable, and related to the time easily seen from the fork-top mounted aircraft clock. A quick check took less time than it does to explain. In any long-distance endurance event such as the ISDT, a rider has a choice of tactics. He can choose to go as quickly as possible all the time with a view to gaining as much time as possible to be used if he strikes trouble. Or he can aim to go as slowly as possible with a view to arriving at each checkpoint with a bare margin in hand. Whilst a lot of riders adopt the former method, I favour the latter. A lot of ISDT problems have been rider-inflicted as a result of pressing-on regardless. I developed a philosophy of reminding myself constantly just how many days of punishment one's machine faced, and the more soft-handed you were the better the chance of the bike surviving the ordeal. That philosophy was even more important for us in this event; completing the ISDT was only part of the job expected of the Star Twins.

From Bruck to the next control at Heiligenblut was a distance of nearly 50 miles on grade two roads, although about nine miles of that proved to be grade one main roads – all wet and slippery. Once more we climbed towards the clouds, this time negotiating one of the highest road passes in Europe; the famous Grossglockner, spiralling upwards, layer upon layer like a ribbon on

Norman Vanhouse passing through a typical Austrian mountain village. The tarmac surfaces were more treacherous when wet than the forest tracks. The glistening surface can be seen in this shot.

the face of the grim, featureless mountainside, to a height of 8,450 feet, well above the snow level, and beyond a layer of cloud to where the sun was shining brilliantly. Although that long gradual climb with the never-ending series of hairpin bends played havoc with small capacity lightweights, including the smaller 250cc sidecar outfits, it was an exhilarating experience on a 500cc twin-cylinder solo. It represented motorcycling at its best with use of the gearbox between hairpin bends maintaining maximum performance, with acceleration and conversely maximum deceleration for each hairpin bend in rapid succession – an almost instinctive, synchronised movement of left hand, right hand and right foot, performed with that deft smoothness which develops with experience and creates a feeling of smug satisfaction. Already that feeling of respect and affinity had developed between man and machine, as though the bike understood what was expected of it and was responding to the best of its ability.

The route had been running in a southerly direction from the Bruck control, over the Grossglockner and down the other side to the check at Heiligenblut, and on south to Winklern where the course turned due east for the check at Gmünd. It was no less than 58 miles between the Heiligenblut and Gmünd checkpoints. This was mostly graded one and two but it did include a few miles of grade four. Where the majority mileage was graded such, the grade four terrain could be tackled with a degree of circumspection by virtue of time gained on the easy stuff.

The 30 minute lunch stop at Gmünd enabled Fred, Brian and I to get together to compare notes, and we all seemed in a happy frame of mind. The mileage to that point was 169, leaving a balance of 111 miles to complete the first day's run. Rain still persisted, on and off, and after leaving the lunch check, the route turned north and once again climbed to 3,600 feet and the next check at Mauterndorf. The check beyond that at Obertauern was even higher at 5,880 feet. Thence to Mandling, 31 miles on and from there it was another long haul of 55 miles to the final check at Bad Aussee. Most of that distance was grade two, but there were a few miles of grade four immediately after the Mandling checkpoint. This was mainly muddy forest track, well littered with rocks and cross gullies which played havoc with the plunger rear suspension which protested with the usual chorus of vicious clonks as a reminder of its limitations.

By then, with over 200 miles behind us, that type of rough terrain with its mixture of surfaces and varying gradients, seemed, if not actually friendly, certainly familiar and not unlike conditions in Wales and Scotland to which we had become accustomed. Quite suddenly the job prospect had been transformed: it was no longer an unknown quantity belonging to an unfamiliar future. The world was now a familiar reality. I felt capable of coping with the worst. Fred and Brian must have felt the same - even though they refrained from putting such thoughts into words.

I arrived back at Bad Aussee with sufficient time in hand to enable me to clock-in on time at 5:16 pm after nine hours in the saddle. Fred and Brian were waiting for me. Like me, they were muddy and dirty, but their broad smiles conveyed more than words could tell. Our first day had gone without a hitch. Much lay ahead but that first day success boded well for the days ahead. We shambled off, Barbour suits unbuttoned and crash helmets slung from our arms, dirty but happy and, in a nearby cafe, celebrated the day's success with a glass of *apfelsaft* before returning to the Hotel Post for a hot bath, a change of clothes and the evening meal.

During the evening, the events and disasters of the day became known. All was not well with many; the day's mileage and conditions had taken their toll, the most dramatic being the casualty rate within the International Trophy contest. Austria, West Germany and Italy had all suffered retirements from their respective Trophy teams – a sad blow to any national team on an opening day. The worst British casualty was the misfortune of Stan Holmes of the official works Norton team when the Featherbed frame of his Norton twin broke and forced his retirement. It clearly was not Norton's year. A few days before he was due to leave for Austria, Rex Young, another Norton teamster who had been selected to represent Great Britain in the Vase 'B' team had been injured in a road accident and was thus a non-starter. Then they lost the services of Jeff Smith whilst out practicing. Now it was Stan Holmes.

Freddie Whittle, the Panther sidecar exponent went out with a leaking petrol tank quite early in the day and worse, from a BSA point of view, David Tye was also in trouble with a leaking tank which required a botched repair with liquid solder. Another blow for the BSA factory team was the inability of Gerrit Brouwer, the Dutch member of the team, to maintain the 10% higher speed schedule. Although he had a trouble-free run, he had dropped 39 marks on time. Of the two British lady riders, Mollie Briggs had a very good day with the loss of but one mark – lost when her Triumph failed to start in the prescribed time at Bad Aussee first thing – but Olga Kevelos, who had won a gold medal in Wales in 1949, had a bad day with a loss of 48 marks on time. She was riding a 150cc Parilla.

So for some the honeymoon was over already. The drama was unfolding. Whilst Fred Rist, Brian Martin and I were viewing events from our untroubled, as yet, vantage point, clearly even the first day had made demands too great for some. We had made the first day without loss of marks. Despite the handicaps imposed by the Star Twin's standard specification, we had been well able to cope. We had a long, long way to go however, and counting chickens in the ISDT is a foolish delusion. But we had proved that the job was possible; that we could face tomorrow with sober optimism.

XXVII. Internationale Sechstagefahrt

DONNERSTAG 18. IX. 1952

1 Tag / Day / Jour / Tappa

Start-Nr. 209

STANDARD-SCHNITT
STANDARD-SPEED
VITESSE DE BASE
VELOCITA
STANDARD

48

See-höhe m	ORT — PLACE		km Zwisch.	km Etappe	km Total	miles Zwisch.	miles Etappe	miles Total	Straßen Güte-grad	%	Zeit / Time Standard Min.	Standard Std./Min.	Team Min.	Team Std./Min.	Notizen
659	**BAD AUSSEE**	Z,T	0.0			0.0					TIME				7.44
511	Obertraun		11.3			7.0									
511	Hallstatt														
509	Gosauzwang		8.7			5.4									
964	Paß Gschütt		12.3			7.7									
	Abzw. Lindenthal		11.8			7.3									
777	**ANNABERG**	Z	8.4	52.5	52.5	5.2	32.6	32.6	II		66	1.06	59	0.59	8.50
750	Niedernfritz		14.3			8.9									
	Kreuzbergmauth														
547	Bischofshofen		14.7			9.2									
853	**MÜHLBACH**	Z	9.8	38.8	91.3	6.1	24.2	56.8	I	— 10	44	1.50	40	1.39	9.34
1351	Elmau														
1071	Birgkarhaus		12.0			7.5									
753	Dienten a. H.		16.7			10.4									
	Taxenbach														
758	**BRUCK / Glocknerstraße**	Z,T	11.1	39.8	131.1	6.9	24.8	81.6	III	+ 10	55	2.45	49	2.28	10.19
1629	Parkplatz Piffkar		19.3			12.0									
2505	Hochtor		13.7			8.5									
1288	**HEILIGENBLUT**	Z	14.8	47.8	178.9	9.2	29.7	111.3	II		60	3.45	54	3.22	11.29
965	Winklern		23.0			14.3									
680	Obervellach		31.8			19.8									
543	Möllbrücke/Altenmarkt		20.3			12.6									
	Lieserhofen	P													
752	**GMÜND**	Z,T,L	18.4	93.5	272.4	11.4	58.1	169.4	I	— 10	105	5.30	95	4.57	1.14
1611	Katschberghöhe		22.3			13.9									
1110	**MAUTERNDORF**	Z	15.3	37.6	310.0	9.5	23.4	192.8	I	— 10	42	6.12	38	5.35	2.22
1738	Tauernhöhe		17.9			11.1									
1004	Untertauern		10.5			6.5									
837	Abzw. Forstau		9.5			5.9									
1000	Forstau														
810	**MANDLING**	Z,T	13.1	51.0	361.0	8.1	31.6	224.4	I	— 10	68	7.10	52	6.27	3.24
1000	Filzmoos		6.1			3.8									
750	Niedernfritz		15.8			9.8									
777	Annaberg		13.5			8.4									
	Abzw. Lindenthal		9.2			5.7									
964	Paß Gschütt		11.8			7.3									
509	Gosauzwang		12.3			7.6									
	St. Agatha														
1012	Pötschenhöhe		11.5			7.1									5.16
659	**BAD AUSSEE**	Z,T	9.6	89.8	450.8	6.0	55.7	280.1	II		112	9.02	101	8.08	

Z = Zeitkontrolle Time-Check Contrôle Horaire Controllo Orario	**P** = Passierkontrolle Route-Check Contrôle de Passage Controllo a Timbro	**T** = Tankstelle Replenishment Ravitaillement Rifornimento	**L** = Mittagessen Lunch Déjeuner Colazione	

Straßen Roads Routes Strade	I	sehr gut	very good	très bon	ottima
	II	gut	good	bon	buone
	III	mittel	fair	médiocre	mediocre
	IV	schlecht	bad	mauvais	cattive

ISDT Day 1 Scorecard for bike 209 - Norman Vanhouse

The Second Day and Night
The British Trophy Team Disaster

During the night it had rained heavily and by the grey early morning hours when riders and officials began to assemble for the start of the second day, it was raining even more solidly, if that was possible. To say that the prospect was dismal, with the surrounding high peaks lost in the masses of cloud cover, was putting it lightly. Prospects looked even more gloomy as the 235 survivors from the day before came under starter's orders. With increased starting problems it became obvious to all that the rain of yesterday, coupled with the frequent change of altitude in the day's route, plus the very low temperature during the night when the machines had very little protection, were combining to adversely effect the ignition equipment. British riders, including factory and national team men, despite the use of waterproofed Wader-type magnetos normally used on special competition machines, were also experiencing starting problems.

The three Star Twins were fitted with standard Lucas magnetos without any protection from water at all, so if anybody was vulnerable, surely it was Fred, Brian and I. So it was with not a little apprehension that we waited our turn to enter the *parc fermé* to collect our bikes and, as the first job, check the contact breaker housing. They proved to be bone-dry. This was no surprise to us really for throughout the previous day they had run faultlessly; they had not missed a beat and always started first kick at every checkpoint. Checking the condition of the spark plugs also proved a mere formality and for the rest of the week, until the speed test at the conclusion of the event, they were not touched again or even inspected. In those days, if it was possible to leave well alone, one did so.

With the balance of the fifteen minutes maintenance time devoted to chain adjustment and the checking of all nuts and bolts for tightness, at 7:44 am I again came under starter's orders. The Star Twin burst into life, crisp and clean on both cylinders without any hint of water or dampness; I was into gear and away on the second day of wet misery. Another day of drama and sensation. The total mileage for the day was 286. But this was split into two parts. There was to be the outward run from Bad Aussee of 166 miles to a control near Graz where riders would be held in check for around six hours. Then they would be despatched on the return trip of 120 miles to Bad Aussee in the dark for the night run which was a feature of the

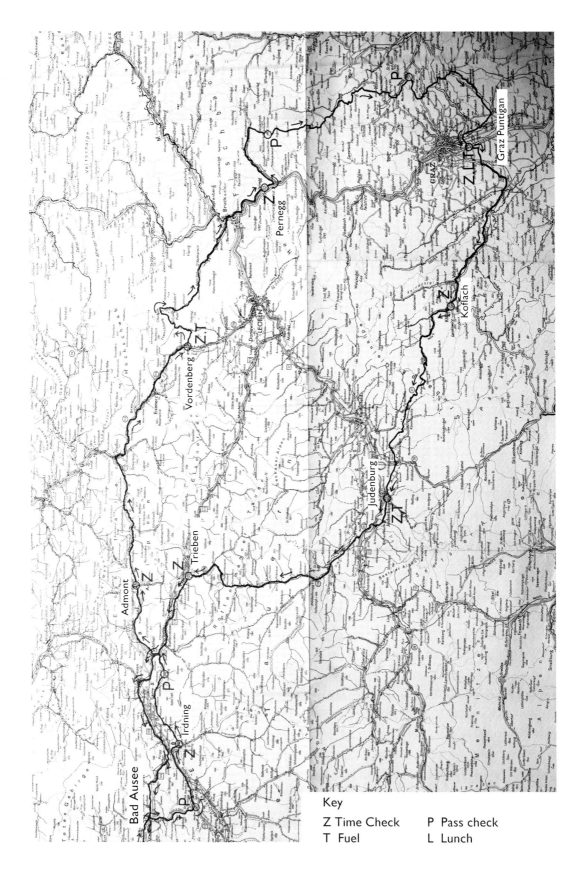

Key

Z Time Check   P Pass check
T Fuel   L Lunch

7:44 am. Norman Vanhouse (209) with foot on the kickstarter awaits the Starter's order. Alongside is a 497cc BMW mounted Swedish rider, Gösta Zalle, who was forced to retire later in the week. Immediatley behind NEV is Len Heath, the British ISDT Trophy and Vase teams manager.

ISDT then. It was not the picnic in those days that many riders of later generations have been led to believe.

With the first check on this second day only 26 miles out of Bad Aussee in an easterly direction, it was a case of getting down to it straight away without any time for warming to the job progressively. The road surface soon deteriorated into muddy tracks and paths through woods and forests where conditions were compounded by the continuous rain. Rocks, cross gullies and tree roots made great demands on the rear suspension which topped and bottomed continuously with a massive clonk similar to a drop hammer in a forge. These sort of conditions prevailed all the way to the first check and beyond, to the second check at Admont, another 21 miles further on. The mud became thicker and thicker, and with it, more and more foreign riders dropped both feet to aid progress through such patches of morass. This approach was unlike most British riders who, on approaching such areas of mud, stood on the footrests and powered their way through. This technique, long-established in the British trials world, was new to the foreign competitors. As each British rider demonstrated the art it was greeted with applause by the assembled and appreciative spectators who had gathered at choice spots.

On one such steep hill, well sprinkled with outcrops of rock, I picked my way through several foreign riders making hard work of it with both feet in action, and my effortless progress with both feet firmly on the footrests and standing up, earned applause from the crowd lining the banks of the hill. The approach to this hill had been rendered very difficult by the need to ford a river at the bottom which was deep in cold water. By the time 200 or more competitors had churned-up the muddy exit from the river, the hill became increasingly difficult for later numbers.

The third check at Vordernberg was another 32 miles further on, and then 28 miles from there to Pernegg. From Pernegg to Graz and the conclusion of the outward run was another 58 miles. The total distance of 86 miles from the Vordernberg check to Graz was atrocious in every respect. It was mud and bogs. Rutted forest tracks and slimey timber bridges where riders were going down like nine-pins. Here and there the odd bent bike abandoned told the story of those who had gone before and become victims of the appalling conditions. There were green-plated numbers of British casualties among them. I had seen Brian Martin briefly at each morning check, but Fred Rist had departed from each before I arrived. There were two sides of the coin, so to speak, riding as the last of three. On the one hand, whilst Fred and Brian stayed ahead it did rather suggest that all was well. On the other hand, whilst they did so, it rather emphasised my responsibility.

Due at the lunch check near Graz at 1:07 pm, I arrived with time to spare, wet, muddy and cold. But the Star Twin was proving more than a match, running sweetly and untroubled - rear suspension apart. Hot drinks were served and sandwiches had been provided. As we relaxed and warmed-up after the cold ride of the morning, stories of the morning began to circulate. The most dramatic was the loss to the Swedish Trophy team of Curth Neblin who had skidded on the slimy main road, crashed into a nearby stone wall and been removed to hospital with head injuries.

Don Evans of the British Vase 'A' team had also crashed. He had previously lost time repairing a leaking petrol tank and in his effort to regain lost time, had been really motoring when he came unstuck. He was still lying in the road unconscious when Don Williams, riding in place of Jeff Smith in the Norton team, came along and stopped to give assistance. This in turn caused Don Williams to lose marks for lateness at the next check. Later in the week however, the international Jury upheld

Norman Vanhouse on MOL 303 tackles a rough forest track.

his appeal and the marks were rescinded. Don Evans too, regained consciousness, remounted and although he lost marks on time, was able to continue his struggle.

Another casualty was Swiss rider Josef Martinelli who slid off the road straight into a deep reservoir along the route. He went straight in complete with his 350cc Condor. Whilst he was able to swim ashore, the bike was beyond recovery. For all I know it may still be there to this day! W.S.G. 'Nipper' Parsons, riding a 500cc Twin in the Ariel works teams, came off and broke the left side of the handlebar right off. News of this prang did not surprise me for at one point, whilst negotiating a badly rutted stretch of track well sprinkled with rocks where discretion was dictated, he rocketed past me like a lunatic. But with the determination of the true professional, he improvised by mounting the clutch lever on the remaining right side of the handlebar to get to the next checkpoint, where luck was with him. The British army back-up crew were at this check and were able to supply him with a replacement handlebar bend.

The West German and Italian Trophy teams were also having a disastrous time.

O. Kollimar of the former lost marks at Bad Aussee when his little 98cc NSU Fox failed to start in the prescribed time. And worse still, during the morning fellow teamster G. Reinhardt went out with machine trouble. N. Grieco of the Italian Trophy team who had been riding a 150cc Parilla, also retired with bike trouble.

Far from creating a feeling of apprehension, such stories of the misfortunes of others, if anything, strengthened our resolve. They were a constant reminder of the severity of the job we were doing; that vigilance could not be relaxed for one second. The natural environment allied with the cruel mood of the elements seemed to be throwing everything at us, and whilst the week was yet still young, there was a mood of optimism - a feeling that from then on both the Star Twins and the riders were proving more than a match.

This midday check was actually sited at Puntigam on the southern outskirts of Graz, where the large industrial organisation Steyr-Daimler-Puch manufactured a range of motorcycles and mopeds. Accommodation for all the riders had been arranged in a brewery (though not the part where the product was brewed or stored) where deckchairs were provided for relaxation and gentle dozing. The heating was turned full on to dry sodden riding suits and hot drinks were available in plenty. But whilst the comfort of the riders received every attention, the welfare of the bikes was completely ignored. Throughout the period of nearly six hours we were there they were parked unprotected in the open where it rained continually. It was hardly the way to inspire confidence for the start of the night run which followed.

Night runs in the ISDT/E have long since been abandoned. They were first introduced in post-war events to test the lighting equipment with which every machine was fitted to comply with the regulations. In the immediate post-war years, British national team selectors took things very seriously and when conducting team selection tests – usually staged in Wales – a night riding section was often included. During the night mileage, the candidates were stopped somewhere on the route and told to carry out some imaginary repair or adjustment against the clock. Consequently, factory riders also took it very seriously and practiced tyre changing in the dark, for example. The experience developed by such experts is best illustrated by citing the great Bill Nicholson who is alleged to have changed his four inch rear inner tube in something like 3 minutes, 30 seconds – in the dark!

The night run did more than test the efficiency of the lighting set, however, for it also challenged the rider's ability to cope with strange country and difficult conditions during the hours of darkness. It also provided a bonus not calculated by the organisers, for with a more generous time allowance (in this instance we had five hours for the 120 miles return to Bad Aussee) there was greater scope for illicit activity when necessary. A good example of this occurred in Wales in 1950, when the rear wheel of Peter Hammond's works Triumph Twin was collapsing, so the team support group led by Allan Jefferies waited just outside Llandrindod Wells until Peter had clocked-out on the night run. The faulty wheel was replaced with a spare and whilst Peter was completing the night section, the original wheel with the official sealing paint was rebuilt by Allan Jefferies. When Peter returned to Llandrindod Wells, the repaired wheel was fitted just outside the town before the final check. Peter experienced no further trouble during the week and went on to gain a gold medal, and Triumph one of the three manufacturers team awards.

With that sort of thing, the important part is not to get found out if one is compelled to break the rules. Indeed, there is a great deal of credit attached to such examples for it is done in the best traditions of overcoming adversity by turning defeat into victory.

On that particular night when we were due to return to Bad Aussee via forest and mountain tracks, in torrential rain and snow, there was going to be precious little time for such heroics. Whilst in the closed-control at Puntigam it had not stopped raining for a moment and as the early numbers came under starter's orders for the night run it was still pouring down unmercifully, and to set the scene I can do no better than to quote Cyril Quantrill who in his report in *Motor Cycling* wrote:

It began in the rain (the night run), it included the crossing of a bad mountain road in fog and snow, and it ran over 'black glass' to frighten even the boldest man on four wheels let alone those on two.

Dramatic prose maybe, but nonetheless pretty descriptive and accurate.

As the early numbers struggled to get some life from their machines it was obvious that leaving the bikes parked in the rain for so long had taken its toll and not a few runners had to resort to push-starting to get the engines to fire. But once again, almost as though enjoying some divine protection, Fred Rist, then Brian Martin got away without the slightest hesitation from the engine. At 6:44 pm as my turn came, it was the same story. A first kick start with both cylinders coming in instantly as though the machine had been stored in a centrally-heated garage in perfect conditions. It really was remarkable. The standard and unprotected ignition equipment - responding faultlessly, in a situation causing problems to even special equipment.

Conditions during the first 21 miles to the first night check at Köflach were comparatively normal. But the rough stuff started in earnest thereafter, heading for the check at Judenburg, a distance of 27 miles over the Stubalpe and Gleinalpe, twisting and climbing through forest tracks to an altitude of over 5,000 feet. Then the rain turned to snow which persisted to beyond the Judenburg check and to the one beyond at Trieben, 30 miles further on. Having run down from the previous altitude of over 5,000 feet, once again the slippery track wound its way up to another 4,000 feet through the Tauern mountain forests.

This area is one of great scenic beauty and in the summer months attracts many Austrian holiday-makers who spend the days exploring the forested heights on foot. On a September night however, mounted on a motorcycle in a snow storm with the hands of the watch ticking away unmindful of the wretched conditions, it was hardly a recommendation for the locality. But it did achieve one thing - it created memories none will forget, such as that of Eddie Dow. Whilst battling with that difficult stretch of forest track in the snow storm, his lights failed. As he came to a standstill in the pitch darkness he heard the drone of an approaching bike, so with the idea of getting a 'tow' by tucking in behind the approaching rider, Eddie kicked his Gold Star into life. As he slipped in behind, he recognised the machine as a BMW. By virtue of the efficient style and verve of the rider, it didn't take Eddie long to realise that he had tucked in behind none other than Walter Zeller, the German road racing ace.

With Eddie carrying number 227 but running on the standard schedule, he did not have the need to progress quite as rapidly as Zeller who with number 244 was running on the higher speed schedule as a member of the German Vase team. If Eddie wished to keep his 'tow' he had no option and probably, as Walter Zeller became aware of another rider slipstreaming him, he maybe tried to shake him off. Both Zeller and his compatriot George Meier (who was also a member of the German Vase team) were equally at home in Enduro events as they were in road racing. So it follows that Eddie Dow had to strain every nerve to stay with the maestro up front who traversed the straight sections of forest track at 70 mph. It also follows that Eddie was on time at the next check. But it was an experience, he later claimed, he had no wish to repeat - ever.

'Nipper' Parsons, who had broken his handlebars during the morning run when he came off, was also in trouble with failing lights. The condition of the works Ariel was also decidedly second-hand as a result of further prangs and his retirement was not far away. Molly Briggs ran her battery flat when trying to assist the one-legged British sidecar driver Harold Taylor, who was at the roadside trying to rectify trouble with his Royal Enfield outfit. Molly had already lost a lot of time clearing a choked jet in the Triumph carburettor when she stopped to help Harold Taylor.

With this combined delay she had only eight minutes to spare at the final check and thus avoided automatic exclusion. Her efforts to help Harold Taylor were in vain. The distributor shaft on the Enfield twin had sheared leaving him stranded on top of the mountain in the snow storm, where he and his passenger had to seek refuge in the nearest *gasthof*.

The remaining 40 miles of the night run from Trieben to Bad Aussee, through Rottenmann, Liezen, Schranz and Mitterndorf were not too bad relatively speaking, with the snow easing off as the altitude dropped, and at about 10:30 pm I slipped into Bad Aussee ready to clock-in at 10:42 pm. I was wet and cold and smugly satisfied. Fred and Brian were waiting for me. We went straight to the hotel for eats, hot bath and bed. It had been a 17-hour day in dreadful weather. But once again the Star Twins' performance had been beyond reproach.

It had been a devastating day for the others however, with the most shattering event, from a British point of view, being the retirement of Bob Manns of the Trophy team. His 500cc Matchless twin had refused to start at the Graz checkpoint after the six hours in the rain. The bike defied all starting efforts for hours. Subsequently the trouble was diagnosed as water in the Wader magneto and the theory was that an over-long breather pipe had created a capillary action. George Buck, the British sidecar driver also went out with ignition failure when his Ariel outfit refused to start at Graz.

British riders in distress were not alone. Quite a number of foreign riders were in trouble including a retirement from the Italian Vase team, with one retirement also from the Swedish team when Nystron and his Royal Enfield went out. There had also been two British army casualties, one being Sergeant V.E. Monk who came off his BSA injuring his leg, and the other being Lance Corporal Jimmy Bray who also came off and retired. Doing his National Service at that time, Jimmy Bray was a very talented scrambles rider from the Midlands. Olga Kevelos retired, thus leaving Molly Briggs as the sole lady competitor.

As a result of the day's activities, the Czechoslovakian trophy team was in the lead. And in the Vase contest, whereas the British 'A' team had dropped 24 marks, the 'B' team of John Brittain, Peter Hamond and David Tye was still clean. And there was a British team on three Star Twins also clean.

XXVII. Internationale Sechstagefahrt

Start-Nr. 209

FREITAG 19. IX. 1952

2 Tag / Day / Jour / Tappa

STANDARD-SCHNITT
STANDARD-SPEED
VITESSE DE BASE
VELOCITA
STANDARD

48

See-höhe m	ORT — PLACE		km Zwisch.	km Etappe	km Total	miles Zwisch.	miles Etappe	miles Total	Straßen Güte-grad	%	Standard Min.	Standard Std./Min.	Team Min.	Team Std./Min.	Notizen
659	BAD AUSSEE	Z,T	0.0						2						7.44
	St. Leonhard								2						
	Anger								I						
	Äußere Kainisch								I						
797	Mitterndorf		16.0			9.9			I.3						
	Durch den Stein														
	Tipschern	P	11.7			7.3	26		I						
668	IRDNING	Z	14.1	41.8	41.8	8.8	26.0	26.0	I	—10	47	0.47	42	0.42	8.31
	Aigen								3						
	Döllach		10.1			6.3			3						
	Lassing							21	2						
634	Selzthal	P	9.9			6.2			2						
641	ADMONT	Z	13.7	33.7	75.5	8.5	21.0	47.0	II		42	1.29	38	1.20	9.13
564	Gstatterboden		14.9			9.3			I						
517	Hieflau		9.6			6.0	32		I						
769	Eisenerz		15.8			9.8			I						
810	VORDERNBERG	Z,T	11.1	51.4	126.9	6.9	32.0	79.0	I	10	58	2.27	52	2.12	10.11
1166	Hieslegg		6.7			4.2			3						
789	Oberort		4.5			2.8			3						
653	St. Kathrein		12.7			7.9			2						
	Berndorf		10.6			6.6	28		2						
487	Bruck a. d. Mur								2						
	Linkes Murufer														11.9
474	PERNEGG	Z	11.9	46.4	173.3	7.4	28.9	107.9	II		58	3.25	52	3.04	
659	St. Erhard								3						
1175	W. H. Teichalpe	P	19.4			12.1			3						
682	Fladnitz								3						
789	Gollersattel		19.5			12.1			3						
520	Gestauda		9.9			6.2			2						
	Albersdorf								2						
444	Bachwirt														
407	Eggersdorf	P													
559	W. H. Bäckenpeterl		15.2			9.4			2						
547	Laßnitzhöhe														
487	W. H. Absenger								2						
	Vasoldsberg														
383	Breitenhilm														
340	Hausmannstetten		20.6			12.8	56		2						
	Liebenau														
347	GRAZ-PUNTIGAM	Z,L,T	9.7	94.3	267.6	6.0	58.6	166.5	34		115	5.25	106	4.50	1.7
350	Tobelbad		8.5			5.3			I						
350	G. Söding		7.3			4.5	21		I						
442	KÖFLACH	Z	19.6	35.4	303.0	12.2	21.9	188.4	I	—10	40	6.03	36	5.26	7.24
1551	W. H. Gaberl		20.1			12.5			2.3						
1115	Purkerhöhe							27	2						
688	Weißkirchen		17.7			11.0			I						
734	JUDENBURG	Z,T	6.3	44.1	347.1	3.9	27.4	215.8	II		55	6.58	50	6.16	8.19
811	Abzw. Pölshals		10.2			6.3			2						
885	Unter Zeiring		6.9			4.3			I						
1053	St. Johann a. T.		13.1			8.1	30		I						
1265	Hohentauern		10.4			6.5			I						
708	TRIEBEN	Z	8.8	49.4	396.5	5.5	30.7	246.5	2 II		62	8.00	56	7.12	9.21
674	Rottenmann		10.9			6.8			I						
650	Liezen		12.4			7.7	40		2						
	Schranz		14.2			8.8			I						
797	Mitterndorf		13.6			8.4			2						
659	BAD AUSSEE	Z,T	13.8	64.9	461.4	8.6	40.3	286.8	II		81	9.21	73	8.25	10.42

Z = Zeitkontrolle / Time-Check / Contrôle Horaire / Controllo Orario

P = Passierkontrolle / Route-Check / Contrôle de Passage / Controllo a Timbro

T = Tankstelle / Replenishment / Ravitaillement / Rifornimento

L = Mittagessen / Lunch / Déjeuner / Colazione

Straßen / Roads / Routes / Strade				
I	sehr gut	very good	très bon	ottima
II	gut	good	bon	buone
III	mittel	fair	médiocre	mediocre
IV	schlecht	bad	mauvais	cattive

Day 2 Scorecard for bike 209 - Norman Vanhouse

The Third Day
The High Casualty Rate Continues

In view of the late finish of the previous day, the starting time for the Saturday, the third day, was put back by one hour, so the first man was not away until 7:00 am. That put my start time at 8:44 am which provided the luxury of an extra hour in bed. This was more than welcome. The weather was much the same, with a steady drizzle replacing the downpour of yesterday, but there was a very cold north wind blowing. The start area was like a sea of mud and the officials found it necessary to redefine the start line more than once.

The first two days had produced 54 casualties. So out of the 260 who faced the starter on the first day, only 206 came to the line on Saturday. The loss of Bob Manns the previous day was a great blow to British hopes and undoubtedly a bitter disappointment for the British team manager, Len Heath, himself a great competitions rider of the pre-war era and one of the masters of his day. Probably the nature of Bob Mann's retirement made it all the more difficult to accept. A mechanical failure can beset the best and rider error too is understandable. But to go out with water in a waterproofed magneto was cruel in the extreme. When Len Heath ruefully observed Fred Rist, then Brian Martin, then myself all kick our standard Star Twins into life that morning without the slightest effort, he must have felt it was ironical in the extreme when he recalled that we had only standard, unprotected magnetos.

I was waiting to be admitted to the *parc fermé* to collect the Star Twin that morning when Len Heath appeared at my elbow, and in a somewhat patronising manner asked me to get out of the way of his team men when they approached me from behind and required to get by. His words were not quite as blunt as that, but his meaning was. I was getting in their way. With his five Trophy team men and six Vase team runners all on the higher speed schedule, most of them starting after me, it meant they were all overtaking me during the first four hours of each day. David Tye with number 259 was the last of the Len Heath men. He started 25 minutes after me and was due to overhaul me just four hours later.

From the outset on the first day I had been conscious of the need to give way to any rider with the green front number plate coming up from astern, knowing full well that they would be British riders on a faster schedule. As far as I was aware I had not caused any such rider inconvenience. But apparently this was not so. There

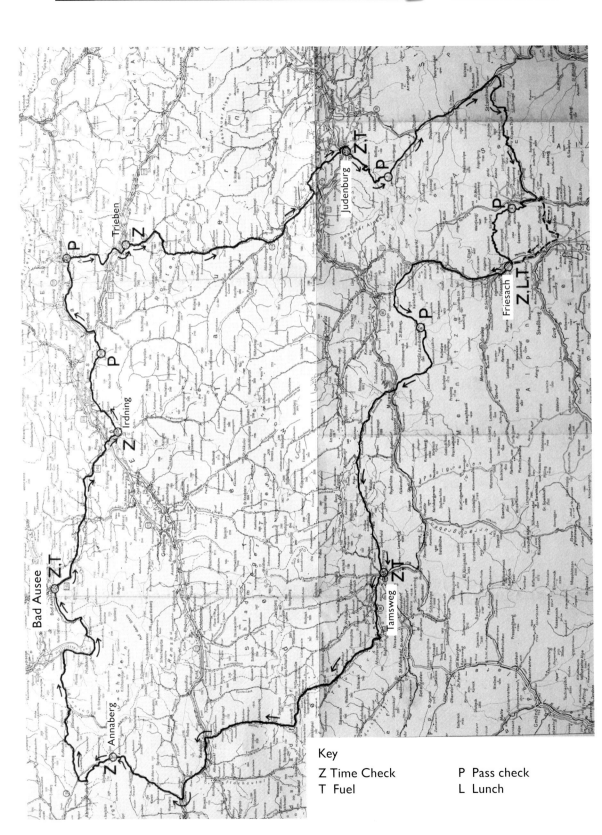

Key

Z Time Check   P Pass check

T Fuel   L Lunch

were those who thought otherwise. True, it could be regarded as a back-handed compliment; I was going sufficiently fast to be difficult to pass. Where there is only a marginal difference in speed, overtaking can be difficult. This can be particularly so in the ISDT where constantly changing conditions can limit opportunities - unless, of course, the rider to be overtaken pulls over at his own expense. This I was not prepared to do. I considered my role as important as the next man's - if not more so. But then even those of us on 500cc machines on standard time were faced with the same problem with smaller capacity models on a lower speed schedule, plus the dreaded sidecar outfits.

It must be recognised that prestige went with any success achieved by the Trophy and Vase team riders and that was all Len Heath was concerned about. Equally Bert Perrigo was only concerned with our success which could bring immediate commercial rewards. It was debatable who was playing the most important role.

Burdened with the dismal thoughts of Bob Mann's failure of the day before, and probably somewhat tantalised by the trouble-free spectacle of Fred Rist, Brian Martin and myself getting away to another effortless start, it must have been a further body-blow to Len Heath to witness Don Evans of his Vase 'A' team drop two marks at the start. Don was in great trouble with a leaking petrol tank plus seized front forks. By the time he had dealt with these problems he had exceeded his starting time, before rushing off down the road in frantic haste.

If that was not enough, poor Len Heath had to gaze in despair as ace rider and captain of the Trophy team, Hugh Viney, prodded away on the kickstarter of his 500cc AJS twin for an agonising minute before the engine reluctantly fired. Aware of the affliction which had struck colleague Bob Mann's machine, Hugh Viney must have suffered agonies of dread and panic before the sweet music of the exhaust restored his customary phlegmatic calm.

After the usual 15 minutes of maintenance and checks I was away at 8:44 am in the wake of Fred and Brian, heading eastwards, leaving Bert Perrigo to watch over the departure of the other BSA runners in whom we had a direct interest. By the third morning I was alone on the start line, my first day starting companion from Sweden with the BMW having retired in the meantime. Gaps were by then appearing in the starting order with sometimes a minute or more elapsing between riders being flagged off. Notwithstanding how many retired, the starting time of those who remained was constant.

The first check of the morning at Irdning was a short sharp 19 miles away to be covered in 34 minutes, but running through Mitterndorf and Schranz on metalled roads it was a gentle warm-up for the more strenuous stuff to follow. The route from Irdning to Admont was over the same route taken on the outward run of yesterday on the way to Graz. At Admont, however, instead of continuing eastwards as yesterday, the route dived south to the next check at Trieben – a check which proved to be very tight. Between Admont and Nagelschmiede, climbing to an altitude of 3,500 feet, the course ran thorough an area known as 'Paradise' with very steep downhill stretches to Kaiserau and Dittmannsdorf. It was extremely difficult and rough; indeed, an Austrian paper report suggested that the riders had no illusions about being in paradise – and that, furthermore, a mule would have been much more appropriate than a motorcycle. Arrival at the Trieben check meant another 30 miles completed with reasonable time to spare.

From Trieben to Judenburg the terrain should have been familiar to us, having covered it only the night before, but having done so in darkness, it was completely strange and unrecognisable – other than climbing to over 4,000 feet on winding, stony tracks and down again on the other side, only to do it all over again through the forests of Rottenmann whose peaks were lost in the leaden clouds above.

I have already referred to the route plotter's optimistic opinion regarding route grading. As far as they were concerned there were no grade four at all during the first two days and no grade three whatsoever during the second day. No doubt weather had made a great deal of difference when grading had been made during the dry sunny days of summer. The severe weather since had altered the whole situation. So it can be fully appreciated that the 55 miles from Judenburg to Friesach which now faced us was viewed with not a little apprehension. It was grade four all the way. All 55 miles of it! If it had been graded thus in kind weather, what could be expected after so much bad weather, we wondered. Actually, according to Eddie Dow, it was not grade four all the way. There was a fair amount of grade three and even some grade two.

There was no doubt about it being hard work, with the need to keep a sharp eye on both the clock and the trip mileage on the speedometer to monitor one's progress, but it did not prove to be as fearsome as expected. The weather may have helped to a degree when it relented to allow a weak, watery sun to break through the mass of ugly grey billowing cloud, revealing the freshly-fallen snow of the night before, which had covered the higher peaks of the Seetaler Alps. We twisted and climbed to Höhenpunkt at 4,700 feet and down the other side through Schmelz and Obdach. Then again the route climbed yet higher to Klippitz-Thorl at 5,300 feet, where the branches of the conifers hung low with the weight of the pure white snow, like decorated Christmas trees in the festive season.

Most of the mileage covered up to that point, a distance of 650 miles since the start of the trial, had been in the rain, which varied from drizzle to violent downpour. It was a condition which turned the job of riding a motorcycle into a grim, almost joyless burden. It rather emphasised man's self-imposed struggle with nature and the capricious elements. There had been brief moments when conditions gave rise to a sense of pleasure and enjoyment - when one was able to delight in the art of riding a good solo with speed and safety uphill and downhill, using the gearbox, throttle and brakes with a deftness and finesse not unlike a craftsman using a good tool. The deep bogs encountered from time to time, on occasions obstructed by struggling sidecar crews, were plain misery without an ounce of pleasure. In striking contrast the winding tracks and forest paths climbing to the dizzy heights of that magnificent Alpine world of space and solitude, were pure magic. Such moments of riding pleasure were stimulated by the superb performance of the Star Twins which evoked, even that early, a sense of gratitude.

After Klippitz-Thorl the mountain track unwound to a more modest altitude, to climb again to 3,700 feet after Lolling and Hüttenberg, through Maria Waitschach and on to the check at Friesach situated at a modest 2,000 feet. I arrived with about eight minutes in hand. That 55 miles of alleged grade four, probably considered by some an anti-climax, had been hard work demanding maximum concentration. According to the route cards, the worst of the week was now behind us. That remained to be seen. The 30-minute lunch stop was sited at this check. Fred and Brian were in good heart and the air of confidence was infectious. Despite this, the morning had produced the usual crop of troubles to others, with an increasing number of bikes bearing witness to the harshness of the environment.

At 2:10 pm after the lunch break, I was into gear and away on the course veering slightly northwest to Neumarkt, St. Lambrecht, Murau and Seethal to the next check at Tamsweg, a distance of 49 miles. Apart from about nine miles of rough going in the area of Murau, it had been quite reasonable, although the occasional stranded machine at the roadside proved there were those less fortunate. From Tamsweg to the next check at Annaberg, a distance of 47 miles, a constantly changing altitude remained as the familiar formula of the daily challenge, and at Tauernhof the track reached the highest altitude of the day at 5,700 feet.

By then the sun was shining brilliantly, with the peaks of the Taurach range of mountains to our left, white and dazzling against a blue sky, with the loftiest peak of Schwarzeck breaking the skyline at 8,600 feet, a magnet for mountain climbers. From Annaberg, where there was sufficient time in hand to tighten the rear chain, the route ran directly north towards Abtenau, then swung due east to Lindenthal and Gosaumuhle, the latter a small Alpine village on the banks of the majestic Hallstatter See. The route ran south around the bottom end of that great shimmering lake, through the small village of Obertraum and so home to Bad Aussee and the final check of the day, to join Fred Rist, Brian Martin and Bert Perrigo, with my arrival thus confirming that we were still intact; still without loss of marks with all three Star Twins still going like clocks, with the engines as sweet and quiet as the day they left Small Heath, 2,600 miles previously.

We were then halfway through the week with 829 miles of the course behind us. The weather appeared to have spent its wrath and was then relenting. If we felt entitled to a mood of optimism, not one of us dared to voice it. A miss is as good as a mile and three days in the clear would count for nothing if things went wrong on the morrow. Our relaxing drink of *apfelsaft* in the little cafe just beyond the *parc fermé* followed, where Fred Rist chatted away with his customary ebullience, amongst rumour and speculation. It was being said that both Jim Alves with the 650cc Triumph and Peter Hammond with the 500cc variant were in trouble with their gearboxes; that gear changing was becoming increasingly more difficult for them. That could affect both the British Trophy and Vase 'B' teams, for Jim was in the former team and Peter in the latter. Norton works teamster Ted Breffitt who left the start line each morning one minute ahead of me, had come a cropper whilst avoiding a fallen Dutch rider, bending the handlebars and a rear damper unit. German rider Werne Haas, riding an Ardie machine, went through a hedge and was taken to hospital for treatment, and a serious loss for the home Austrian Vase team occurred when one of their riders came off and broke a leg.

From the International contest point of view, there was a ripple of drama when it became known that the dour, dependable Czechs, riding unspectacularly and as dependably as the railway trains of days gone by, had dropped marks and lost their clean sheet. Although R. Dusil with the 250cc Jawa had dropped two marks, the team still headed the Trophy contest with ease from our British team with a loss of 200 marks. The British Vase 'B' team was still clean along with the teams of West Germany and the Dutch 'A' team. The British Vase 'A' team had lost 24 marks up to that point. Of the many manufacturers' one-make teams, only three remained un-penalised - BMW, CZ and the British Triumph team. Several club teams remained un-penalised including the Birmingham M.C.C. which we three riders were representing.

XXVII. Internationale Sechstagefahrt

SAMSTAG
20. IX. 1952

3 Tag / Day / Jour / Tappa

Start-Nr. 209

STANDARD-SCHNITT
STANDARD-SPEED
VITESSE DE BASE
VELOCITA STANDARD

48

See-höhe m	ORT — PLACE		km Zwisch.	Etappe	Total	miles Zwisch.	Etappe	Total	Straßen Güte-grad	%	Zeit Standard Min.	Std./Min.	Team Min.	Std./Min.	Notizen
659	**BAD AUSSEE**	Z,T	0.0						I						8·44
797	Mitterndorf		13.8			8.6	⑲		I						
	Schranz		13.6			8.4									
668	**IRDNING**	Z	3.0	30.4	30.4	1.9	18.9	18.9	I	— 10	㉞	0.34	31	0.31	9·18
	Aigen								3						
	Döllach		10.1			6.3			3						
643	Lassing ~~TIGHT~~	P							3						
641	Selzthal	P	9.9			6.2			2						
1086	Admont		13.7			8.5	㉚								
	W. H. Nagelschmiede		5.3			3.3			3-4						
	Dietmannsdorf														
708	**TRIEBEN**	Z	8.6	47.6	78.0	5.3	29.6	48.5	I·II	+ 10	㉘	1.40	59	1.30	10·24
1265	Hohentauern		8.8			5.5			2						
1053	St. Johann a. T.		10.4			6.5			I						
885	Unter Zeiring		13.1			8.1			I						
811	Abzw. Pölshals		6.9			4.3	㉜		I						
	Pöls														
734	**JUDENBURG**	Z,T	12.2	51.4	129.4	7.5	31.9	80.4	I	— 10	㊽	2.38	52	2.22	11·22
	W. H. Reiterbauer								2						
1442	Höhenpunkt		9.7			6.0			2						
	Abzw. In der Schmelz	P	3.4			2.1			4						
1273	St. Wolfgang		2.7			1.7			4						
874	Obdach		6.2			3.9			4						
715	Bad St. Leonhard								2						
	Abzw. Klippitz-Thörl		17.1			10.8			2						
	Kiening		4.4			2.7			2						
1642	Klippitz-Thörl ~~TIGHT~~		10.1			6.3			2						
979	Lölling		8.1			5.0			3						
	Abzw. bei Hüttenberg		7.5			4.7			2						
1154	Maria Waitschach	P							4						
	Baierberg					�55			4						
	Krauping								4						
	Olsa								4						
637	**FRIESACH**	Z,T,L	19.1	88.3	217.7	11.9	54.9	135.3	IV	+ 25	⑬⑧	4.56	124	4.26	1·40
	Neumarkt		17.8			11.1			I						2·10
1072	St. Lamprecht	P	13.0			8.1			3						
919	Murau		15.5			9.6	㊽		4						
	Seethal								I						
1021	**TAMSWEG**	Z,T	31.9	78.2	295.9	19.8	48.6	183.9	II		㊾	6.34	88	5.54	3·48
1110	Mauterndorf		10.8			6.6			I						
1235	Tweng		10.2			6.3			2						
1738	Tauernhöhe		7.7			4.4	㊼		I						
1004	Unter-Tauern		10.5			6.5			2						
856	Radstadt		10.3			6.4			I						
750	Niedernfritz		11.8			7.3									
777	**ANNABERG**	Z	14.3	75.4	371.3	9.0	46.9	230.8	I	— 10	�85	7.59	77	7.11	4·13
964	Abzw. Lindenthal		8.4			5.2			2						
509	Paß Gschütt		11.8			7.3	㉝		3						
511	Gosauzwang		12.3						2						
511	Hallstatt								2						
659	Obertraun		8.7			5.4			3	II						
	BAD AUSSEE	Z,T	11.3	52.5	423.8	7.0	32.6	263.4			㉖66	9.05	59	8.10	5·19

Z = Zeitkontrolle Time-Check Contrôle Horaire Controllo Orario	**P** = Passierkontrolle Route-Check Contrôle de Passage Controllo a Timbro	**T** = Tankstelle Replenishment Ravitaillement Rifornimento	**L** = Mittagessen Lunch Déjeuner Colazione

Straßen / Roads / Routes / Strade		
I	sehr gut	very good	très bon	ottima
II	gut	good	bon	buone
III	mittel	fair	médiocre	mediocre
IV	schlecht	bad	mauvais	cattive

Day 3 Scorecard for Norman Vanhouse

Top, the first day, ready for the off. Eddie Dow (227) on the B34 Gold Star at the start line. No 228 is the Horex of Ernst Hurin of Switzerland. Below left, Brian Martin, centre, paddles his way through the frequently encountered mud and right, with the Star Twin's plunger suspension hard at work he swoops downhill through the pine forests. (Photos from BSA Competition History by Norman Vanhouse, published by Haynes Publishing)

Above left. Later in the week a well muddied Eddie Dow awaits his morning start time. Dow's reconnaissance notes of the ISDT routes proved very valuable to the Star Twins team. Above right, Brian Martin prepares for yet another ISDT day in the Austrian Alps accompanied by John McNulty. Below, Brian Martin, with rear wheel airborne, tackles another forest track. (Photos from BSA Competion History by Norman Vanhouse, published by Haynes Publishing)

The Fourth Day
Over the Handlebars

Although a Sunday morning, it was back to the early 6 am start for the hard working officials and competitors with early numbers. Another 18 riders had fallen by the wayside during the third day, thus leaving 188 to face the official starter on this, the fourth day. It was a beautiful morning of brilliant sunshine, but bitterly cold. During the night the temperature had dropped to well below freezing point and this filled the hearts of many with dread, for the bigger four-stroke models with dry-sump lubrication - and also the Royal Enfields with their wet-sump lubrication – would have greater starting difficulties than the small capacity two-strokes mainly used by the Continental riders.

Sure enough, when their starting time came, both Don Evans and Johnny Brittain had great difficulty in persuading their Enfield twins to fire, and both exceeded the time allowance and incurred penalty points. Thus the British Vase 'B' team lost its clean sheet and the Vase 'A' team went further into debt. Poor Len Heath suffered further torment when Hugh Viney pumped the kickstarter of his AJS twin for nearly three minutes without the slightest response, until with but two seconds only to spare it came into life and carried him across the second start line. Not surprisingly, Jack Stocker of the Trophy team with the massive 700cc Royal Enfield also had his work cut out to get the big twin under power, but by then Len Heath must have been drained of emotion, for Dick Clayton of his Vase 'A' team had been excluded. During the previous day's run he had had the misfortune to break the front fork yoke of his 500cc Matchless but nonetheless had managed to stay on time and remain un-penalised.

During the night, Bob Mann's 500cc Matchless which had failed to start the night run and had been excluded, had been cannibalised for its perfectly sound top fork yoke. In the 15 minutes maintenance time Dick Clayton set about fitting this yoke to his Matchless – no small task which in fact took him beyond his start time. He still had the stubborn engine to kick into life, and having watched him kick his heart out to no avail, the officials stepped forward and said, "It doesn't matter: you cannot go on: you are excluded - you have broken the official seal on the front forks". Len Heath was another man short.

Although the engine oil in our Star Twins was also thick by virtue of the low

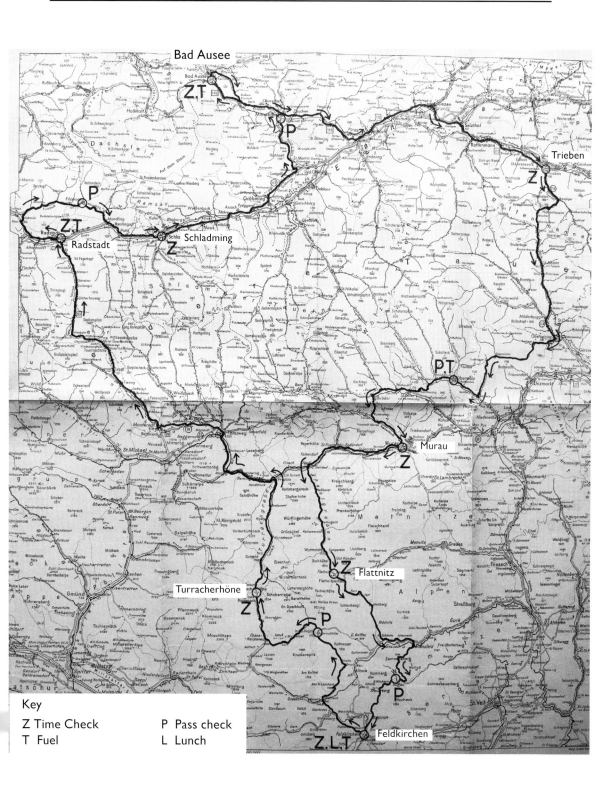

Bad Ausee

Trieben

Radstadt

Schladming

Murau

Turracherhöne

Flattnitz

Feldkirchen

Key

Z Time Check

T Fuel

P Pass check

L Lunch

temperature, nonetheless we had no difficulty in kicking them over and getting them started. With over 2,500 miles on the clock by then, it was clear they were nicely run-in and that much freer than the 'specials' transported from England. Undoubtedly the assured start we experienced each morning so far raised our ego and confidence enormously. It created a calm frame of mind which enabled us to start the day on the right foot in order to tackle the rigours that lay ahead. The combination of a lovely morning and a Day of Rest brought out crowds of spectators who gathered to wave us through their attractive villages with timbered and white-walled houses topped by great sloping eaves, which also provided protection for the piles of wood neatly chopped in readiness for the winter months ahead. Window boxes bursting with geraniums created almost unreal splashes of vivid colouring which seemed to glow in the sunshine.

The first check of the day was situated 42 miles away at Trieben which had been the location of the second check on yesterday's route, but whereas then we had left Bad Aussee on the road running south to Mittendorf, this time we were heading north out of the town on the road for Grundlsee. Within a few miles however, the route swung right round and headed south through Anger and Aussere Kainisch to rejoin the route taken yesterday. Then it deviated from that route just short of Irdning by turning north just beyond Unter-Grimming and kept along the north side of the River Enns as far as Liezen. Again the route swung south, crossing the River Enns before heading for Rottenmann and the next checkpoint at Trieben. The roads were dry and the mileage had been the easiest of the whole week to date, with little variation in altitude. It was a period of respite, it seemed, demanding little concentration, but to bring us back to reality we were faced with climbing up to Hohentauren with the massive peaks of the Rottenmanner range of mountains towering above us in both directions.

We climbed and descended, passing through tiny hamlets with magical names, Sankt Johann am Tauern, Pirkwiesser, Franzl, Grieswirt, Jokelwirt and Oberzeiring to name but a few, all looking like views on picture postcards, their little churches with thin pointed pencil-like steeples, situated at varying altitudes up to 3,000 feet. All the way to Oberwölz and the next check at Murau the world was dominated by towering peaks which probed the skies at over 8,000 feet. It was a mighty landscape, powerful enough to distract anyone's attention. Maybe I was getting over-confident and a little careless, when suddenly it happened. I was off.

It is difficult to recall just how it happened. It came as a rude shock and a reminder that like everyone else, I too was fallible. I think it was on the downhill

Two contrasting machines at a checkpoint. The British Army Team's BSA Gold Star mounted Captain Osmond (191) alongside Worcester Auto Club's Johnny Morris (125) on his 197cc DMW. Both riders went on to win Silver Medals.

stretch on the way to the Murau check. It might have been on the run down to the check at Feldkirchen where the half-hour lunch stop was sited. Whatever the geographical location, it was a fast and exhilarating downhill track through a pine-scented forest with tree roots and ridges and loose gravel. It was enjoyable and demanded good path-picking when suddenly, over a short sharp ridge, the front wheel landed untrue and broke away. The wheel crabbed onto full lock and I went straight over the handlebars, bending the front competition number plate flat across the headlamp. The bike came to a crunching stop as I picked myself up with a spasm of fear. A quick check revealed no damage to the front forks, the most vulnerable part of the machine, and apart from a bent footrest and the flattened number plate, all was well. There was no other physical reminder of my foolish lapse. It was a sobering experience which clearly de-tuned me for a time, and with my ego

*Norman Vanhouse following a fast downhill swoop through one of the many grand Austrian forests. This
stretch was also utilised during the night run. Such tracks, with their many cross-gullies gave the Star Twins'
rear plunger suspension a very hard time.*

somewhat chastened I carried on, thankful that nothing untoward had happened to the Star Twin to inhibit its performance from then on. It was another forceful reminder that there can be many a slip; that concentration should be willed on the immediate present and those few yards of terrain in front of you.

From Murau it was a short run of 22 miles to the next check at Flattnitz, but whereas this had been graded three on the route card, it proved to be easier than that with plenty of time to spare. But the 27 miles to the lunch check at Feldkirchen proved much stiffer, with several miles of grade four going in the area of Kotschendorf and Lind where the course climbed to 3,300 feet before descending to 1,800 feet at the lunch check. Both Fred and Brian were fine, so it had been only me who had put things at risk that morning.

After the lunch break, with 141 of the day's mileage behind us, the route turned in a northerly direction with 28 miles to the next check at Turracherhöhe, the highest point of the day's route at 5,700 feet, and this stretch too contained several miles of severe grade four going. From the next check at Radstadt was a long haul of 52 miles and whilst it proved to consist of narrow, twisting climbs and descents on loose, stony surfaces well sprinkled with cross-gullies and water courses, it wasn't too demanding despite the fact that the area had not previously been included in the route. Along the Turracher Pass, the route meandered through the tiny hamlets of Tamsweg, Mauterndorf and Tweng, all dwarfed by the mighty peaks of Scharreck, Weisseneck and Schwarzeck where the snow-capped peaks vied with each other, the highest at about 8,500 feet.

Beyond the Radstadt check the course turned in an easterly direction for a distance of 22 miles to the Schladming check, before curving north in the direction of Bad Aussee and the conclusion of that day's run. But somewhere between the Radstadt and Schladming checks where the course was narrow, leaving little room for overtaking, we were blessed with the unnerving spectacle at very close quarters of a machine going up in flames and shrouded in a great pall of black smoke. It was a Royal Enfield. That much could be seen as we squeezed past the obstruction to hurry on our way. It proved to be Don Evans' bike. He had been fighting a losing battle all day with his leaking petrol tank. Then he was further delayed with a tyre blow-out. It was whilst he was striving to make up lost time after changing the punctured inner tube that the leaking tank, no doubt aggravated by Don's forceful efforts, suddenly got worse and ignited. The bike was a complete burn-out. Len Heath's Vase 'A' team was another man short. Ted Usher on his 500cc AJS twin was now the sole survivor.

At 5 o'clock I rode gently down the cobbled streets of Bad Aussee ready to clock-in at 5:12 pm. As usual both Fred Rist and Brian Martin were there with helmets removed and Barbour jackets undone, waiting for 'the third man' so to speak. Fred was as exuberant as ever. He had not fallen off his bike all week and was the only one of us not to have done so. He was undoubtedly a superb rider who always rode with a polished and unflurried skill, and was one of the finest ISDT riders to come out of the British Isles. We sauntered to the little cafe for our customary *apfelsaft* and gathered the scraps of news going.

Phil Mellors of the official Ariel factory team had retired with gearbox trouble at the end of the Turracherhöhe Pass, so with 'Nipper' Parsons already out, this left only Bob Ray of the Ariel trio still going - and as he was a member of the British Trophy team - that was a blessing. Also a member of the Trophy team, Jack Stocker on the 700cc Royal Enfield, was in constant trouble with a leaking petrol tank and was applying liquid solder at practically every checkpoint. It was rumoured that Bob Ray had been delayed when a wooden bridge had collapsed but had been allowed the time this had cost. By the time the later numbers arrived the bridge had been by-passed.

The gear selection problems of the Triumph boys put paid to Peter Hammond, thus causing the loss of one Triumph team man and the loss to the British Vase 'B' team which had been clean hitherto. And yet another sad blow for Len Heath, John Giles the third Triumph team man, riding in his first ISDT, was also complaining of the same gear selection problems.

On the International front, the West German trophy team had been completely decimated when their last man retired during the day, with the Italian trophy team also losing another man. The West German vase team of George Meier, Walter Zeller and Hans Roth on their big black BMWs seemed to ride rough-shod over all opposition with typical ruthless efficiency and had not dropped a single mark. They seemed bent on revealing the folly of their countrymen in using small capacity machines for the more-important Trophy contest.

XXVII. Internationale Sechstagefahrt

Start-Nr. 209

STANDARD-SCHNITT / STANDARD-SPEED / VITESSE DE BASE / VELOCITA / STANDARD 48

SONNTAG 21. IX. 1952 — 4 Tag / Day / Jour / Tappa

See-höhe m	ORT — PLACE		km Zwisch.	Etappe	Total	miles Zwisch.	Etappe	Total	Straßen Güte	%	Zeit Standard Min.	Std./Min.	Team Min.	Std./Min.	Notizen
659	**BAD AUSSEE**	Z,T	0.0												7.44
	St. Leonhard														
	Anger														
	Äußere Kainisch														
797	Mitterndorf		16.0			9.9									
	Schranz		13.6			8.4									
659	Liezen		14.2			8.8									
674	Rottenmann		12.4			7.7									
708	**TRIEBEN**	z	10.9	67.1	67.1	6.8	41.6	41.6	I	−10	(76)	1.16	68	1.08	9.0
1265	Hohentauern		8.8			5.5									
1053	St. Johann a. T.		10.4			6.5									
917	Abzw. Ober Zeiring		11.8			7.3									
	Ober Zeiring														
966	W. H. Fasser														
1001	Fasser		5.3			3.3									
1340	W. H. Hochecker		8.7			5.4									
828	Oberwölz	P,T	10.9			6.8									
815	St. Peter am Kammersberg		9.4			5.8									
933	**MURAU**	z	17.6	82.9	150.0	10.9	51.5	93.1	I	−10	(94)	2.50	85	2.33	10.34
837	Lutzmannsdorf		16.3			10.1									
927	Stadl														
1390	**FLATTNITZ**	z	18.6	34.9	184.9	11.6	21.7	114.8	III	+10	(48)	3.38	44	3.17	11.22
793	Klein-Glödnitz		15.5			9.6									
701	Weitensfeld														
	Kötschendorf														
1019	Lind		11.8			7.3									
737	Gogau	P	7.3												
556	**FELDKIRCHEN**	Z,L,T	8.4	43.0	227.9	5.2	26.7	141.5	III	+10	(59)	4.37	54	4.11	12.21 / 12.51
811	Himmelberg		9.4			5.9									
1102	Urschwirt														
795	Bad St. Leonhard														
1596	Sirnitz														
1086	Hochrindlhütte	P	16.1			10.0									
	Reichenau		10.7			6.7									
1763	**TURRACHERHÖHE**	z	7.3	43.5	271.4	4.6	27.2	168.7	IV	+20	(65)	5.42	59	5.10	1.56
915	Predlitz		19.6			12.2									
1024	Tamsweg		15.0			9.3									
1110	Mauterndorf		10.6			6.6									
1235	Tweng		10.2			6.3									
1738	Tauernhöhe		7.7			4.8									
1004	Untertauern		10.5			6.5									
856	**RADSTADT**	Z,T	10.3	83.9	355.3	6.4	52.1	220.8	I	−10	(95)	7.17	86	6.36	3.31
1000	Filzmoos	P	19.0			11.8									
810	Mandling		6.1			3.8									
749	**SCHLADMING**	z	9.9	35.0	390.3	6.2	31.8	242.6	II		(44)	8.01	40	7.16	4.15
776	Gröbming		18.9			11.7									
608	Tipschern		6.0			3.7									
	Durch den Stein														
797	Mitterndorf	P	11.7			7.3									
659	**BAD AUSSEE**	Z,T	13.8	50.4	440.7	8.6	31.3	273.9	I	−10	(57)	8.58	51	8.07	5.12

Z = Zeitkontrolle / Time-Check / Contrôle Horaire / Controllo Orario
P = Passierkontrolle / Route-Check / Contrôle de Passage / Controllo a Timbro
T = Tankstelle / Replenishment / Ravitaillement / Rifornimento
L = Mittagessen / Lunch / Déjeuner / Colazione

Straßen / Roads / Routes / Strade:
I — sehr gut / very good / très bon / ottima
II — gut / good / bon / buone
III — mittel / fair / médiocre / mediocre
IV — schlecht / bad / mauvais / cattive

Day 4 Scorecard for Norman Vanhouse

The Fifth Day
Near Catastrophe at Wasserboden

With another 6:00 am start and 248 miles in store for the remaining 168 riders to face the starter on the fifth day, the weather might be described as back to normal, with cold, drizzling rain from first light. This became steadily worse during the day until the heavy rain nearly brought the trial to a complete standstill mid-morning at a point about 60 miles out from the start.

With a further 20 riders out of action, the total casualties to date stood at 92, a number which contained not a few British riders including the experts of Len Heath's national teams whose problems continued to compound daily. As usual, I might say, Fred, Brian and I got away to good starts and with the supreme prize appearing that bit closer, any confidence we felt or showed was that much more justified. Bert Perrigo did not have much to say each morning. Clearly he had complete faith in us and left us to get on with the job. He seemed to hover about the *parc fermé* within reach should his assistance be required. Assistance, it must be understood, only of the moral and advisory type whilst in that official enclosure.

By then I had not touched the spark plugs for days. At every checkpoint a single prod of the kickstarter crank was enough. The tick-over of all three models was as sure and steady as the day they left the factory. In comparison to the carnage taking place with the factory specials, the performance of these standard Star Twins was supremely ironical. If they failed without doing another mile, they had already covered themselves in glory.

Once again heading away from Bad Aussee and my 7:44 am start, there was no time to play with this morning, with the first check at Bad Ischl a mere 15 miles along the route in a northerly direction through the very rough Steinberg Pass via Altaussee, Blaa-Alm and Rettenbachalm. Having reached this first check with a few minutes to spare, clocked-in and set off on the next leg, the route then swung round easterly in the direction of the next check at Altmunster. This was another 28 miles of reasonable going devoid of mountain climbs or altitude until we reached the control point on the banks of the Traunsee at its northern end. This is a large lake bordered on the one side by peaks of over 5,000 feet which, on this murky morning, were lost in the swirling clouds above.

By now the pouring rain had turned the job into a grim chore, pleasureless and

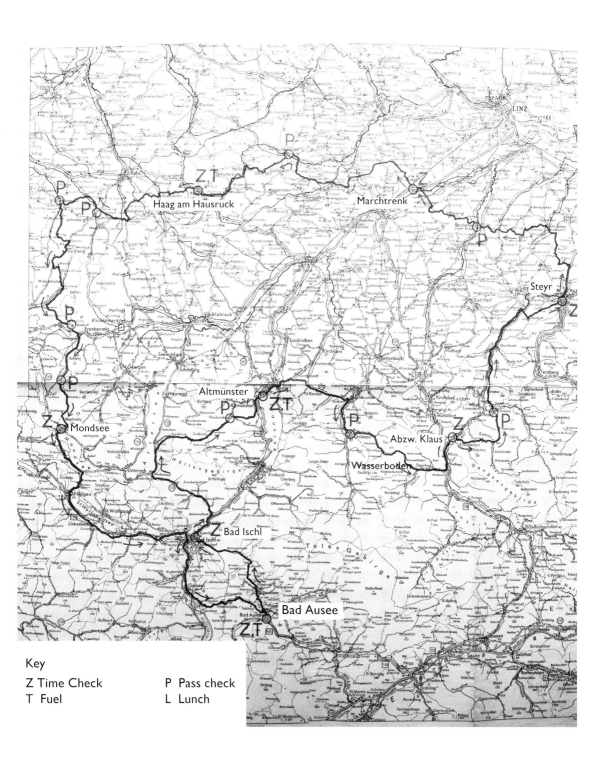

Key
Z Time Check
T Fuel
P Pass check
L Lunch

unrewarding. Altmunster came and went as did the small town of Gmunden, and a further 15 miles on, the town of Grunau, whilst heading slightly south for the Steyr Valley and the next checkpoint. But before most of us were to reach that check, we were destined to face a crisis of dramatic proportion which fate seemed to hurl at us like some final throw of the dice aimed at sorting the men from the boys. It happened in the vicinity of Wasserboden, and once again I cannot do better than quote from Cyril Quantrill's *Motor Cycling* report:-

> During the morning, amazing scenes were witnessed at Wasserboden near Frauenstein in the Steyr Valley. A rapidly deteriorating mud lane led through a foot-deep water splash and then snaked upwards over a greasy hillside with a gradient of 1 in 4. Beneath the grease was genuine Colmore Cup mud and the first arrivals began to fall off as soon as they attempted an ascent. Then the heavy German sidecars arrived to add to the congestion and when Bob Ray reached the hill it was blocked by the sidecars and a score of fallen solos in various stages of exhaustion. Bob Ray, after one abortive attempt, took to the grass bank and made a flat-out-in-second gear ascent. Other riders were quick to follow his example and soon the expanse of green meadow was being cut-up by spinning rear wheels. In the circumstances it is not surprising that many arrived late at the lunch check.

It was reported in one Austrian magazine that the two German sidecar drivers Kraus and Klankermeier actually fitted snow chains to their rear wheels in an effort to surmount the obstacle - but still to no avail.

Just prior to reaching this hill, not knowing what lay around the corner, Hugh Viney of the British Trophy team overtook me in the normal course of events. With riding number 233 and running on the higher speed schedule, he was due at that point at 9:56 am after two hours of riding. On the standard schedule I was due at that point at 10:00 am after 2 hours 15 minutes of riding. Thus we were both on schedule. We both turned off the main road in line astern onto this muddy track, round a bend and into the water splash swollen by the heavy rains of the week. Beyond the stream crossing was a quagmire of mud created by riders carrying the water up the bank as they emerged from the deep water. Still in line astern we rounded a bend and the sight which met my eyes I will never forget.

The narrow muddy track went straight up the hillside at an ever-increasing gradient and on both sides it was surrounded by steeply sloping grassy meadows. It looked like a great sports arena complete with terrace after terrace of seats and at the top fringed by a forest of conifer trees which divided the battlefield from the

Norman Vanhouse (209) having already passed the sidecar oufit in the distance, prepares to pass German rider Robert Poensgen (119) riding a 197 cc Tornax. Poensgen's start number was 45 minutes earlier and he finished the week with the loss of 93 marks. The nature of many of the forest tracks being liquid glutinous mud is clearly shown in this picture.

sky above. For the scene that met my eyes was indeed like a battlefield strewn with casualties.

All this was taken in like a flash. The track was choked with struggling and exhausted riders, solo men and sidecar crews, pushing and heaving in clouds of blue smoke. To get up by the track was out of the question. My instant reaction was to follow Hugh Viney. At that time there was no better trials rider in the world. He possessed a supreme and polished talent and the ability to secure grip which defied others. He too had seen in one quick glance that the track was out of question and as he shot up the bank to the right, I followed. But that was the last I saw of Hugh Viney on that hill, or indeed all that day. Having hit the grassy bank I was immediately beset with acute wheel spin and as I lost momentum I was forced to turn downhill to my left to regain lost momentum, find a gap among the stranded riders on the track, and dive up the left bank with the momentum thus gained - a type of tacking, or bank-to-bank technique often used with success in sporting trials.

The moment I hit the gradient square on, all forward progress ceased as violent wheelspin dug deeper and deeper until the bike rested on the low-slung silencers and the wheel spun helplessly. By dint of prodigious and strenuous physical effort I managed to haul the bike, an inch at a time, until my strength began to wane and I lost what little progress I had made, And as I weakened with the bike sliding backwards, the silencer outlets dug into the sodden turf and jammed solid with mud. With the bike resting on the silencers I got my screwdriver from the tank-top tool kit and laboriously poked mud from each silencer outlet, at the same time recovering a little from the physical exertion.

Whilst waging my private battle, I had been vaguely aware of willing spectators pushing both sidecar outfits and solo riders up the hill. This was outside assistance, the penalty for which was exclusion. Whatever happened, I had vowed to avoid such outside help. But as my physical reserves drained away my resolve weakened also. The top of the hill seemed as far away as ever and it appeared that on my own I wasn't going to make it. So having cleared the mud from the silencer ends I no longer resisted the assistance so freely offered, and with this outside help I once again made forward progress, rear wheel still spinning and both legs working hard to maintain the momentum gained. By then I was living in a world of my own. I was not really aware of other competitors. The bottom of the hill seemed a lifetime away. I was almost oblivious of things around me, and uncaring. Such were my bitter thoughts as the gradient eased and my struggles and exhaustion

Norman Vanhouse on the standard production BSA Star Twin (MOL 303 No.209) negotiating one of the many sections of glutinous mud resulting from the heavy rain and snow which plagued the 1952 ISDT in Austria causing many retirements as a result.

gradually grew less. With the time I must have lost, it had all come to nothing after all. Everything that had gone before had gone down the drain. That dreadful hill had ruined the lot. Heaven knows where Fred Rist and Brian Martin were. They must have had similar problems. But there was no sight of them. As I cleared the top of the hill and rode onto the firm track which curved off through wet, dripping trees with my composure returning and my thoughts less distraught, I glanced at the clock on the fork top, then checked the distance to the next control and the time due there on the route card, and couldn't believe my eyes. I could still do it! All was not lost after all. And it had been so chaotic on that hill, I reasoned with myself as once again I got cracking, that it would not be possible to know who had and who had not received outside assistance.

The reaction was sheer joy, rather like being reprieved no doubt, and even the weather no longer mattered. I arrived at the check with a few minutes in hand, as Fred and Brian had done before me. The rain continued to pour down as we headed for the lunch check at Steyr which was reached after the route had swung north at Molln, and for half-an-hour we re-fortified ourselves with hot drinks and sandwiches, recounted our different stories and noted the large number of competitors arriving very late, obviously as a direct result of the debacle at Wasserboden.

From the lunch break at Steyr, with the next check 28 miles away, the route ran through a never-ending series of narrow, winding lanes in a westerly direction through Dietachdorf, Hofkirchen, Neuhofen and Weisskirchen to the check at Marchtrenk. Together with the next stretch of 31 miles to the check at Haag am Hausruck, it proved an easy two hours of riding, which further helped me to recover from the traumatic experience of the morning. Then it was another 50 miles of narrow, twisting lanes and tracks to Mondsee, situated on the northern tip of the lake of that name which was grey and uninviting, as was the famous St.Wolfgangsee eight miles further on where the lake separated us from the picture-postcard St.Wolfgang and its renowned White Horse Inn. The route had already swung south at Mettmach and Bad Ischl which we had gone through on the outward leg in the morning, the day's route having completed a circle we had traversed in an anti-clockwise direction. From there it was but a few miles south to Bad Aussee to complete the day's run.

The end of that day really concluded the severe part of the event. We had covered 1,350 miles of mountain roads and passes, forest tracks, rivers, gullies, bogs and glutinous mud. Those who had survived that wet and testing ordeal had good cause to be happy and elated. We were as good as home and dry (although the latter seemed most unlikely). The one-hour speed test on the morrow, the final day, would be the climax, and success would depend largely on the mechanical health of one's machine. Really, for the only time that week, the rider would play a secondary role.

Although I was happy to finish the day without loss of marks along with Fred and Brian, thus retaining our clean sheet as a team, I had this niggling doubt in my mind. Even if the outside assistance I had received did not come to official notice and I collected a gold medal, my conscience would not be clear. I had defaulted. But this problem of conscience was solved for me when after long hours of deliberation which went on into the night, the International Jury elected to delete that section which included the ill-fated hill near Wasserboden. Those who had lost marks as a result of the massive delays encountered had them rescinded. My conscience was clear.

But it was another sorry day for Len Heath and his men. Left with top gear only on his 650cc Triumph, Jim Alves had given up the struggle, making our Trophy team two men light. This British misfortune, however, was of benefit to the Austrian Trophy team who moved up into second place. John Brittain of the Vase 'B' team also retired about 50 miles from the final check at Bad Aussee when his engine failed. It was rumoured that this engine failure was a direct result of using a thinner grade of oil to ease the starting on cold mornings at that high altitude.

Two German competitors had come unstuck during the day. One, the sidecar driver Ernst who hailed from Nuremburg, collided with a lorry and sustained injuries which forced his retirement, whereas compatriot Kramer carried on to the finish despite sustaining injuries when he collided with a horse and cart. Compared with the days that had gone before, the casualty rate was a modest seven retirements. This left a total of 161 competitors at the final check. One of these was unlucky next morning when his bike refused to start. So the final tally to face the starter on the last morning was 160.

Having clocked-in at 4:35 pm and sauntered to the little cafe, we indulged in two glasses of *apfelsaft* by way of celebrating. Even if the trial was not yet over, certainly the worst was behind us and the Star Twins remained as good as new.

XXVII. Internationale Sechstagefahrt

Start-Nr. 209

STANDARD-SCHNITT / STANDARD-SPEED / VITESSE DE BASE / VELOCITA STANDARD   **48**

MONTAG 22. IX. 1952   **5 Tag / Day / Jour / Tappa**

See-höhe m	ORT — PLACE		km Zwisch.	km Etappe	km Total	miles Zwisch.	miles Etappe	miles Total	Straßen Güte-grad	Straßen %	Standard Min.	Standard Std./Min.	Team Min.	Team Std./Min.	Notizen
659	**BAD AUSSEE**	Z,T	0.0												7·44
723	Alt Aussee		10.8			6.7	(15)								
902	W. H. Blaalm														
630	Rettenbach Alm														
469	**BAD ISCHL**	Z	13.4	24.2	24.2	8.3	15.0	15.0	III	+ 10	(33)	0.33	30	0.30	8·17
	Weißenbach am Attersee		18.5			11.5									
603	Forstamt		15.1			9.4	(25)								
	Neukirchen	P													9·13
439	**ALTMÜNSTER**	Z,T	11.3	44.9	69.1	7.0	27.9	42.9	II		(56)	1.29	50	1.20	
494	Gmunden		18.2			11.3									
	Scharnstein - Abzw. Mühldorf	P	6.6			4.1	(32)								
527	Grünau		11.4			7.0									
940	Wasserböden														
525	Steyrling														
	Abzw. Phyrnpaß														
	Bundesstraße		8.1			5.0									10·22
414	**ABZW. KLAUS / HERMANNSCHMIED**	Z	6.4	50.7	119.8	4.0	31.4	74.3	III	+ 10	(69)	2.38	62	2.22	
	Frauenstein														
	Ramsau														
444	Molln	P	14.4			9.?	(27)								
	Abzw. Haunoldmühle		8.2			5.1									
320	Pichlern		11.5			7.1									
307	**STEYR**	Z,L,T	8.3	42.4	162.2	5.2	26.4	100.7	II		(54)	3.21	48	3.10	11·15
310	Dietachdorf		16.0			10.?									11·45
340	Hofkirchen i. Traunk.	P	14.1			8.8	(28)								
592	Neuhofen a. d. Krems		10.3			6.4									
302	Weißkirchen														
304	**MARCHTRENK**	Z	4.1	44.5	206.7	2.6	27.8	128.5	II		(56)	4.27	50	4.00	12·41
356	Krenglbach		15.1			9.4									
335	Grieskirchen	P	15.6			9.7	(31)								1·43
504	**HAAG am Hausruck**	Z,T	19.0	49.7	256.4	11.8	30.9	159.4	II		(62)	5.29	56	4.56	
51?	Pattigham		14.9			9.2									
	Kemating	P													
463	Meltmach	P	16.6			10.?	(50)								
660	Stelzen		8.6			5.5									
570	Pöndorf	P	18.8			11.7									
655	Hasiau	P	10.4			6.5									3·23
493	**MONDSEE**	Z	10.4	79.7	336.1	6.5	49.5	208.9	II		(100)	7.09	90	6.26	
481	Scharfling		9.1			5.6									
	St. Gilgen		4.8			3.0									
54?	Strobl		11.8			7.3									
	Bad Ischl		11.7			7.?	(40)								
	Kaltenbach														
4?	Lauffen														
54?	St. Agatha														
101?	Pötschenhöhe		17.1			10.?									4·35
65?	**BAD AUSSEE**	Z,T	9.6	64.1	400.2	53.8	248.7		I	− 10	72		65	7.31	

Z = Zeitkontrolle / Time-Check / Contrôle Horaire / Controllo Orario

P = Passierkontrolle / Route-Check / Contrôle de Passage / Controllo a Timbro

T = Tankstelle / Replenishment / Ravitaillement / Rifornimento

L = Mittagessen / Lunch / Déjeuner / Colazione

Straßen / Roads / Routes / Strade		sehr gut	very good	trés bon	ottima
	I	sehr gut	very good	trés bon	ottima
	II	gut	good	bon	buone
	III	mittel	fair	médiocre	mediocre
	IV	schlecht	bad	mauvais	cattive

Day 5 Scorecard for Norman Vanhouse

The Sixth Day
A German Disaster

Waking that morning for this, the last day of what could be described as an epic ride, one was aware of that inner feeling of excitement and apprehension. It was butterflies in the stomach I suppose, for we were within an ace of the success we had not dared to think about too much, and which had always seemed a long way off and out of reach. Nevertheless, our mood was one of confidence, despite the weather, true to form, being wet and cold and cheerless.

With the first man away at 6:00 am and Fred Rist due to follow at 7:36 am, Brian Martin at 7:41 am and myself at 7:44 am, it was probably generally known by then that we were the sole surviving British team of any composition still un-penalised.

When Fred was admitted to the closed control at 7:21 am and collected his bike for the usual 15 minutes of maintenance, he pottered about the machine, checking this and checking that with his customary exuberance and self-confidence, like the true professional he was. He was a fine example - not only to Brian and I, but to all others. Whilst his Star Twin was plastered with five days of Austrian mud, its condition was still impeccable. There was not one dent or scratch to mar the elegance which lay beneath that covering of honourable mud. Once more and for the last time, at 7:44 am I came under starter's orders. The Star Twin purred into life as readily as ever, as both those of Fred and Brian had done minutes before. It was a phenomenon the lugubrious Len Heath must have viewed with envious disbelief as he surveyed the remnants of his tattered force that morning. Of the British Trophy team only Hugh Viney, Bob Ray and Jack Stocker remained. Ted Usher was the sole survivor of the Vase 'A' team. David Tye the sole survivor of the Vase 'B' team.

With just 77 miles to go for the speed test at Salzburg, the route ran due west from Bad Aussee, heading for the first check at Scheffau some 37 miles away, round the northern tip of the Hallstatter See and along its west shore for a few miles, before diving west again. Although narrow and winding all the way to Salzburg, the metalled roads, graded two on the route card, were little more than a warm-up for the speed test to follow; almost a parade of the week's survivors. Going through the villages of Golling, Sankt Koloman and Hallein, the mountain road was dwarfed by mighty peaks thrusting skywards to 8,000 feet and more, the self-same mountain country which had protected Hitler's retreat at Berchtesgaden, a short

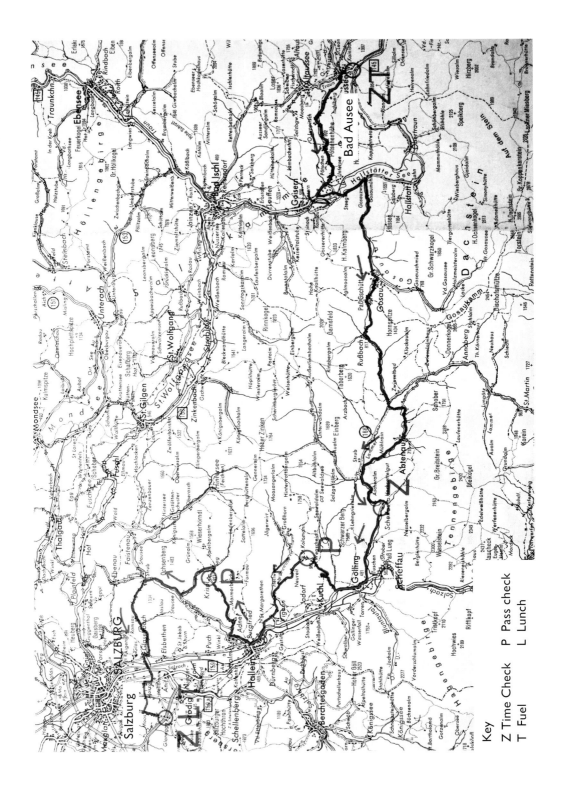

Key

Z Time Check   P Pass check
T Fuel   L Lunch

distance away. At Stause the route veered south-west to avoid the music festival city of Salzburg, then headed for Kreuzung and the Moosstrasse autobahn, which was closed off for the speed test scheduled to start later that morning.

Due to clock-in at 10:19, I arrived with time to spare as both Fred and Brian had done, and as had been the case at the end of each day's run, the machines went into a closed-control area until 15 minutes before we would be called upon to complete one, conducted lap of the 3.48 mile circuit. The plan of this closed circuit resembled a sardine tin key, with two parallel straights of autobahn connected at one end by a hairpin bend. At the other end, running in an anti-clockwise direction, it ran up a sloping access road, turning left over the top of the autobahn, then left downhill and along the reverse lane of the straight and back to the hairpin. This was rigged by marking an access gap with straw bales, with the surface of the access gap consisting of good old-fashioned stone-sets.

With over an hour to play with, the scene was not unlike the start of any Continental Grand Prix. Everybody had converged there. All the Trade back-up vehicles and personnel had congregated together with team managers, trade representatives, club and FIM officials. Banners and buntings added colour and atmosphere to that cold but dry setting, for although low rain clouds threatened from above, it had dried up since we left Bad Aussee. At 11:30 am we were given access to our bikes once more, which allowed us the usual 15 minutes for final adjustments before setting off on the conducted lap.

In our case, other than a final check of nuts and bolts, we replaced the original set of spark plugs with a harder set, keeping the originals to go back in after the test. At 11:45 am the whole entry jostled for places as the official car took us round for that one lap of familiarisation. Having done that, once again, we three on the Star Twins had a long time to wait, since the entry was split into various groups. The first group consisted of smaller capacity models up to 250cc, with the distance to be covered in the hour depending upon the engine size, so the smaller 75cc models were faced with 34.80 miles in the hour, and the 250cc models required to cover 52.50 miles.

The next group was made up of 350cc solos and over. Next to run were the sidecar class, and finally a group comprising all the teams which had tied on performance in their respective classes. This last group would thus 'race' each other in order to resolve the tie. We were to take our place in the latter group. Out of a grand total of 66 teams of various types which had started the trial on the previous Thursday, there were just five teams tying on performance - all with no marks lost. These were three club teams from Germany, one club from Sweden and one British club team - ourselves. The winning team would be the one to improve on the set average for the capacity class by the greatest margin. With the Maudes Trophy as our main objective and not the club team award, we had no intention of going out there to 'race'. We would be required to cover 62.64 miles in the hour, and that is what we would aim at. No more.

Having completed the one conducted lap, we returned to the pit area to pass away the time whilst the other groups did their stuff. Then, suddenly, like a bolt from the blue, it was panic stations. Brian Martin's petrol tank was leaking, and quite badly. This would not have been the first retirement of the week brought about by petrol tank failure. Now one of the Star Twins was in severe trouble. We were still under FIM *parc fermé* rules - there was no time or allowance for repairs. Brian Martin could be eliminated at this late stage! Bert Perrigo shot into action. Firstly he supplied some liquid solder to be applied to the offending leak, then he recruited the help of the Major in charge of the British army back-up group, and it was arranged to have petrol available on his Jeep to be driven to any point around the outside of the circuit should Brian's tank run dry during the hour's high speed test. A constant watch would be set-up from the moment he got underway. This was high drama and threatened Brian's gold medal hopes, the BSA team's clean sheet, and with it the whole Maudes Trophy attempt. Remember the test objective was to enter and complete the ISDT, and then ride the machines back home afterwards.

Nothing else could be done apart from top-up Brian's $3^1/_2$ gallon tank immediately prior to starting the one-hour stint. In the meantime, all we could do was try to relax and watch the other groups complete their hour. One of the first riders forced to a standstill in the lightweight group was British rider M.G. Shepard who, though stopping to change a spark plug, nevertheless continued and completed the whole trial on his 125cc BSA Bantam. Although not gaining an award, his was a fine performance completing that sort of week on such a basic lightweight machine. Another lightweight man in trouble was Karl Devoty of Austria who, with grim determination, completed the whole hour with the broken right hand side of the handlebar of his Puch jammed between his thigh and the petrol tank in a way which enabled him to operate the twist-grip. Italian rider Pasolini came off his Aermacchi and required medical treatment, and Swedish rider Gosta Nyberg with a 244cc N.V. completed the whole hour with broken front forks and went on to qualify for a gold medal.

Although there were no teams in the lightweight group 'racing' to gain time on the scheduled speed, nonetheless most of the riders assisted the performance of their small machines by adopting a prone riding position to reduce the frontal area by flattening themselves along the top of the tank, saddle and pillion seat, with legs trailing behind like boys on toboggans charging down frozen slopes. The Czechoslovakia Trophy team scorned such exhibitionism, riding round in close formation with a display of unpretentious and purposeful style. There was no need to risk blowing up their CZ and Jawa models: they were all set to collect the International Trophy that evening.

Although the British Trophy and Vase teams had suffered more than their fair share of problems and disappointments during the week in the mountains, their riding standard and technique became a major talking point of the event, and a great deal of praise and admiration was voiced and written about their superb style.

Bob Ray in particular, with his Ariel twin, many times had electrified and stunned the spectators with his aggressive style - fast, feet-up and faultless. Before the week was out, many Continental riders - including the Czechs - tried adopting the 'English way' as they termed it. It was probably one of the early post-war opportunities that European riders had of seeing how expert British riders scorned steep muddy hills. Although every single rider in our national teams that year was a supreme artist, among the best ever produced by this country, Bob Ray in particular came in for unstinting admiration. Whilst his flat out in 2nd and flat out in 3rd with feet on footrests technique was well known in Britain, it came in for a great deal of comment in Austria because he was the first of the British superstars to hit the scene and at times he left the spectators gasping with admiration.

Ironic then, even tragic, that whilst our riders covered themselves in glory with individual ability, team-wise the results were a dismal failure.

After the lightweight machines had finished their one hour stint, it was the turn of all solo machines of 350cc capacity and over, which therefore included most of the British competitors with the exception of ourselves. It also included the German Vase team of George Meir, Walter Zeller and Hans Roth on those indomitable-seeming BMWs, up to that point the only un-penalised national team in the entire entry. Surely the Vase was theirs. Nothing could stop them it seemed. But it was not to be. As the whole pack of large-capacity machines got underway with the BMWs of Meier and Zeller zooming off with that beautiful throaty roar, sounding as healthy as ever, that of fellow teamster Hans Roth stayed silent. As the pack of riders disappeared and the noise died away in the distance, a dramatic silence seemed to envelop that one lonely figure still pumping away, with long regular swings on the transverse kickstarter crank of his recalcitrant BMW. He swung that starter crank without stop until he could swing no more; until dripping with perspiration and completely exhausted, he was forced to concede defeat. The BMW had given up the ghost. It was a traumatic scene to witness. The Vase had slipped through the fingers of the German team at the eleventh hour, after a commanding performance throughout the week. Later reports indicated that the valves of the BMW had burnt out.

David Tye, the lone British Vase 'B' team survivor and BSA factory team man also caused a minor stir when he overdid things on the cobbled-surface hairpin on one lap and fell off. Fortunately he did no damage and remounted to complete the trial and collect a gold medal. Mollie Briggs, frequently referred to in the Austrian press as 'that English Amazon', survived the rigours of the week, and whilst without reward, completed the speed test and the event, to the delight of those who saw her riding the 500cc Triumph with professional neatness and determination. She too contributed to the prestige of the British riders in the event.

Witnessing the disaster befall the, until now, dominant German national team did little to calm BSA nerves. Brian's leaking tank was a huge concern. Still overcast but with the rain continuing to hold off, our turn eventually came as we lined up with the other four club teams who had retained clean sheets throughout the week. This was an exclusive squad of fifteen riders who between them had not lost a single mark, and who would now be striving to gain a time advantage to determine the destination of the club team award. With Brian Martin's petrol tank topped-up at the last moment, we were off. It had been arranged for Bert Perrigo to give us the thumbs-up signal when we were lapping at the required time of approximately three minutes per circuit, which would give us 62 miles in the hour – rather slower than George Meier and Walter Zeller who, in the previous group, had completed their quickest laps at 78 mph for the sheer fun of it.

With the Maudes Trophy our main objective, it would have been madness to have attempted any speed higher speed than was necessary; nevertheless, we were the fastest three on the circuit in that group, trailing each other line astern, lap after lap, overtaking the smaller capacity bikes in the group running on a lower speed schedule. Each lap the figure of Bert Perrigo emerged from the crowd of spectators bordering the course with the desired thumbs-up signal. Suddenly, when about half-way through the session in the wake of Fred Rist with Brian Martin bringing up the rear, one of the cylinders on my Star Twin cut out. In less time than it takes to tell, I had leaned over to find one plug lead adrift, snapped it back into position and resumed position at the rear of the trio. And thus we circulated until the 18 laps required had been completed and we were flagged off. Towards

The ISDT Sixth Day.
From the left, (77) Gotleib Haas, Germany, 175 Maico; (209) Norman Vanhouse, BSA; (71) Karl Ludwig Westphal, Germany, 173 Maico; (202) Brian Martin, BSA; (180) Otto Sonsburg, Germany, 250 DKW; all rounding the circuit hairpin during the Speed Test. Minimal crowd control in 1952!

the end of the session Brian had to turn the petrol tap to the reserve position. As he came to a standstill at the finish and took a quick look in the tank, it was seen to be bone dry. He would not have managed one more lap. The distance covered during this final speed test, even taking into account the larger rear sprocket, would have needed no more than 1½ gallons of fuel. Although benefiting from Perrigo's liquid solder, the remaining 2 gallons had been lost during the test, liberally covering the machine and rider. Rather more petrol than had actually passed through the Amal carburettor itself. Good fortune had smiled during this final test!

Then it was noticed that my petrol tank was also seeping petrol, but much less so than Brian's had been before the application of liquid solder. This leak had developed during the speed test, and could be attributed to the higher engine speed I had used in each gear before changing up in order to maintain the same speed as Fred Rist. It must be recalled, however, that the very rough nature of the course in the Austrian

Success written on faces. Brian Martin, Norman Vanhouse and Fred Rist. A picture taken immediately after completion of the ISDT - on production machines and the only British team to lose no marks throughout the week.

Alps had given rise to a great many petrol tank failures during the week. If I had changed-up, say 500 rpm sooner with each gear change during the speed test, and avoided the high-frequency vibration, I feel sure the tank would have been fine. For the same reason I had lost the primary chaincase filler cap.

Of the five club teams without penalty, the three German teams finished one, two, three; having increased on their schedule speed by the greatest margin. The Swedish team was fourth and we were last. The Württemberg team came out as victors with a margin of 22 seconds over the second placed German team of Südbayern 'A', with the same club's 'B' team in third place. It is significant that the smaller capacity models found it much easier to gain on their schedule speed on that flat type of circuit than bigger models with a higher speed. With our three Star Twins we gained a total of 9 minutes, 3 seconds on our set time - an average of 3 minutes, 1 second per rider. The winning German team on small capacity models

A brief moment to relax in the evening sunshine but once again under the ACU Observer's eagle eye. The ISDT finished and the Star Twins now looking somewhat more than two weeks old - ISDT number plates still in place. The next day was to see the start of the European and Scandinavian run of the Maudes test. Left to right, Fred Rist, Brian Martin, John McNulty (ACU Observer), Norman Vanhouse.

saved no less than 30 minutes, 39 seconds - an average of 10 minutes, 13 second per rider. It is thus fairly certain that had we elected to go for the club team award it would have been futile with the tie-breaker based upon that formula.

But all that was of no consequence. It was immaterial. We had done it. We had completed a few miles short of 1,500 on one of the toughest International Six Days of recent years: an event severe enough to claim the retirement of no less than 102 of the 260 who had faced the starter on the first morning. Of the 158 who finished the course, 84 qualified for gold medals. Of this total, only 17 golds went to British riders, and of these, great credit must go to Don Evans of Worcester who took over the Jeff Smith factory Norton at short notice when Jeff was prevented from starting. One of the most meritoriously-earned gold medals of the British contingent was undoubtedly that of S.E. 'Buster' Cunningham who without any support at all as a private entry, survived the daily grind on his 500cc AJS single with unspectacular persistence. He was the sole private British civilian rider to win a gold medal that year.

The British Army contingent had also come out with much credit, with gold medals going to Captain Eddie Dow, Captain David Miles and Sergeant R.A. Rhodes. With a loss of 10 marks Captain D.C. Osmond collected a silver medal and the remaining Army finishers, Sergeant Rowthron and Fusilier Nield, both collected Bronze medals. *(The full results are shown in Appendix 1, p182)*

Back to Bad Aussee we went, by the straightforward, main-road route at a speed to suit our mood and not the dictates of a route card and the relentless demands of a clock. That evening we attended the formal presentation of trophies which took place in the Civic Hall, complete with the town band and local civic leaders all on the stage, together with officials of the organising club and members of the FIM International Jury. There were the usual speeches, the main ones being those of Doctor Manfred Mautner-Markhof, president of the *Österreichische Automobil, Motorrad und Touring Club*, the Austrian national body who carried out the organisation of the trial, and by the steward of the FIM Herr Michel Tavernier, who thanked everybody connected with the event and congratulated Czechoslovakia on their double victory, for in addition to the trophy win, the German debacle at the speed test had also given them victory in the Vase contest.

Needless to say it was a very happy evening. National parties were grouped together and identified by their national flag. The wine and beer flowed, and even those with less to celebrate warmed to the atmosphere and enjoyed the occasion. As the only British team of any composition to retain a clean sheet, I suppose we three should have been the happiest Brits in the room that night. We had good reason to be, but it was rather sobering to reflect that our job was only two thirds done. Next day, Wednesday, would see us back in harness on three Star Twins which had already made motorcycling history. The full extent of our accomplishment could only be measured by events which lay in the future. And we had no way of knowing, or even guessing, that what we had just completed would never again be repeated.

Not by a British manufacturer for sure.

And probably not by any other motorcycle manufacturer either.

XXVII. Internationale Sechstagefahrt

DIENSTAG 23. IX. 1952

6 Tag / Day / Jour / Tappa

Start-Nr. 209

STANDARD-SCHNITT
STANDARD-SPEED
VITESSE DE BASE
VELOCITA
STANDARD

48

See-höhe m	ORT — PLACE		km Zwisch.	km Etappe	km Total	miles Zwisch.	miles Etappe	miles Total	Straßen Güte-grad	Straßen %	Zeit — Time Standard Min.	Zeit — Time Standard Std./Min.	Zeit — Time Team Min.	Zeit — Time Team Std./Min.	Notizen
659	**BAD AUSSEE**	Z,T	0.0												7·44
1012	Pötschenhöhe		9.6			6.0	③⑦								
	St. Agatha														
509	Gosauzwang		11.5			7.1									
964	Paß Gschütt		12.3			7.6									
715	Abtenau		15.0			9.3									
488	**SCHEFFAU**	Z	10.1	58.5	58.5	6.3	36.3	36.3	II		⑦③	1.13	66	1.06	8·57
481	Golling														
851	St. Koloman	P	16.7			10.4									
	Neureit														
468	Vigaun														
469	Hallein		11.6			7.2									
482	Adnet														
927	Krispel	P	9.8			6.0	④①								
710	W. H. Sag														
	Stausee														
450	Glasenbach		18.4			11.4									
435	Hellbrunn														
433	Morzg														
442	**KREUZUNG**	Z,T,L													10·19
	Moosstraße-Autobahn		9.0	65.3	123.8	5.6	40.6	76.9	II		⑧②	2.35	74	2.20	

Z = Zeitkontrolle / Time-Check / Contrôle Horaire / Controllo Orario

P = Passierkontrolle / Route-Check / Contrôle de Passage / Controllo a Timbro

T = Tankstelle / Replenishment / Ravitaillement / Rifornimento

L = Mittagessen / Lunch / Déjeuner / Colazione

Straßen / Roads / Routes / Strade		
I	sehr gut	very good	trés bon	ottima
II	gut	good	bon	buone
III	mittel	fair	médiocre	mediocre
IV	schlecht	bad	mauvais	cattive

Day 6 Scorecard, Norman's final Scorecard with no points!

us schwedische Beiwagengespann Thörnblom auf BMW 500 (103) beim Be-
ingen des Geländestückes der „Kaiserau".
ser Walter Krammer mit seinem Mitfahrer auf Puch 250 (6). Am Wege rechts
nipuliert der Italiener Strada an seiner Rumi (40).
ranschaulicht uns das schwierige Geländestück bei der Auffahrt nach Maria-
aitschach, Keitel und sein Beifahrer helfen der Zündapp 600 durch Schieben
ch (115). Die Aufnahme vermittelt eindrucksvoll die großen Strapazen, die
Mensch und Maschine bei dieser Prüfung gestellt wurden.
g das Gelände des englischen Truppenübungsplatzes auf der „Schmelz"
gen Obdach, gerade beim Passieren von drei Teilnehmern. Man sieht auf
r Aufnahme, bis zu welcher Höhe es in der Nacht zum dritten Fahrtag
schneit hatte.

*Forest tracks in the snow at the 1952 Austrian
ISDT (from Auto Touring October 1952,
reproduced by courtesy of OEAMTC)*

Wie in der Beschreibung des 4. Tages vermerkt, handelt es sich bei nachfolgenden Aufnahmen um den erwähnten Steg, welcher als Provisorium über die Wasserrast gelegt wurde. Die Bilder zeigen sehr deutlich, in welchem Zustande dieser Wegbehelf von den Teilnehmern angetroffen wurde und auf welche Art der einzelne Fahrer über dieses Hindernis hinwegzukommen versuchte.

1 Der Holländer van Wees auf CZ 150 im „Kreisverkehr". 2 zeigt den Schweden Ring auf einer BMW 500, wie er auf seine Art das Hindernis umfährt.

Bild 3 und 4 stellen ein und denselben Fahrer dar. Links wie er vor der Rast stürzt, und rechts, wie er die Maschine aufzurichten versucht.

Conditions were tough at the 1952 Austrian ISDT! (from Auto Touring October 1952, reproduced by courtesy of OEAMTC)

Up To Scandinavia

End to End in Germany

With the conclusion of the ISDT, the three Star Twins once again came under the control of John McNulty, the ACU observer, and he resumed his authority from the moment the trial finished at the end of the one-hour speed test. As has already been made clear, during the run-out from Birmingham until the bikes were handed over to the officials of the trial, the machines had been in the lock-up every night with the garage doors sealed. The same conditions applied during the trial, for each night they were parked in the closed-control which was not acc essible to us. From the moment we arrived back at Bad Aussee from Salzburg and the speed test, the three models went into a private lock-up garage and the doors were sealed. So whatever work was needed to be done on any machine, it would be done under observation and recorded - and used in evidence.

Next day, Wednesday, along with all the other competitors packing their bags and leaving for their homes in all quarters of Europe, we prepared to leave Bad Aussee

Bad Aussee, Austria. The 1952 ISDT completed. Three Gold Medals won. The only British team to lose no marks. The trio now start the long ride to Oslo in Norway to complete the Maudes Trophy adventure. A crowd gathers to watch their departure. From the left are: Fred Rist, Brian Martin, Norman Vanhouse.

as soon as possible. But first there was work to be done. Enquiries produced the information that there was a welding specialist in the town who was quite willing to have a go at repairing Brian Martin's petrol tank. It was decided to get him to treat my tank at the same time. Although a minor seep, unless dealt with then, almost certainly it would get worse during the following days. So it was a case of all hands on deck removing both tanks, draining petrol and swilling out with water. When repaired all traces of water had to be removed before re-filling.

The missing primary chaincase cap was replaced on my Star Twin together with the rear light bulb, and a frayed rear light cable on Brian's bike was also replaced. The hard grade spark plugs fitted for the speed test were replaced with the original plugs on all three bikes. And that was the sum total of battle damage inflicted by the abuse to which those standard motorcycles had been subjected over 1,456 punishing ISDT miles. It was a remarkable performance by any standard.

If George Savage's Austin A70 car had been well-loaded on the outward trip, then that of Bert Perrigo, as we left Bad Aussee to head for Germany on the final phase of the test, was even more so. In addition to John McNulty, who always occupied the front passenger seat in the interests of a clear view, there was Bert's wife Cherry and the official photographer Alan Blowry who had flown out from England and joined us in time for the start of the ISDT. Four adults in the car, plus the luggage of seven people - it was going to be quite a trip for the A70!

During the six days of the trial the enemy had been a combination of the natural alpine environment, plus the unforgiving elements activated by the remorseless hands of the clock. From now on, time alone would be the enemy. With the Maudes Trophy as the objective, any ACU-observed test to be eligible for this prestigious award needed to be completed by the 30th September in any given year. With our departure date from Bad Aussee being September 24th and the stated destination of the observed test being Oslo, we had only six days at our disposal. Failure to reach Oslo by the 30th would mean defeat. This final phase then, if anything would be more finely balanced. Arrival at Oslo was actually fixed for Monday 29th September, so having devoted time to petrol tank repairs before starting out, we had just five and a half days in which to cross Germany from end to end, and get through Denmark, Sweden and Norway. There was no margin for delay of any description.

From then on it was a case of 'into wind' as Bert Perrigo so aptly put it, leaving behind Bad Aussee for the last time, then bathed in warm sunshine, and heading for Salzburg and the Munich autobahn. Having left Austrian soil behind, the scene of so many triumphs and disasters, and reached the autobahn, we began our long trek north in that buoyant frame of mind which comes with success. The Star Twins were going better than ever; like oiled silk, swift and sure; smooth and responsive like living things in tune with our mood. With the sun to our left, we aimed for Munich with the needles of the speedometers hovering around the seventy mark with the green A70 bringing up the rear, hour after hour with the six exhaust pipes producing a turbine-like hum of musical quality.

Munich, the home of BMW, where no doubt at that very moment as we passed on our triumphant way there must have been long faces already conducting a post-mortem of the failure of Hans Roth's machine the day before, disappeared in our wake, as we aimed for Stuttgart and our stop for the night. Augsburg came and went and finally we turned off the autobahn and headed for our hotel, having completed 292 miles since leaving Bad Aussee, despite the delayed start.

Thursday morning dawned wet and raining and after a good breakfast, we climbed into our riding gear, withdrew the Star Twins from John McNulty's nightly 'quarantine' and again headed for the autobahn a short distance from the hotel. After a few miles to give the Twins time to warm to their task, it was back to the effortless cruising speed of 70 mph, heading for the Rhineland of Germany. As the day grew longer, names associated with the industrial might of modern Germany marked our progress like key milestones – Karlsruhe, Ludwigshafen, Darmstadt and Frankfurt. To by-pass such industrial areas without hindrance or loss of time was a luxury at that time not enjoyed in the United Kingdom. That, perhaps, was the one good thing Hitler did, when he initiated the programme of motorway construction which made such progress as we were then making, not only possible, but pleasurable as well. Without the autobahn our crossing of Germany would have taken much longer, and no doubt also proved tedious.

With motorway travel now an everyday thing for all who use motor vehicles, it is regarded by many as a boring method of covering ground, but in that situation, despite the rain, it was a wonderful relaxation in contrast to the riding we had been doing during the ISDT, where maximum concentration had been required every yard of the way; where every bend could conceal pitfalls and dangers. Here on the autobahn, it was almost like riding by instinct, knowing what the riders in front would do, whilst one's thoughts were allowed to range at will, almost oblivious to the wet world around us. It was proving to be the easiest part of the whole trip.

The day's destination was Düsseldorf where we were to be met by Albert Thomm, the BSA dealers in Erkrather Strasser, who had also arranged our accommodation for the night. So having passed Cologne on our left, we turned off the autobahn and

Right. Norman Vanhouse and Brian Martin check odometers during a refueling stop during the post-ISDT section of the test.

Below. Team leader Fred Rist lightens proceedings during the refueling stop. Brian Martin on MOL 302.

headed for the centre of that bustling and busy town situated on the river Rhine. After our stay in the Alpine world of Austria with its idyllic villages scattered among the lush valleys and on the slopes of mighty mountains, Dusseldorf came as a rude reminder of the industrial and commercial realities of the modern world to which we belonged. It was the usual pleasant evening, with our hosts making every effort to make our short stay a happy one.

Next day, Friday 26th September, was destined to be the highest daily mileage of the whole trip, with Flensburg, over 400 miles north at the German-Danish

The team are about to set out on one of the days of German riding. The machines are looking less pristine than when they left the factory. Left to right, Fred Rist, Norman Vanhouse, Brian Martin.

frontier, as our destination. That it was again wet and raining almost goes without saying; indeed, in his report that day, John McNulty described it as very wet. But by then our spirits were immune from such trivia as a spot of bad weather; by then we were spurred by that light which had at first appeared as a small speck at the end of a long dark tunnel, and that now loomed large and bright.

Having bid farewell to our German hosts at Dusseldorf, we headed north for Essen but we rejoined the autobahn before reaching that town - a place I had last seen in 1945 when it was a desolate wasteland of rubble still 'housing' people who had survived the wholesale destruction. With the engines warmed-up, it was again full-steam ahead, hour after hour at a steady 70 mph, which the engines despite the lower-than-standard top gear, seemed to revel in. Across the sweeping wolds of Westfalia with the vast vistas of forest land stretching to distant horizons, we pressed on past Gelsenkirchen, Dortmund, Hamm and Bielefeld and the area including Herford, Bad Oeynhausen and Bad Salzuflen, familiar to me as a result of my war days with the 21st Army Group Headquarters stationed in that locality.

It was pleasant indeed in that area of Germany, and with the rain having stopped and the needs of the inner man becoming apparent, we pulled off the autobahn at a convenient point and indulged in a wayside picnic with food supplied by the hotel we had left that morning. But it had to be a quick one. Although making good time there was still a long way to go, so without wasting any time, it was a case of getting back on the autobahn and making full-steam for Hannover and Hamburg. The sunshine again disappeared and by the time we reached Hamburg and the end of the autobahn network, the rain was back with us, and as we headed across Holstein for Neumünster and Kiel, it got steadily worse.

With the day's mileage in excess of 300 at that point, and as the rain fell steadily harder, I think it began to have an effect on our resilience. Enough is enough. There seemed no end to it. Surely the rain had to stop sometime? But it did not. Later that evening as we ran through the streets of Flensburg, having travelled through Eckernförde and Schleswig in a mood of dreary indifference with all our earlier enthusiasm having long since disappeared, the rain descended in violent torrents with the roads awash. Policemen on traffic point duty wore great ankle-length waterproof coats, as similarly attired pedestrians splashed their way about like ducks on a village pond. It was awful.

We had covered 413 miles since leaving Dusseldorf that morning, and crossed the 1,000 miles of Germany in just two and a half days. A tribute to the autobahn network, and to the Star Twins at a time when they had already completed around 4,000 miles. It was virtually a final test of 1,000 miles at a speed of 70 mph. Remember also that we were pulling the low, sidecar ratio top gear. This did bring its effects, for once again there was a slight leak just beyond the weld on Brian Martin's fuel tank which would require treatment when possible.

It seemed a very wet world that evening, but as always, once inside that warm and welcoming hotel with its aroma of good food percolating the friendly atmosphere, our spirits bounded back. By the time we had enjoyed a good meal, and chatted over the events of the day (for the first and only time left to our own devices) we could have done it all over again – almost!

Into Scandinavia

Whilst the heavy downpour of the evening before had subsided during the night, when Saturday September 27th dawned it had actually stopped. By the time we had dressed for the road again, with a good breakfast inside us, and with the roads only wet, our prospects did not look bad at all. It is true that once underway with but a few miles of the day covered, the rain was with us yet again – but innocuous and inoffensive by recent standards. The day's mileage too would be less than half of yesterday's total, with Copenhagen the destination a mere 186 road miles away. The day promised to be about as demanding as a garden party on a fine summer's day.

Just beyond Flensburg we passed out of Germany, through the Customs barrier and into Denmark where we headed due north for Aabenraa, and Kolding where the road turns abruptly east and over the narrow straights which separates the mainland from Fyn. From there it was on to Nyborg where we were due to catch the ferry across the narrow stretch of sea known as the Store Belt which separates Fyn from the main island of Sjaelland. Having caught the ferry, we relaxed for a time, breathing the sea breezes blowing down from Kattegat which is protected from the North Sea itself by that long strip of mainland Denmark, like some huge breakwater jutting out into the ocean. After the short relaxing ferry crossing, it was back into Barbour suits ready for the landing at Korsør and the next leg to Copenhagen.

As we went ashore, much to our delight, we received a very warm welcome by a reception committee organised by the Danish BSA distributor and headed by the principal himself, Mr. H. V. Hansen; he was also accompanied by his son who, at that time, was completing his national service in the Danish army and was thus dressed in khaki. The welcome they gave us was warm and friendly. They spoke excellent English and there was much laughter and humorous banter. This, to our party, was the front door to Scandinavia and the welcome we received at that front door left a deep and lasting impression of sincere friendship. The atmosphere of courtesy and cordiality created at that time, prevailed from then on all the way to Oslo. The attitude of our hosts was partly motivated by a business responsibility. But their interpretation of that responsibility came from the heart. It was sincere and genuine. They were wonderful people. They made the last chapter of our epic ride all the more memorable.

We were guided and escorted from there to our hotel in Copenhagen and the conclusion of yet another trouble-free day's run. As far as our hosts were concerned, the day was yet young and they had no intention of wasting the hours that remained. Having spent a happy time with them getting to know more about unfamiliar Scandinavian seafood dishes, the younger Mr. Hansen insisted on showing off the delights of the nightspots of his native city which, like most late night drinking places the world over on a Saturday night, did not seem unduly short of customers with the means of keeping them in business. Certainly our host did his best. How many places we patronised that night I can no longer be sure. I don't even think I was sure at the time. What time we got back to our hotel is another point which is very vague. But I can remember climbing out of the taxi which dropped us off outside our hotel. It had been rather a splendid night. Rather on a par with that one at the Cafe Veska, back in Bad Aussee, a lifetime ago.

By Copenhagen our mileage had topped 4,500. The whole operation thus far had been remarkably successful. It is true it wasn't quite over. Almost over, nonetheless, bar the shouting. So a little celebrating on that Saturday night seemed harmless enough. Next morning, having said goodbye to our very good Danish friends, and gone aboard the ferryboat for the hour's trip from Copenhagen to Malmo in Sweden, it was rather a different story. I had already abstained from breakfast and as the boat ploughed through the swell of that narrow strip of green-coloured sea known as The Sound, I was forced to the conclusion that the degree of celebration which had seemed so harmless was in reality self-inflicted punishment. Never again, I vowed.

By the time the boat edged its way slowly towards the landing stage at Malmo, with that green sea left behind, colour began to return and with the Barbour suit once more at the ready I felt capable of climbing aboard the Star Twin for the very last lap. The weather, believe it or not, was fine, and there on the quayside was another Copenhagen-like welcome, this time laid-on by Mr. A.B.E. Fleron, the BSA Swedish distributor supported by a veritable entourage of hospitable companions. Whilst we had 196 miles to cover that day in order to reach Gothenburg, time no longer seemed to be against us and we felt quite happy to dally and enjoy the hospitality provided, including a rather splendid lunch of various Scandinavian dishes. My rapid recovery, fortunately, permitted me to do lunch full justice.

When we drifted from the hotel to Bert Perrigo's car to once again don our riding gear, the public square in which the hotel was situated seemed full of people and motorcyclists and we had to struggle through the crowds to reach the bikes. As a result of our success in the ISDT, Mr. Fleron had done a good local public relations job, and the centre of attraction was, in fact, us and our three Star Twins. A squad of riders from the local motorcycle club had also been organised, and with a one-time Olympic sprinting champion leading the way mounted on an immaculate Sunbeam S7, we were escorted on a guided circuit of the city. It was all rather fun, made more so by the warm sunshine.

All good things have to come to an end, and rather reluctantly we bade our farewell to our friends, and with the Sunbeam S7 rider escorting us as far as the outskirts of the city, we left Malmo behind, heading north for Gothenburg. On dry roads with a clear sky above, and the well-loaded Austin A70 bringing up the rear as faithful and reliable as the silver Star Twins which set the pace, the miles slipped away with effortless ease. Driving on the more familiar left hand side of the road as at home, the fifty miles came up on the milometer. Then 100 miles was reached, having motored through Ängelholm, Laholm, Halmstad and Falkenberg, with the waters of Kattegat fusing with the clear sky of the horizon far away on our left hand side. With 150 miles coming up on the dial, through Varberg and on to Kungsbacka, then with a few miles short of 200 since leaving Malmo, we entered the outskirts of Gothenburg where we were to stay the night.

That evening we were entertained to dinner by the area BSA dealer who had booked a table at a very exclusive restaurant, complete with orchestra which played soft music whilst the clientele dined, supped wine and mellowed to the atmosphere. When it became known to the orchestra leader that there was a party from England dining there, he gently switched to familiar British tunes, and before the night was out we had responded by singing the words of those we knew. It goes without saying that, by special request, we had to oblige with the most famous chorus of all, 'Tipperary'.

And then it was time to rest. It had been a lovely evening, thanks to the hospitality of the warm-hearted people who live in those cold climates of Scandinavia. Tomorrow we faced the last day of our marathon. There remained 210 miles between us and the total success which was surely ours. It is true that slips between cup and the lip have been known and with just two days left in which to qualify this test for recognition in 1952, such a thing could happen to us. But we knew it wouldn't. By then our confidence in the Star Twins was supreme. The confidence in our own abilities, likewise, had been reinforced by success.

Monday morning in Gothenburg presented the opportunity to get a little more welding done on Brian Martin's petrol tank, so after a relaxing breakfast, a couple of hours were devoted to that job. When it was completed and with no other work needed on the Twins, we donned the riding gear, packed the car, kicked the machines into life, settling them into their usual sure steady tick-over,

Travelling through Scandinavia, and another day starts with a group of interested spectators. Norman Vanhouse, (left) with Brian Martin (centre), and Fred Rist. The ever-present ACU Observer John McNulty is behind Brian Martin's right shoulder. Vanhouse and Rist have retained their ISDT number badges on their Barbour jackets. Note also that despite the accumulated road and ISDT grime on the bikes, the Star Twin's BSA tank badges are wiped clean and clear for all to see, most clearly seen on Fred Rist's bike.

waved goodbye to those who had made our stay so enjoyable and threaded our way through the traffic of Gothenburg out to the open highway and with clear blue skies, once more heading north. So we progressed through Uddevalla and Strömstad with the great open stretches of the Norwegian Skagerrak visible to our left until it disappeared in the distance and the North Sea beyond. After a few hours of pleasant and uneventful riding we left Sweden behind, crossing the mighty, bridge-spanned gorge into Norway where we followed the coastal road through Sarpsborg, Fredrikstad and Moss and thence to Oslo. This, the final leg of the journey which had taken us from Birmingham, right across Europe and then all the way up to this northern clime, was probably the most attractive and enjoyable of the entire trip, with the road winding its way alongside quiet lakes with mirror-like surfaces which reflected the blue sky above, and fringed with forests of scented firs and spruce. The whole countryside seemed to glow with a soft golden warmth, as though making us welcome and apologising for the crude behaviour of the elements further south.

During the day we covered about 50 miles on rough, un-surfaced roads with pot-holes and ball-bearing like surfaces, dry and dusty where each bike spewed-up a plume of dust like spray from a high-powered speedboat. The car, in its turn, also created a billowing cloud in its wake which seemed to hang suspended long after we had passed. Whilst this picture remains sharp and clear in my mind, after all these years I cannot be sure if that stretch of unmade road ran through Sweden or Norway, or perhaps both.

Nonetheless, the roads ran through remote stretches of unspoiled countryside dominated by lake and forest land which appeared devoid of traffic and people. We seemed alone in the world, heading for the Arctic Circle. Then having regained metalled roads with signs of habitation increasing by the mile, we toured gently round a bend in the road where overhanging trees cast soft shadows, and there at the roadside beneath a signboard proclaiming the outskirts of the city of Oslo, sat two Norwegian policemen astride their patrol motorcycles, awaiting our arrival to escort us to our final destination. As we stopped, parked and dismounted to exchange formal greetings, we were fascinated by their police motorcycles. They were identical to our own - BSA Star Twins. Neither party could speak each other's language; but the mutual pleasure the meeting had created was obvious, and the admiration we had for each other's mode of transport was also mutual.

So with that official police escort we were spirited with speed and great efficiency through the traffic of Oslo to our final destination - the elegant hotel which was to be our base for the next two nights. And there to meet us was a tall, quiet man of modest charm and dignity, Mr. Erling Sande, a gentleman of warm sincerity which no doubt fitted his role as the head of the concern that distributed BSA motorcycles throughout Norway with a network of fifty dealers. He was the epitome of kindness, tinged with a touch of shyness. During the years to come when we had the pleasure of meeting again many of the friends we had made on this trip – usually on the occasion of the International Motor Cycle Show at Earls Court, London – it was meeting Erling Sande again which gave the most pleasure.

After the usual photographic session and dealing with all the questions put to us by the assembled press reporters, the crowd gradually dispersed as once more John McNulty placed the Star Twins in quarantine, sealing the garage doors from his never-ending supply of sealing wire.

That evening, hosted by Erling Sande and his wife and daughter, was the most memorable of the whole trip. It was almost like a banquet which went on for hours, in convivial company which seemed to respond to the unique nature of the occasion. Fred Rist, a natural raconteur, was on top form. Normally his repertoire on such occasions was without peer. This time he really excelled and finished up singing verse after verse of 'Steamboat Bill' to everyone's delight. Thereafter it was regarded as Fred's signature tune, and Erling Sande never forgot it.

Inevitably the evening came to an end. It had provided that sort of happy-ever-after ending favoured by story writers. Hospitable, warm and generous, Erling Sande had endeared himself and the city of Oslo to us in a way which gave the names a touch of magic.

The Speed Trial

When we awoke on Tuesday September 30th, the world of Norway was bathed in sunshine, the fourth sunny day in succession. The weather had clearly relented and in recognising that it had rather overdone things since our departure from Birmingham, was determined to seek forgiveness. It was the final day of the test; a test destined to make history.

After breakfast, whilst once more we climbed into our travel-stained Barbour suits, John McNulty withdrew, for the final time, the three Star Twins from their nightly solitary confinement, making them available to us for the usual instant first or second kick start. With Erling Sande leading the way we motored gently to an airfield some 50 miles from Oslo – an airfield constructed by the Germans during their occupation of Norway during the last war, and no longer in use. There we were met by two officials of the Norsk Motor Klubb, Mr. Skramstad and Mr.H.N. Rood who had already set up the timing apparatus, a bank of electrically operated chronometers similar to those used in the Helsinki Olympic Games. These were required to test the maximum speed performance of each Star Twin. This was to be the final act.

We spent fifteen minutes refitting the harder set of spark plugs we had used for the one-hour test at Salzburg, adjusting the rear chains and increasing the tyre pressures. Then we again warmed up each bike ready for the final dash down the concrete ribbon of track. In turn each Star Twin would complete two standing start one-quarter mile runs, one in each direction, followed by two flying start runs in both directions.

Fred Rist went first with the standing start runs and accomplished identical times of 17.9 seconds on both runs, which was remarkable. His mean average was therefore 49.99 mph. Brian Martin followed with a painfully slow run in one direction of 19.9 seconds as a result of a particle of dirt floating about the well of the main jet. Before making the return run, he cleared the jet and romped back with a time of 17.4 seconds, a speed of 51.44 mph, but the slow outward run reduced his

Brian Martin (MOL 202) prepares for the ACU Maudes Trophy final speed test at Oslo Aerodrome. Norman Vanhouse, mostly hidden, awaits his turn on MOL 303.

average speed to 47.97 mph. My outward run was a good 17.7 seconds (50.56 mph), but the return run was slightly slower at 18 seconds (49.71 mph), giving me a mean of 50.15 mph.

Over the flying quarter mile which followed, Fred Rist returned a mean speed of 82.12 mph. Brian Martin excelled with a speed of 84.43 mph, but my speed was a disappointing 80.27 mph. Before I entered the timed section I knew that something was amiss because the engine was not gathering speed in the gears as it should have done. Twice I veered off before entering the timed strip in order to clear the main jet. On the third attempt I kept going, but I still felt that the engine was not revving as freely as I knew it could. The standing start runs had showed that my machine was just as fast as the other two, and I am satisfied that, despite my efforts to clear the jet, there still remained a grain of dirt which limited the engine RPM.

Brian's fastest run was at 85.23 mph compared with 83.63 mph of Fred Rist and my fastest at 82.12 mph. The potential of each bike must have been virtually identical but at about fifteen years younger than Fred and I, Brian was lighter in weight and slimmer which gave him an advantage. That more-or-less identical performance at the conclusion of the observed test also emphasised the remarkable achievement of each model, and I was convinced at the time that each machine could be turned round to do it all over again. I was less sure about the riders!

To round off the official test, John McNulty took a ride on each machine in turn, in order to pronounce them safe and in road-worthy condition. Then, with a touch of finality, he produced the chemical with which to check all the dabs of sealing paint he had applied at the outset in order to identify original components. He announced each model as legal and law-abiding, and was fully satisfied. We were also.

The 1952 BSA ACU-observed test was over. During the period of the test each machine had covered a total of 4,958 miles. By the time we boarded the boat next day to head for Newcastle, the speedometers had clocked up the 5,000 and by the time we got back to the factory in Birmingham the totals had gone up to 5,200 miles for each machine. The only trouble of any consequence had been the leaking petrol tanks experienced by Brian and myself. All three engines had remained one hundred per cent oil-tight throughout the test. We had even completed the entire test on one set of spark plugs – other than the harder set used for the speed tests at the end of the ISDT and at Oslo. Present day ISDT/E riders may have great difficulty in believing that fact, but it is true.

When studying ACU-observed tests of later years, it should be recalled that the entire BSA operation was carried out by three riders only. When it was all over, Fred Rist, Brian Martin and I had every reason to be proud of what we had just accomplished. During the three weeks of riding we had developed a tremendous respect for those wonderful Star Twins, the product of British labour back home in Birmingham. Bert Perrigo did little more than congratulate us with formal handshakes, but while mostly a man of few words who always called a spade a spade, I am sure beneath the surface he was a very proud man. This was the result he had planned for and, indeed, expected. That is why he selected the riders he did. He knew that we were capable and his confidence never wavered - despite the severity of the ISDT and its high casualty rate among our compatriots.

The result was merely a product of good planning. He knew it could be done. We had only done what he knew we could do. It was as simple as that. But even Bert Perrigo could not appreciate just what those standard Star Twins went through during the period of the ISDT in Austria. The BSA colour film made of the whole test gives little idea of the true severity because the photographer could only get to

Norman Vanhouse, Fred Rist and Brian Martin on the three BSA Star Twins. This picture was taken in Oslo at the end of the trial.

those parts accessible by car. The film gives no hint of the bogs and mud; the rocks and gullies and the constant punishment absorbed by those plunger rear-sprung frames.

Only those competitors who completed the entire course can understand the nature of those Star Twins' accomplishment. Given the same conditions today, over 60 years later, it is uncertain whether modern one-off specials could achieve the same, let alone straight from stock, standard products like those Star Twins which could have been bought by anyone over the shop counter.

So it was back on the bikes and back to Oslo for yet another superb and relaxing evening, though we saw little of John McNulty that night for he had his reports to conclude, one to go with him when he flew back to England the following day and

October 2ⁿᵈ 1952. All three riders looking pensive - but the whole job had been completed successfully by this point! Awaiting disembarkation from Olsen Lines M.S. Blenheim, the Oslo to Newcastle ferry. Left to right, Brian Martin, Norman Vanhouse, Fred Rist.

one for Bert Perrigo to bring back and post should anything befall the aircraft on which John would be flying.

Next morning, 1st October, we said goodbye to John McNulty who was being transferred to Oslo airport by the kind offices of Erling Sande and his staff. He had been a good friend, and had been one of us, despite carrying out his official duties with meticulous impartiality; he had made it quite clear right at the outset that if the certified test was to mean anything, then he had to carry out his duties without fear or favour. He had done so with fastidious care and proved a credit to both himself and the Auto Cycle Union whom he represented.

By midday we ourselves were on the move, making for the Fred Olsen Shipping Line berth at Oslo docks to catch the M.S. Blenheim bound for Newcastle-upon-Tyne. With the car and bikes aboard, we waved our final farewells to the charming Erling Sande and his family who had come to see us off, and as the Blenheim slowly pulled away, they were gradually lost to sight in a sea of waving arms of other people doing likewise.

Quite suddenly we were alone - the six of us - Bert and Cherry Perrigo, Alan Blowry, Fred Rist, Brian Martin and I. We had 24 hours in which to relax and unwind. To snooze, to eat, to drink and to socialise among ourselves until we arrived at Newcastle the following day. For some time we were content to stay on deck and admire the superb Norwegian views as the ship took a meandering course down the confined, narrow strip of Oslofjord, with its tree-lined banks on either side, broken by small hamlets with square-shaped churches only a short distance away, reminding us of the road we had used a couple of days before. Beyond the strip of Fjord which separates Horten on the west bank and Moss on the east bank, the inlet gradually opened out into the Skagerrak strait, and thence to the open North Sea where the ship gathered speed – and with it came the movement which can upset humble land-lubbers before the necessary sea legs have been acquired.

Although we had enjoyed a splendid five-course dinner the night before, by morning, the sea was less considerate and it seemed doubtful that some could do full justice to the fine array of help-yourself buffet breakfast which included pickled fish. Whilst my appetite was doubtful, that of Fred Rist could only be described as robust, and he more than made up for the shortcomings of others.

By midday the grey industrial skyline of Newcastle appeared through the misty distance and gradually, as the M.S.Blenheim slowed down, the quayside grew larger and came sharper into focus, until with the familiar ringing of the ship's bell and shouting of many instructions, the ship tied-up and the disembarkation commenced.

The BSA Maudes Trophy team land at Newcastle on its return from Oslo in October 1952. The welcome party at Newcastle consisted of Fred Rist's father and his friends Mr & Mrs Bartlett. Left to right; Norman Vanhouse, Mrs Bartlett, Brian Martin, Cherry Perrigo, Bert Perrigo, Fred Rist, Fred Rist's father, Mr Bartlett.

We were welcomed by Fred Rist's father who was accompanied by two old friends of Fred, Mr. and Mrs. Bartlett, and this was a pleasant surprise. Fred came from that area of England but had not lived there since pre-war days. So after a quick coffee and exchange of news it was time to bid farewell to Fred's father, friends, and photographer Alan Blowry who left the group to catch a train to London.

We once again kicked the Star Twins into life and headed south through the county of Durham and across the vast broad acres of Yorkshire, that county which has produced an army of top-grade trials riders since the early days of motorcycling; thence through Derbyshire to the east Midlands and so to Birmingham. Right to the last minute the Twins never missed a beat, purring as sweetly as the day they left the factory, having upheld the faith placed in them in a manner which surely would defy emulation in the years ahead.

It was late afternoon with the factory still humming with production activity and noise when we slipped down Armoury Road and came to a stop outside that proud office entrance that no longer exists. Our arrival made no more impact than the departure had twenty-five days previously – was it only twenty-five days? It seemed a lifetime ago. I think a couple of managers left their desks to meet us. And stand and gaze at three Star Twins which as the years went by, grew in reputation and stature.

Three BSA motorcycles, which as C.E. 'Titch' Allen put it, 'created one of the great legends of the ISDT'.

October 1952 - BSA Armoury Road factory - 4,958 miles including 1,500 miles of the 1952 ISDT and three ISDT Gold Medals. From the left, Brian Martin, Fred Rist and Norman Vanhouse display the covetted ACU Maudes Trophy with the project architect, BSA Competitions Manager Bert Perrigo standing behind.

Claiming The Maudes Trophy

Merely because we had completed what we regarded as a very successful ACU-observed test, did not mean that the Maudes Trophy would come our way automatically. It was up to the ACU Competitions Committee. They required the time to convene and study John McNulty's test report and decide if the test had been, in their opinion, sufficiently meritorious to justify the award of the Trophy. We knew, of course, that no other tests had been undertaken that year, so there had been no competition to weigh against ours. It was purely a case of judging our test on its merits. It would not be unreasonable to suggest that it probably did not take the committee long to decide. General reaction in the Press to our test did rather suggest that when the announcement of the award came some ten days later, it had been little more than a formality.

When the formal announcement came, it was the signal for the BSA advertising and publicity people to pull out the stops in preparing all the material required in order to exploit the success to the full. It would be the first time the Maudes Trophy had been awarded since Triumph had won it pre-war, and BSA made the most of that fact. Apart from conventional advertising in the motorcycle press, including double-page colour spreads, a booklet outlining details of the test and results together with a selection of pictures taken was produced and distributed to dealers worldwide in record time. Entitled, very aptly, 'The Machines you might have bought', together with a souvenir book-marker, it was ready for general distribution at the International Motorcycle Show which opened at Earls Court, London on the 15th November 1952.

The colour cine film taken from leaving Birmingham until that point we lost the first photographer in France, and then from where it was resumed by the replacement photographer who joined the party at Bad Aussee, of course took rather more time to be processed and edited. When it was completed it proved to be

BSA gained extensive publicity from the Maudes Trophy and ISDT Golds. (The Motorcycle, 6 November 1952 MotorCycling, 6 November 1952 and BSAs advertisement at the time shown above)

a superb film which even today 60 years later, will stand comparison with modern productions. Many copies of the film were distributed throughout the world for use of BSA distributors and of the twelve celluloid copies retained for use in the United Kingdom, only one survives as far as I am aware. I saved this from the scrapheap when BSA Small Heath folded at the end of 1971.

The official presentation of the Maudes Trophy to the BSA company took place on Friday 14th November, which was Press Day at the Motorcycle Show at Earls Court. This took place in a dining suite of the Royal Automobile Club at Pall Mall, London, presided over by Professor A.M. Low, the distinguished Chairman of the Auto Cycle Union at that time, who presented the large silver trophy to James Leek, O.B.E., Managing Director of BSA Cycles Ltd. Sales director Stan Digby who had seen us off from Small Heath at the start of the test, also attended the function, as did the three riders. It was easy enough for Fred Rist and I to attend, but less so for

November 14th 1952. Maudes Trophy Presentation Luncheon at the Royal Automobile Club, London. Professor AM Low, Chairman of the Auto Cycle Union of Great Britain, addresses the three BSA riders. From the left, Professor Low (ACU), S F Digby (BSA Sales Director), James Leek (BSA Managing Director), Norman Vanhouse, Fred Rist, Brian Martin.

Brian Martin. By then he was in khaki undertaking his National Service. He had to report for National Service before the test started, but by dint of high-level string pulling (I assume), he was deferred long enough to take part in the test. Presumably string-pulling was again resorted to in order to get him at Pall Mall for this very special occasion.

On the subject of Brian Martin, who went on to become Competitions Manager at BSA for a period of ten years or so including the time when Jeff Smith won the World Motorcross Championship in 1964 and 1965, I cannot resist recounting how, having returned from Newcastle on the Star Twins on that Thursday afternoon back in October, Brian just had time to get hold of a 'proper' competition model and rush down to the West Country on the Friday for the trade-supported National West of England trial. The three weeks on the Star Twin had done him no harm. It might have done him a deal of good. He then rushed back to the Midlands for the Worcestershire Grand National on the Sunday – which he won!

Following the presentation of the Maudes Trophy at Pall Mall on the Friday, we attended a very big social function at the Park Lane Hotel on the Saturday, attended by some two thousand BSA motorcycle and bicycle dealers, when Fred Rist, Brian Martin and I were presented on the stage, along with the five members of the BSA bicycle road racing team which had won the Daily Express 'Tour of Britain' cycle race. 1952 was quite a year for BSA!

Obviously, the Maudes Trophy was proudly displayed on the BSA stand throughout the Motorcycle Show period, together with Fred Rist's model. Although not scratched or dented at all, Fred's bike looked more the part, because unlike Brian and I, he had had the foresight not to clean the mud from the rims of either wheel at the start of the speed test at Salzburg.

Soon after, another little celebration took place on the stage of the BSA works canteen back at Small Heath when a representative of the Esso Petroleum Company presented a high-quality canteen of cutlery to each rider, in recognition of the Esso tie-up with the test. Other than one occasion in the Russian zone of Austria where Esso fuel was unobtainable, we had used their petrol throughout.

A month or two later an official dinner was organised by BSA at a pleasant hotel, in Monkspath just outside Birmingham, to which all directors, senior managers and factory foremen were invited, to mark the success to which they and their departments had contributed directly or otherwise. On this occasion, Brian Martin was unable to attend, so it was left to Fred Rist and me to do the speech-making on behalf of the riders. Senior management attending that night, many of whom

December 1952. BSA Official Maudes Trophy Dinner, Monkspath Hotel just outside Birmingham. All BSA Directors, Senior Managers and Factory Foreman present. Norman Vanhouse (standing) addresses the gathering on behalf of the three riders involved. On his right sits James Leek (Managing Director BSA Cycles Ltd.), a man hugely respected by the author for his significant contribution to the British war effort through his leadership of BSA's armaments production. In the foreground sits the coveted Maudes Trophy.

having long since passed on, included Bert Hopwood who became widely known over the years for his design contributions to the British motorcycle industry, and subsequently during his retirement as the writer of 'Whatever Happened to the British Motorcycle Industry?'. With so much top-brass about the place that night, it was quite an illustrious gathering of devoted and able men who, in their respective roles, had helped to make the name BSA truly great in those days. I was both proud and honoured, but nonetheless apprehensive, to sit next to the great James Leek for the occasion. His major contribution to the British war effort whilst head of the mighty BSA empire during the Second World War has never been fully acknowledged publicly. At that time he was still a man of immense authority.

By then Fred Rist had already left the employment of BSA to set-up his own

March 1953. Esso Divisional Sales Manager A.Launder makes a presentation of a canteen of cutlery to the riders in recognition of the Esso supported successful BSA ISDT Maudes Trophy project. Left to right are Norman Vanhouse, unknown, Brian Martin, A. Launder, Fred Rist. Location: BSA Works Canteen, Armoury Road.

motorcycle retail business in Neath, South Wales, so the 1952 ACU-observed test was his last official ride for the factory with which he had links since pre-war days while a regular soldier in the British Army. After the war he had made his home in Birmingham in order to become one of Bert Perrigo's team in the factory competitions department. First time out in the factory team he hit the headlines by winning the Colmore Cup Trial, the first post-war trade-supported national trial. Thereafter, along with Bill Nicholson and others, he contributed to the most successful competitions period ever experienced by BSA.

For several years after leaving BSA, Fred amused himself with a spot of sand racing on the great sandy beach at Pendine in particular, and his performance there, I understand, was one of those things that had to be seen to be believed, for he adopted a technique which was both spectacular in the extreme and highly successful.

With Brian away in the army and Fred down at Neath selling motorcycles, of the three riders involved in the Maudes Trophy story, there remained only myself on the spot at Small Heath. This meant that as motorcycle clubs up and down the country requested the loan of the Maudes film and a visit of one of the riders in person to talk about it, it always fell to me to fill the breach. Then during the club dinner season for several years after, I was invited to more and more clubs as guest of honour, and given the honour of presenting their awards. On these occasions the praise voiced by so many, if anything, grew with the passing of time.

Already, from a distance, the victory was beginning to assume even greater proportions than it had when in immediate focus.

One of the first things to be done on return to the factory was an engine strip of each Star Twin for expert examination. This was carried out by the highly respected David Munro M.I.Mech.E., M.S.I.A, one of the senior Engineers with the company. His subsequent report is reproduced in full following this chapter. The excellent condition in which he found each engine supports my claim that the Star Twins were going as well at the end of the test as they had been in the beginning and throughout. It had not been imagination playing tricks. The last paragraph of the report states:-

> In all my long experience I have seldom seen engines strip so beautifully, and certainly never before on completing a test as severe as that from which these three Star Twins have emerged so triumphantly.

That really says it all. One can even detect a hint of surprise and possible disbelief in the measured tones. Nonetheless it was all very true and very real. It was the first post-war ACU-observed test carried out by any manufacturer[1]. It was the first time the Maudes Trophy was presented post-war. And history now records that it was the last time it was ever awarded to a British manufacturer. Not a few people claim that it was the most profound ACU-observed test of them all. Having researched the test objectives and results of those that had gone before and those which came later, who am I to disagree?

The merits of the BSA test of 1952 had been patently obvious to most impartial

---

1   On the 11th of August 1950, J.H.Dale, a private individual from Auckland, New Zealand, registered his 1948 350 cc GS/1 Matchless with the ACU for a petrol consumption test. In 8 hours, 3 minutes, 48 seconds he covered 51 laps and 2.5 miles of the MIRA test circuit near Nuneaton, UK, a distance of 156.163 miles on a half-gallon of petrol. Where conditions permitted the motorcycle was allowed to coast with the engine stopped.

observers. So much so that Graham Walker, Editor of *Motor Cycling*, one of the two respected and revered weekly journals of those days, was prompted to pre-empt the ACU announcement when he wrote the following in his edition of 9th October of that year:-

> We congratulate the team of BSA riders who have just completed a 5,000-mile ACU-observed test which included a faultless performance in the ISDT. It was a courageous undertaking for, as those manufacturers who support competition events are all too aware, the adverse publicity in failure can sometimes exceed the benefit gained by success. Until the observer has delivered his report and the latter has been considered by the appropriate committee, it cannot be stated categorically that the Maudes Trophy will be awarded for this most meritorious performance; but if it is, then certainly it will have been well earned.
>
> The value to our industry in demonstration of what standard British machines can do under conditions of official observation is great; it is to be hoped that the renewed interest in the Maudes Trophy competition created by this test will encourage other manufacturers to enter the lists next year.

Graham Walker's advanced judgement of the test proved to be correct and in line with the official ACU view, so whilst his premature congratulations and views preceded the formal ACU announcement, he forestalled a possible offence by the use of ethical prose. The essence of his stated views, however, was the hope and desire that other British marques would demonstrate their standard products in a similar manner. To a certain extent his hopes were realised, for only twelve months later two further tests were undertaken, with a third in May 1954. With both the former tests taking place after September 30th, 1953, it meant that when it came to September 30th 1954, the ACU had no less than three tests to judge.

There seems little doubt that the BSA success had stimulated interest in the observed-test formula as a means of publicity. But it also seemed likely that the BSA test of 1952 had set a very high standard by which those that came after would be judged.

If that was the case then it was a pity, for as the years went by, the frequency of the ACU-observed tests declined until today, at the time of writing, they have become virtually extinct. And thus it could be claimed that as well as stimulating new interest in the series, they also helped to kill-off the series.

The glamorous make-up and sensational success of BSA in 1952 had made it very difficult for others to follow in a similarly convincing style, but then the same thing had been said after the Triumph success of 1939. It was claimed that the standard set then would discourage attempts post-war. This may have been true although I seriously doubt it. The immediate post-war years had been a seller's market for the British industry, and whilst budgets were allocated for advertising and promotions, they had been devoted mainly to traditional press advertising plus the established and convenient platform provided by competitions and road racing. Furthermore, after six years of war, it took time to get things back to normality with management levels up to full strength before there was time available to look ahead to more elaborate promotions.

As market leaders with a worldwide network of dealers requiring all the promotional support possible, it was inevitable that BSA, above all others, should again look to such a promotion in furtherance of BSA prestige. To some extent they had a responsibility and they were to be praised for facing up to it, knowing as well as anybody in the industry, just as Graham Walker stated in that editorial, that the adverse publicity in failure can sometimes exceed the benefits gained by success.

In facing up to that responsibility which was rewarded with success, BSA not only earned direct benefit for themselves - they earned additional prestige for the entire British motorcycle industry, enhancing its reputation throughout the world. Such individual success brings fringe benefits to others engaged in a like business.

Such successful tests as those of Triumph in 1939 and that of BSA in 1952 are difficult to follow and emulate, let alone improve on. Novel ideas with a newsworthy angle but based on a sound demanding test routine which can be readily and officially observed, are not easily come by. It is said that this was the view held after the Triumph success in 1939. Nonetheless, BSA came to the conclusion that what Triumph could do, BSA could do – and even surpass. And they did just that.

In the years that followed the BSA epic of 1952, eight observed tests were undertaken and concluded without the ACU presenting the coveted Maudes Trophy to any of them. None of the tests were failures as such, but conversely none of them could have been considered sufficiently meritorious for the ultimate recognition. Could it be that none of them measured up to the BSA standard?

It was to be no less than eleven years before the Maudes Trophy was removed from the luxurious showrooms of BSA at Small Heath – and for the first time in its long history presented to a foreign manufacturer. That surely, was a portent of things to come. The famous trophy had been out of sight – and perhaps out of mind – for far too long. To present it after such a long lapse could well stimulate renewed interest and establish it once again as the keenly sought-after trophy it had always been.

There may well be a view held today that such observed tests are no longer capable of testing modern motorcycles. To find the answer to that we need only look at the two occasions when the trophy was awarded during the 1970s, when the participants encountered troubles galore. Or could it be that it is felt that such undertakings are dogged by too many imponderables and uncertainties? For that is just what I was told by one company executive when advocating such a promotion aimed at raising the prestige of certain models.

To all those company executives of the past who had faced up to such self-same gambles over and over again, that surely is the most profound compliment of all.

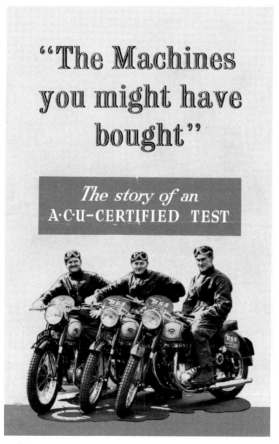

The Cover of the BSA produced Maudes brochure with the advertising message
'The Machines you might have bought' and which highlighted the Technical Report reproduced on p124.

Report of the Examination of BSA Star Twin Engines after 1952 ACU Observed Test

By D.W. Munro, M.I.Mech.E., M.S.I.A. – BSA Technical Engineer

After this extremely severe test a certain amount of wear might have been expected, but an examination of the moving parts of the engine reveals a negligible amount. At the same time, the various bearing surfaces are found to be in wonderful condition, and this is clearly seen in the untouched photographs. Take the pistons, for example, the bearing surfaces on the rear or thrust sides of the piston skirts are well-nigh perfect *(see below)*, showing uniform distribution of contact area without high spots, and entirely innocent of those burnish marks which indicate distortion or high local unit pressure. There is no evidence of piston tilt, since there was a noteworthy absence of slap during the tests, this was only to be expected.

The piston rings have developed exquisite bearing surfaces, and the top lands show by their almost complete freedom from carbon deposit, that their nicely generated contact surface just 'fit' the cylinder bores adequately under the maximum temperature conditions attained. It is evident from this that additional heat transfer area becomes effective during full throttle work, with a consequently superior temperature control when it is most needed.

The cylinder bores have been polished during the large mileage of the test to a mirror finish, but without appreciable wear, and one of the pictures clearly shows the piston tracks, with a slight smear of carbon, amounting to little more than a stain, beyond the upper reaches of the rings. As was to be expected with this carefully designed cylinder unit, there is no evidence or witness of distortion.

Among the most highly stressed parts of a motorcycle engine are the valves and their seats. One of the photographs *(left)* shows how well the valve seats in the cylinder head have stood up to the gruelling conditions imposed. On the inlet side they are virtually as new, and even the exhaust seats which had to endure for so long the fiery blast of high-power combustion, are so unscathed that a slight touch with grinding paste would completely restore them, and , even untouched, they are fit for many more miles of faultless service.

The small amount of carbon deposit inside the cylinder heads, and on the sparking plugs, indicate that carburation and lubrication conditions were perfectly suited to the engines, and to the work they had to perform, and the freedom from distortion, which is so notable a feature of the cylinder barrels, is also conspicuous on the heads. In all my long experience I have seldom seen engines strip so beautifully, and certainly never before on completing a test as severe as that from which these three Star Twins have emerged so triumphantly.

Number 209, Norman Vanhouse's bike MOL 303 at the end of the ISDT. This, and the other photos above are taken from the BSA brochure 'The machines you might have bought'.

What Happened Next: BSA Star Twin - MOL 303

When BSA won the Maudes Trophy in 1952 nobody could possibly have predicted that it was to be the last such British success for at least sixty years. History may yet prove it to be the last British Maudes Trophy success ever. Similarly, when all those people at BSA were basking in the glory propagated by the wealth of BSA competitions activity and success in those heady days, no one could have forecast that nineteen short years later the Small Heath factory would be still, silent and empty of all the family who had helped to make the name of BSA great. And worse still, with the passing of a further five years or so, the factory would be razed to the ground, with the remnants of the once great establishment looking like neglected gravestones in a gaunt and silent cemetery – a cemetery full of past ghosts.

If the eventual monopoly of the Japanese motorcycle manufacturers could have been foreseen, maybe the management of such companies as BSA might have been encouraged to preserve, as living examples of motorcycle engineering progress, various models which had created pride and prestige. But in those successful days, there was no room for such sentiment. BSA was a public company concerned only with the harsh commercial realities and decisions to influence the well-being of the company trading into the future. What had gone before was of little consequence – unless it had a bearing on future prosperity.

Thus, whilst the current range of production motorcycles was always displayed in the plush, carpeted showrooms on the first floor of the main office block at the head of Armoury Road, BSA maintained no museums of past models. Had they done so, almost certainly room would have been made for at least one of the history-making Star Twins of 1952, to stand alongside other BSA machines which had made their mark before them. Instead, when they had served their purpose, all three Star Twin bikes used in the successful Maudes Trophy operation were disposed of in the normal way – sold to either employees or BSA dealers. I have no idea just when they left the Small Heath factory for the last time. After our return from Oslo, and the subsequent presentation of the Trophy, the riders were reunited with the bikes one more time for further publicity photographs. Once Fred Rist's bike, MOL 301, had been displayed at the Earls Court Motorcycle Show in 1952, I cannot recall ever again seeing any of the three machines.

Long before the British motorcycle industry floundered and the highways of the world became thronged with Japanese products – the latter a situation which in itself has nurtured and accelerated the great nostalgic interest in British bikes – there were enthusiastic individuals who, without thought of commercial gain, devoted their spare time to what the industry itself had not done; researching the past history of the industry and its products and, in achieving the latter, unearthing, reclaiming and restoring old models long since left to rot.

Future generations will owe much to these enthusiasts and it is difficult to know when and where it all started. There will be those who will recall Captain Jim Hall who, during the years of the Second World War, devoted much spare time to unearthing all sorts of long forgotten and near rusted-away relics from the past that had been dumped away in old barns and farm buildings. No doubt starved of general interest editorial for his weekly magazine, Graham Walker, as Editor, devoted significant space to Jim Hall's activities in *Motor Cycling*, but then Graham Walker himself proved to be a keen devotee of the cause.

But there is one name above all, that of C.E. 'Titch' Allen, as founder of the Vintage Motor Cycle Club (VMCC), which is more synonymous than any other with the foundation and development of the vintage movement and, in so doing, bringing to the forefront the glorious history of the British motorcycle industry and the wide diversity of its products. Inevitably, the growth of the Vintage MCC attracted commercial interests which moved to exploit the potential of what is now regarded as the classic period of motorcycling, with the result that we now have more devotees chasing fewer examples of classic bikes, which have thus acquired the value and glamour of rare objects.

With the interest in vintage motorcycles thus fermented by Titch Allen and his ilk, it is only natural that the example they set by restoring and displaying their work, gave rise to the thoughts of others in providing a permanent home for such beautiful objects. So the time of motor and motorcycle museums arrived, and one of the earliest and probably the best was established by Lord Montagu at his ancestral home at Beaulieu in Hampshire, a combined museum with Graham Walker as the original curator. This highly successful museum was later to acquire national status, and must have inspired others to follow suit, for since then many other such museums have evolved throughout the country.

One such person probably influenced by this trend was Roy Richards, a Birmingham business man who opened his sophisticated and specialised National Motorcycle Museum (NMM) just south of Birmingham in October 1984. He first had visions of creating such a museum complex in the mid-1970s, and with his long-term plan before him, he recruited skilled enthusiastic individuals for the purpose of acquiring classic British motorcycles from all over the country and then proceeding to restore them to original mint condition for eventual display in the proposed museum.

In embarking on the mechanics of the job long before he had tackled and overcome the problems imposed by location and planning authorities, Roy Richards displayed considerable faith and determination in bringing his plans to fruition. Long before the legal obstacles had been overcome, restored bikes were being completed and loaned for display at such exhibitions as the International Motorcycle Show at Earls Court and at the National Exhibition Centre at Birmingham. And one such Richards' restored model loaned for the classic bike display at Earls Court in August 1978 was an immaculate 1952 BSA Star Twin, with the registration number MOL 303, fitted with three green oval competition-type number plates inscribed with the words, 'Standard BSA undergoing 4500 miles 7242 Kms ACU Certified Test'. The restored model was faithful in every detail, and when I first saw it, for indeed MOL 303 was the Star Twin which I had ridden back in 1952, it was like turning back the hands of a clock.

Discovery of this historic model was one of those chances dreamed-up by fiction writers, such was the improbability, and full credit goes to BSA enthusiast Colin Wall, a member of the Vintage MCC, who was persuaded by Roy Richards to give up his telephone engineering job to join his team of British bike restorers. In his new role of full-time restorer, Colin got to know all sorts of places where old bits and pieces could be found. One such place was a small motorcycle shop, long since closed down, which was situated on the main Bristol Road in Selly Oak, Birmingham, just a few hundred yards from the old Ariel factory.

During one of his several visits there, when the partners running the business were clearly experiencing cash-flow problems, Colin was offered a virtually bare BSA frame at a give-away price. Although not looking for such a frame at that moment, the price was so right, Colin was unable to resist the bargain, so there and then he piled the frame into his pick-up and took it home. It was complete with front forks, but they were non-standard, with the lengthened tubes beloved of chopper builders. Already fully occupied with other rebuilds due for completion, the old BSA frame was dumped in the open and virtually forgotten for around six months. Until one day, one of the partners at the Selly Oak business brought round some items Colin had agreed to buy, to help clear the stock prior to the shop's final closure. And almost as an afterthought, he gave Colin the logbook which belonged to the BSA frame he had purchased six months previously.

Now in possession of a logbook with registration number, and engine and frame numbers, Colin's interest was kindled. What about the engine from that frame he wondered? No, that had been sold months before – to an individual living in the Stirchley area of Birmingham. He decided it might be worth following-up so he visited the address of the person who had bought just the engine, only to learn that most of the engine had been used. Only the crankcase halves remained. The owner was quite willing to sell these but the asking price was a little high, so having made a mental note of the number stamped on the crankcase half, Colin departed empty handed. When he got back home he compared the number in his head with that on the logbook. To his delight they tallied. It was now obvious that if he was going to restore that old BSA he would need those two crankcase halves, so back he went and after some bartering, agreement was reached, and he came away with the desired crankcase. The number, clearly visible, was AA7S 2570.

He was still unaware of what he had come by and having got to know Bob Currie, the motorcycle journalist and vintage bike authority, he casually mentioned that he had bought some parts from a 1952 BSA Star Twin. Just as casually Bob remarked that it was with Star Twin models that BSA had won the Maudes Trophy in 1952. At that point the name Maudes Trophy meant nothing to Colin Wall. But Bob's comment had registered for, during that night whilst in bed the remark began to ring a bell in the deep recesses of his mind. He could vaguely remember once seeing a picture of three riders sitting astride three BSA models with one clutching a great silver trophy. Was that what Bob Currie had been referring to?

Thus inspired he donned his dressing gown, went downstairs and began thumbing through old back numbers of the *Motor Cycle* magazine until he came to the Earls Court Show number on November 13th 1952. And there it was! A double-page BSA advertisement depicting three riders on Star Twins, a composite spread made up from shots of the riders taken at different times during the test, with only one broadside view of any of the bikes with the registration number clearly visible. And that was the picture of myself with an Alpine mountain background – on MOL 303. That was it! For the first time Colin realised just what he had come by and after confirming the exciting news with Bob Currie, he set about the job of restoration with renewed enthusiasm.

I had no knowledge of all this until about March or April 1978 when, for the first time, Colin contacted me to verify certain specification details and then, soon after, to invite me round to inspect his magnificent handiwork. When the restoration was completed I was invited to the Vintage MCC annual race meeting at Mallory Park in May of that year with a view to riding MOL 303 round the circuit in the traditional parade. I in turn contacted Brian Martin and Bert Perrigo. I also tried to contact Fred Rist living in retirement in Devonshire with a view to completing the trio of riders, but Fred was out of the country and couldn't make the event.

So, on 7th May 1978 both Brian Martin and I rode Star Twin MOL 303 round Mallory park and, I must say, rather more sedately than we had ridden those bikes on occasions back in 1952. It was a unique experience which gave me a great deal of pleasure. Apart from being featured in a classic bike line-up at Earls Court later that year, the machine was virtually moth-balled until it took its place with around four hundred other exhibits at the opening of the National Motor Cycle Museum in 1984.

But what of the years between 1952 and Colin Wall finding the remnants of the old bike? Well, in September 1980 *The Sunday Mercury* published a picture of Fred Rist, Brian Martin and myself taken before we set out on the ACU-observed test in 1952. This picture prompted a letter from a Mr.J. Gatehouse of Hall Green, Birmingham which appeared in the following week's edition and ran:-

> *The photograph on the 'Biking' column September 29th of the three BSA motorcycles and riders brought back memories of my motorcycling days. I owned one of the BSA Star Twins in the photograph, ridden by Norman Vanhouse, with which BSA won the Maudes trophy in 1952. In 1953 they were displayed at exhibitions, and in 1954 I bought MOL 303 from Handley's of Birmingham. I rode it solo for one year, then coupled it with a Swallow Jet 80 sidecar. My wife and I covered many miles in it until I parted with it in 1966.*

I have no knowledge of the exhibitions to which Mr. Gatehouse refers, but it is clear that the Star Twin gave him twelve years of loyal service – eleven of those years with a sidecar attached – having purchased the bike from the motorcycle business at the bottom of Suffolk Street in Birmingham set-up by that great TT rider Wally Handley.

What happened to MOL 303 after Mr. Gatehouse disposed of it in 1966 until Colin Wall found the remains in 1976 remains a mystery. But this is of no consequence. What really matters is that Colin has put new life into a classic model which will perpetuate a living legend for many years to come.

'The Machines You Might Have Bought'

Reg. No.	Engine No.	Frame No.	Rider
MOL 301	AA7S 2577	ZA7S 35946	F.M. Rist
MOL 302	AA7S 2563	ZA7S 35963	B.W. Martin
MOL 303	AA7S 2570	ZA7S 35979	N.E. Vanhouse

MOL 303, now restored at the National Motorcycle Museum

Last Words by Graham Vanhouse

Norman Vanhouse was to ride MOL 303 once again, this time in the National Motorcycle Museum grounds. The occasion was the large BSA Centenary Event held at the museum in July 2003. Norman rode MOL 303 alongside John Cooper on his 1971 Race of the Year winning BSA Rocket 3 in front of the assembled crowds.

Then on the 16th September of 2003, a massive fire ripped through National Motorcycle Museum buildings destroying around 70% of the museum's buildings and around 400 of the motorcycles on display, including many unique and prize exhibits. One of these bikes was MOL 303. This historic machine was fire damaged beyond recognition. The museum founder and staff had only one response to this disaster – to rebuild the museum and restore the damaged machines, and to do so as quickly as possible.

Colin Wall, now Chief Restorer at the museum, set his son Wesley (also a motorcycle restoration expert) the task of restoring BSA Star Twin MOL 303. In an impressive timescale of a little over 12 months the Museum re-opened its doors on the 1st December 2004. In this time frame a restoration of 400 machines would have been impossible. But a significant number had been restored, and MOL 303 was chosen as one of the first to be tackled. When he had finished his detailed restoration in 2004, Wesley telephoned NEV and arranged for NEV to meet him and be the first to witness once again the restored machine. And the chosen meeting point? Armoury Road, Small Heath in Birmingham - the home of BSA , and from where MOL 303 had first emerged in 1952 some 52 years earlier. Once again it was a fantastic restoration and a tribute to the Star Twin's unique heritage. Judging from both its track record and its NMM custodians MOL 303 has always been destined to survive whatever is thrown at it and will be around forever!

Finally, NEV passed away in May 2011. His funeral cortège included Ariel, BSA and Yamaha machines organised by the Kings Norton Motorcycle Club (of which NEV had held various roles over the years including President) to represent the marques closely associated with NEV throughout his sporting and working years in the motorcycle industry.

The funeral cortège was met at the crematorium by Colin and Wesley Wall, with MOL 303. The Star Twin was fired-up and provided a great focal point and fine tribute.

Part 2

Maudes Trophy History 1923 - 1994

Observed Trials and the Start of the Maudes Trophy

From the earliest days of the British motorcycle industry, manufacturers had been keen and willing to demonstrate the reliability and potential of their standard production motorcycles. In so doing, they had come up with many novel and ingenious tests repeated, from time to time, with certain variations. Initially, of course, when competitions and long-distance endurance events came into being, such events provided an ideal means of testing the reliability of manufacturers' machines with the added bonus of publicity in the event of success. As with all forms of competition, specialization creeps in, which then becomes progressively more expensive. Even during the very earliest days of the twentieth century, over the three-year span of the International Motor Cycle Cup Races held on the Continent, non-standard machine specifications and rule breaking were rife. In these events, held in 1904, 1905 and 1906, the motorcycles were limited to a maximum weight of 110 pounds (50 Kg). This encouraged flimsy and unsafe contraptions.

At this time in Britain the Motor Car Act of 1903 had raised the speed limit on the roads to 20 mph, but the Act also stipulated that racing on the roads in England, Scotland and Wales was illegal. However, although part of the British Isles, the Isle of Man's own government, the Tynwald, were able to pass their own Acts, and with much foresight in recognising a great opportunity, arranged to close the public roads in order to stage road racing. The governing body for British motorsport, the Royal Automobile Club, thus organised the first car racing on the Island in 1904, this being trials for the annual International Gordon Bennett (of the *New York Herald*) Cup car races that had commenced in 1900.

Motorcycle road racing was similarly restricted to the Continent, thus putting British motorcycle manufacturers and riders at a clear disadvantage. To address this, the Auto-Cycle Club, the forerunner of the Auto-Cycle Union (ACU) followed the lead of the car brigade and what followed in 1905 and 1906 were the first motorcycle road races on the Island, which were trials for the International Cup races.

The framework for the first TT races in 1907 quickly evolved, organised by the Auto-Cycle Union. The ACU were keenly influenced by the experience gained in that early European series, and the principle established was one to foster, not hinder, the development of sturdy, economical roadster machines. Thus the maximum weight limit was scrapped, but in the interests of commercial factors, a limit was imposed on engine size and on the amount of fuel allowed for each competitor to cover ten laps of the 15-mile St. John's course. The object was to encourage any maker to enter his standard production roadster, and the trophy donated by the Marquis de Mouzilly St.Mars was named the Tourist Trophy. You couldn't get anything more clearly defined than that. However, it was recognised in due course that the fuel ration imposed was hindering machine development, contrary to the original principle of running the races as an aid to development. Thus the fuel restriction was scrapped. Then in 1911, again in the interests of further development, the races were moved to the Mountain course used to this very day in the Isle of Man.

Development progressed rapidly. And the era of one-off specials for events of a specialised nature had arrived. Only a few manufacturers were prepared to spend capital and factory facilities on producing special racing machines and instead, preferred the more economical policy of using standard production motorcycles for any form of competition or promotion. Indeed, there were those who argued that the public preferred to see machines available to them over the counter put through various forms of endurance testing. There were also manufacturers who were convinced that such activity was much more meaningful than any grand prix victory achieved with extremely expensive specials bearing no resemblance to their standard product.

As the years went by, the road and track racing specials were produced by a declining number of makers, with the majority of manufacturers preferring to use their commercially-produced machines in various endurance events and promotions. It was soon understood that it was not enough to claim in advertising that a certain feat had been achieved. Nor was it enough to invite the press to witness and report on such things: ideas on reporting vary widely and things can appear rather differently through an alcoholic haze. What was needed was an independent and impartial observer to verify the claimed performance as an honest statement of fact.

Thus was born the series of endurance tests officially observed by an official appointed by the Auto-Cycle Union (ACU) who would subsequently issue a certificate detailing the objectives and results of the test undertaken, with all problems and any replacements used duly logged and recorded. It could be good. It could be bad. It would be there for all to see. This honourable arrangement has stood the test of time, and the names of manufacturers who have submitted their products to this form of public scrutiny, some of them over and over again, reads like a who's-who of the British motorcycle industry since its formation.

Right at the head of this galaxy of names, most of which make up that colourful, tapestry-like backcloth to the glorious past of the British industry, was the name of Phelon & Moore, makers of the Panther motorcycle which undertook the first ACU test on the 11th August 1911. This was to be a 1,000 miles trial of a 3.5 hp Phelon & Moore motorcycle 'without the use of a tool'. Bold stuff no doubt in those distant pioneering days. As fate would have it, this inaugural test failed with but 591.5 miles of the target completed. The reason for failure reads quite dramatically for it states that 'a collision with a telegraph pole stay in avoiding a restive horse brought the trial to a sudden termination'.

In the wake of Phelon & Moore came Clyno, Win Precision, Humphries & Dawes (OK Union), Scott, Ivy, Wilkin, Coulson-B, The Excel, AJS (A.J.Stevens), McKenzie, Edmund, Dunelt, Hack, Dorway Sidecars, Clement, Harper Runabout, Rudge-Whitworth, Quadrant, Warrier, Norton, Kenilworth, FN (England), BSA, Raleigh, Douglas, Francis-Barnett, Ariel, Triumph, Radco, New Hudson, Fleet Three Wheelers, and in 1936 BMW. A number of the names listed did not take up the challenge until after the First World War, which put an end to all such activities for the duration. But once hostilities ceased, development of motorcycles in those early post-war years forged ahead. Road racing machines became increasingly specialised, which in turn made officially-observed tests of endurance even more attractive than before.

The Maudes Trophy: Attempts and Winners

And so it came about that in 1923 with a view to stimulating interest and support in such tests Mr. Pettyt, the proprietor of Maudes Motor Mart of Great Portland Street, London, donated a silver challenge trophy to the ACU as an annual award.

With three other branches of the business in the provinces – one in Paris Street, Exeter, another in Wolverhampton Street, Walsall, and finally one in Prince of Wales Road, Norwich - it is clear that Mr. Pettyt had a close interest in the sport, apart from his eye for business, because he had already previously donated a shield to the Surbiton Motor Cycle Club as the premier award in their annual Maudes Shield Trial.

Initially, the trophy donated to the ACU was called the Pettyt Trophy but subsequently it was renamed more appropriately the Maudes Trophy, and as such was destined to play quite a role within the British industry.

From 1923 onwards it became a highly prestigious and sought-after trophy and for several years the ACU was faced with a major task in selecting what was considered the most meritorious of the many tests undertaken in each period of twelve months. The peak year for tests was 1927 when no less than 31 manufacturers submitted products for an observed test. By 1936 the total had dropped to 15 tests in the year, and in 1939 just three. Perhaps the observed test was getting too elaborate and specialised.

The following is an account of the Maudes Trophy winners, and also a number of the more significant attempts reflecting the competition for the award as well as some of the rather more bizarre entries! Given that there were several hundred ACU observed trials it is not possible to give an account of every attempt.

1923 Norton Maudes Trophy Winner

The growth of ACU-observed tests of standard production motorcycles had been stimulated in part by the development of specialised racing machinery, in which sphere Norton Motors were already active and reasonably successful, it is paradoxical to some extent to observe that it was Norton who won the Maudes Trophy when first presented in 1923 – and then proceeded to win it four years in succession. It would seem that Norton believed in having a foot in both camps! The 1923 attempt involved running a 490cc ohv model for 12 hours at Brooklands, in the process of which they gained records for the number of miles travelled in 7, 8, 9, 10, 11, and 12 hours and the highest average speed over distances of 500, 600 and 700 miles, the latter averaging 64.02mph.

1924 Norton Maudes Trophy Winner

This time Norton used a Big Four 633cc model with a sidecar. The object was to travel from Land's End to John O'Groats and back, twice, and also to make 20 ascents of the notoriously steep Porlock Hill. They covered 4088 miles in 18 days.

1924 Raleigh Cycle Company Attempt

The Raleigh Cycle Company set the pace in 1924 when Hugh Gibson, using a 7 hp Raleigh V-twin combination covered 3,400 miles in just under twelve days in a clockwise direction round the coast of the British mainland, simultaneously with Marjorie Cottle tackling the same route anti-clockwise on a Raleigh 2.75 hp lightweight solo model. It was this outstandingly successful epic which inspired C.E. 'Titch' Allen to emulate the format 30 years later (see p154)

1924 BSA 'fastest time up Snowdon' Attempt

BSA assembled four riders with a bike each with which to climb Snowdon. At that time, the fastest climb of any type of motor vehicle had been achieved by a 10 hp BSA car with a time of 49 minutes, 5 seconds. The test objective was to beat that time.

The four riders were Harry Perrey, George McLean, George Savage and Harold Briggs. Three of them rode 350cc ohv models but George McLean rode one of the little 250cc Round-Tank models. When the party assembled at the foot of Snowdon on the 14th May, the weather was dreadful which delayed the start of the climb until the afternoon. When they eventually got going, Harry Perrey and George McLean set out to climb the mountain via the railway track, which they actually used, bumping from sleeper to sleeper. George Savage and Harold Briggs set out on the much rougher, and very narrow in places, mountain path.

Harry Perry was first up in 24 minutes, 6 seconds with George McLean only a little over six minutes astern. Having experienced a very rough ascent, George Savage made the climb in 41 minutes, 8 seconds with Harold Briggs only one and a half minutes inside the hour.

It had been a convincing demonstration – but the ACU had been more impressed with the Norton observed test of that year, so the Maudes Trophy went to Bracebridge Street, yet again, for the second time.

1925 Norton Maudes Trophy Winner

This time a 588cc ohv bike and sidecar was used. They started off with a 3,915.5 mile road test and one hour speed test under ACU observation. Following this they ran the bike around Brooklands for 12 hours which resulted in world records at exceeding 54 mph for 10, 11, and 12 hours driving, and the same speed for 600, 900 and 1000kms.

1925 BSA attempt

In January 1925 BSA arranged for the ACU to purchase from BSA dealers at random up and down the country, the parts required to assemble a Model L 350cc sv machine. The dealers from whom the parts were purchased had no knowledge of what was going on (or so it is alleged) and all parts were available to the ACU within three days. The object of the exercise, of course, was to demonstrate the over-the-counter availability of BSA spare parts. The complete machine was assembled at the ACU headquarters in Pall Mall with the job being completed in 4 hours, 44 minutes. To prove that the model was a runner, it was then taken on a 104-mile, cross country route in Kent and Surrey, on the way taking in several well-known steep hills.

Then to illustrate that such top-grade spares service was not confined to current production models, BSA repeated the exercise three months later with the object of assembling an obsolete 1914, 557cc sv model. Again, all the parts required were available within three days from unsuspecting dealers. The machine was assembled and given the same 104 mile test run. It might be fair to comment that the intervening 1914-1918 war years had restricted technical innovations with a number of the components used on the 1914 model still in use immediately after the war. This test was not of an arduous nature and, strictly speaking, although officially observed by the ACU, could not be termed Maudes Trophy standard.

1926 Norton Maudes Trophy Winner

1926 was the last of Norton's wins. This year they again used the 588cc ohv model and sidecar, with Phil Pike driving. After competing in the International Six Days Trial in which he won a gold medal, the outfit was handed over to the ACU official when, without any work being done on it, it was driven across country from Brooklands at the end of the ISDT to Dinas Mawddwy in central Wales where Phil Pike proceeded to climb the infamous Bwlch-y-Groes hill no less than 100 times in succession. These were not accomplished in one day, however, with 60 climbs completed in 9 hours 15 minutes on the 15th September and the remaining 40 climbs completed in 7 hours 22 minutes the following day. With 100 climbs of the Bwlch under his belt, Phil Pike turned the outfit north to Edinburgh; there he promptly turned round and rushed down to Land's End and back up to Plymouth where the observed test finished. He had covered a further 1,535 miles, including the 100 climbs of Bwlch-y-Groes, over and above the severe mileage completed in the ISDT. That was over 85 years ago before design had advanced beyond rigid frames, girder front forks, hand gear-change and narrow section tyres; and the roads, long before the development of by-passes and motorways, were often badly surfaced, badly cambered and far from straight. They must have been men of iron in those days, with immense will power.

1926 BSA attempt

In spite of the two previous failures to lift the Maudes Trophy, it seemed BSA were determined to succeed and break the Norton stranglehold, so they lost no time in 1926 by inviting the ACU observer, Arthur Bourne, to visit their Redditch factory in January to select a 350cc ohv sports model at random from the stock of like models. This done, the model was ridden to the Birmingham factory by Arthur Bourne where it was fitted with a BSA sidecar. Next day, after a few laps of the test track round the company's sports ground at one side of the great factory, Harry Perrey blasted off to Wales with Arthur Bourne as the sidecar ballast. The destination was the notorious, un-surfaced and challenging Bwlch-y-Groes where the target was to be 100 consecutive ascents and descents of the winding hill. They only had time to do 60 consecutive climbs that day, but the remaining 40 climbs were completed the following day. It was a most convincing performance by the redoubtable Harry Perrey.

Although they beat Norton to it by nine months when Phil Pike also did 100 climbs of that demanding hill, and with a more powerful engine than the BSA, the Maudes Trophy still went to Norton. In that instance, it will be recalled, Phil Pike had already completed the ISDT with his 588cc Norton outfit when he did his 100 climbs and then went on to complete another 1,535 miles on the road after the climbs.

With three disappointments, it could be that BSA became disheartened. Whatever the reason, they made no further ACU-observed tests for nine years. Whilst not participating themselves they probably astutely noted the efforts and results of those who did. Meanwhile, throughout the 1920's and 1930's, they were achieving more than their fair share of success in one-day sporting trials and the six days of the Scottish and the International.

1927 Ariel Maudes Trophy Winner

Ariel used their 557cc sv model with sidecar for their attempt. They ran for 5,000 miles without stopping the engine in a time of 251.5 hours using a route in the Cheltenham, Gloucestershire district.

1927 Shell-Mex Attempt

1926 was not the last time that the Norton name was involved in an ACU-observed test however, for in 1927 the Shell-Mex company undertook a test involving a line-up of twelve machines of various makes including two Nortons. The test involved a public road mileage of 1,403 plus 600 miles of high speed work at Brooklands when Hubert Hassell put in the fastest lap at 80.36 mph on a Norton 490cc Model 18.

1928 Ariel Maudes Trophy Winner

For this attempt Ariel used a 248cc and a 497cc ohv stock models. They covered 10,003 miles in 22 days plus a 1 hour speed test at Brooklands, all without a decoke. Speed test figures were 47.92 mph and 52.21 mph respectively. The road test mileage was carried out in the Cotswold hills.

1928 Shell-Mex Attempt

In a similar test to that attempted in 1927, a line-up of 15 varying makes, including just a single Norton was assembled. This time, however, the fastest Brooklands lap was recorded by a 980cc Brough Superior with a lap speed of 88.08 mph.

1929 Dunelt Maudes Trophy Winner

From 1929 it is reasonably true to suggest that the ACU-observed test became the province of those manufacturers who had adopted a non-racing policy, with Ariel, BSA, Triumph, and Panther dominating the series from then on. However in 1929 it was Dunelt who took the coveted trophy with a truly remarkable performance. One of their 350cc ohv single-cylinder models covered no less than 25,000 miles in 23 days, representing an average speed of 45.14 mph. This was only possible on a closed circuit and thus they journeyed to France to utilise the high-speed circuit of Montlhéry. Even today, it would take courage to set out to better such a performance, despite the sophisticated advantage of the modern motorcycle.

1929 Ariel Maudes Attempt

Along the way, gimmicks, to some extent, were inevitable, the prime example probably being when Harry Perrey assisted by Ted Thacker, crossed the English Channel in 1929 on an Ariel motorcycle mounted on a pair of floats. It was the 497cc ohv single-cylinder. As the old time comedian Stanley Holloway might have put it, 'there were no wrecks, and nobody drowned'. Good publicity maybe, but it proved very little, if anything, from the motorcyclist's point of view.

1930 Dunelt Maudes Trophy Winner

The Dunelt 496cc ohv model was the star in 1930 with a high speed test on the TT course at the Isle of Man. An astonishing 350 laps were completed, totalling 13,199 miles at an average of 34.82mph using a team of seven riders over a period of 18 days - but there was no riding at the weekends! The March weather in the Isle of Man was as unpredictable then as now, as the ACU Observers report makes clear:

> Weather for a great part of the time was intensely severe with heavy falls of snow and high winds on the mountain causing drifts up to 3 feet in depth. Snow also fell on lower parts of the course and for a week ice on the roads was plentiful. Gale force winds, much rain and low cloud on the mountain made visibility very bad throughout at intervals.

During the test the Dunelt was involved in an accident when the bike collided with a car at Ballaugh Bridge. The rider was unhurt, however the machine 'sustained considerable damage' but was repaired on the road. There were also a number of other spills during the test as a result of the road conditions. Dunelt's amazing achievements had repercussions 43 years later when BMW undertook a similar marathon in the Isle of Man (see p170)

1931 Ariel Maudes Trophy Winner

Ariel entered seven models for seven different tests of performance. Some of these were more publicity stunts than tests of the motorcycle (decarbonisation in seven minutes for example), but overall it was an interesting concept, if not quite in the same class as Dunelt's efforts in the previous two years.

Test 1. Model MB 350cc sv. Seven hours of endurance testing at Brooklands track.

Test 2. Model MF 350cc ohv. Seven shillings economy run.

Test 3. Model VB 550 sv. Seven minutes decarbonisation test.

Test 4.   Model VG 500cc ohv. Seventy miles in one hour at Brooklands race track.

Test 5.   Model SB 550cc sv. Seventy minutes non-stop road test on each gear.

Test 6.   Model SG 500cc ohv with sidecar. Seven non-stop climbs of each of seven test hills.

Test 7.   The engine of the 600cc four cylinder model to be started by seven boys under fourteen years of age. All started at the first attempt with the exception of one which started easily on the second attempt.

1932 Not Awarded

1933 Triumph Maudes Winner

The publicity-seeking Harry Perrey, now with Triumph, went to Brooklands with one of the new Val Page-designed 650cc vertical twins, complete with Triumph sports sidecar, and covered a distance of 500 miles in a time of 8 hours, 17minutes at an average speed of 60.28 mph. A pretty convincing speed for a standard combination 80 plus years ago.

1934 Phelon and Moore Maudes Trophy Winner

In the general performance test of 1934, Phelon & Moore put one of their 248cc ohv Red Panther models through a number of tests including one lap of Brooklands undertaken without the rider touching the handlebars! The other test results included:

Economy:	115.7 mpg at an average speed of 35.5 mph.
Steering:	The driver completed one lap of the track without touching the handlebars.
Hill climbing, braking and starting	21 non-stop ascents and descents of the test hill were made, one with the additional weight of an adult male pillion passenger. A re-start on the 1 in 4 section of the test hill, and on this section the driver brought the machine, with gear in neutral, to rest by the independent application of each brake.
Acceleration and speed:	Flying half-mile, 28 seconds @ 64.28 mph; Flying quarter mile, 12.2 seconds @ 63.38 mph; Standing start mile, 23 seconds@ 39.13 mph.
Accessibility:	The back wheel of the machine was removed in one minute 16 seconds.

1935 Not awarded

1936 BSA Attempt

After nine years, BSA must have felt more than capable of winning the Trophy, for when the new 500cc Empire Star model needed promoting for the 1936 season, another ACU-observed test was considered to be an ideal medium.

So for November 1935, a two part test was planned. The first part would be 500 miles at Brooklands with a target of 70mph. This would be followed-up with 1,000 miles on the road, taking in well-known test hills along the route. The 500 miles at Brooklands would be done by Jock West and Ted Mellors, both highly successful racing men, plus Fred Povey of trials riding fame. With the 500 miles completed in less than seven hours, the target speed was comfortably exceeded with an average of 73.31 mph.

For the 1,000 miles of public roads which followed, the saddle was shared between Jack Amott and Bill Walker, both being expert riders from the factory. The route followed embraced the famous West Country main road hills of Porlock, Lynton and Beggars' Roost. In Gloucestershire they digested both Birdlip and the Nailsworth Ladder and in Wales the inevitable Bwlch-y-Groes, before heading for the Lake District where the passes of Kirkstone, Whinlatter and Honister were brushed aside. It had been a trouble-free trip right from the word go; the original tyres had been used throughout and the overall petrol consumption including the high speed work at Brooklands exceeded 50 mpg.

In respect of achieving stated targets and the nature of the success, this test was as good any. Yet for some obscure reason, the ACU did not award the Maudes Trophy at all for 1936. With BSA it was proving to be a classic example of 'if at first you don't succeed…'. And try again they would, in 1938.

1936 Not Awarded

1937 Triumph Maudes Trophy Winner

When the Triumph Engineering Co. of Coventry won the Maudes Trophy for the second time in 1937 they introduced a new dimension to observed tests by arranging for the ACU to purchase at random the three machines required for the test directly from dealer's stocks. (In fact BSA had done something similar in 1925, but had not won the Trophy, see p138).The ACU was supplied with a list of 38 Triumph dealers from whom to obtain the bikes. It had been decided to use three Tiger models of different capacities. In due course a 250cc Tiger 70 was purchased from Walter Brandish & Sons Ltd. (after whom the famous high-speed corner in the Isle of Man TT is named); a 350cc Tiger 80 was obtained from Glanfield Lawrence of London and the 500cc Tiger 90 came from Colmore Depot, Birmingham.

After being prepared, all three machines were transported to Donington Park and given a little gentle running-in. In spite of bad weather delaying the test by a day and with a great deal of rain and water on the track, they persevered and finally Ted Thacker completed 79 laps on the Tiger 70 at an average speed of 50.72 mph. Allan Jefferies riding the Tiger 80 completed no less than 89 laps at an average speed of 57.43 mph. But Freddie Clarke riding the Tiger 90 experienced various problems, including running out of road, and only managed 84 laps at a speed of 54.41 mph.

Next day, the machines were transported down to Surrey and Brooklands where they completed three laps of the outer circuit with the second flying lap timed. The 250cc Tiger 70 lapped at 66.39 mph; the 350cc Tiger 80 lapped at 76.03 mph and the 500cc Tiger 90 at 82.31 mph. The outcome of this observed test was based purely on speed performance, a formula which had brought Triumph success in 1933 for their first win.

1938 BSA Maudes Trophy Winner

Just as in 1935, BSA selected a 500cc Empire Star to make the attempt, but this time it would be partnered by an M21 combination. Both machines were to be selected at random from dealers' stocks as Triumph had done the year before, and there were no less than 1,100 names on the list from which the final choice would be made. The Empire Star was selected from the BSA stock at Sandums of Tottenham, London and the 600cc sv M21 came from Godfreys of Great Portland Street, London. With the ACU observer in charge, the M21 was taken to the factory in Birmingham to have a sidecar fitted and, at the same time, change the engine sprocket to provide sidecar gearing.

With the test getting underway from Wembley Stadium and with road racer Ted Mellors pressed into service to ride the solo, they headed west into Wales for that Bwlch-y-Groes incline which seemed to draw Maudes entrants like a magnet. The M21 sidecar outfit was driven by R.A. Harris, an employee of the factory, with the observer E.B. Ware in the sidecar. The initial stage of the test, after travelling across Wales, was to accomplish 20 consecutive ascents and descents of the hill. With that dealt with, they had to make for Brooklands track in Surrey. Once there, the object was six hours of continuous running on the outer circuit. Both machines went like watches and at the conclusion of the stipulated six hours the Empire Star had completed 127 laps. This gave an average speed of 58.59mph including a fastest laps of 72.71 mph. The combination completed 100 laps which gave an average of 46.12mph including a fastest lap of 50.58mph. They had also been timed over a flying kilometre. The solo's speed was 78.94 mph and the sidecar clocked a handsome 56.26 mph. (It must be remembered that we are writing about a 600cc side-valve single cylinder of nearly 80 years ago).

With that high speed chore completed it was back across country to the Welsh terror near Dinas Mawddwy for another 20 consecutive climbs of the Bwlch. When that was successfully accomplished, there was still more to come. One more trick up the sleeve, so to speak. They drove back to London where the fourth and final phase of the test was enacted. This consisted of making an east to west crossing of London with both bikes fixed in top gear: to be followed by a south to north crossing in the same condition. For this final demonstration of flexibility, the sidecar outfit was driven by David Munro, the highly respected BSA Engineer, whilst the solo was ridden by no less than Jimmy Simpson, the road racing ace famous for his innumerable record laps and ability to break the heart of so many racing bikes. In this instance, the heart of the Empire Star was as stout at the end of the test as it had been at the start.

With this elaborate test having taken place during the February of that year, BSA had to wait seven whole months before receiving the glad tidings. They had done it. They had won the Maudes Trophy at long last. They had won it for the first time.

1939 Triumph Maudes Trophy Winner

It now seemed like a battle royal between BSA and Triumph. The Coventry factory had won the illustrious trophy in 1937. Now BSA had won it in 1938. Clearly they both resolved to win it in 1939 and probably made early plans to be implemented as soon as possible at the turn of the year. We now know that these early events in 1939 proved to be the last act before the curtain came down on peacetime activities and put an end to such keen inter-factory rivalry, but at the time, Triumph could not get back in the hunt quick enough. With the hope that the worst of the winter would be over by the end of February, they fixed the 27th of that month as the start date.

It was to be another high-speed demonstration with two machines selected at random from dealers' stocks. Not surprisingly they decided to use the Speed Twin and the Tiger 100 sports variant. The Speed Twin was purchased from Horridge

& Wildgoose of Sheffield with the Tiger 100 coming from George Bryant's of Biggleswade. The plan was a total of 2,000 miles on the public road coupled with an intermediate period of six hours of continuous high-speed running at the Brooklands track. With R. Ballard riding the Speed Twin and W.J. Nichols the Tiger 100, the public road mileage was achieved by rushing up to John O'Groats which was reached on the Wednesday having left Coventry on the Monday. Then it was south of the border again all the way down to Land's End which was reached on the Saturday. Sunday's riding routine was a gentle 157 miles from Exeter to Weybridge ready for the six hours of lapping Brooklands on the Monday. For this part of the job, four racing men were assembled – David Whitworth, Freddie Clarke, Ivan Wickstead and Allan Jefferies. It could be argued that it is wrong to describe Allan Jefferies as a racing man. He wasn't, in the true sense at that time, but he certainly qualified for the title in the Isle of Man Clubman's TT during the post-war years.

At Brooklands on Monday, the Speed Twin lapped very consistently at just over 74 mph for the first five hours and by the completion of the six hours, the average speed had gone up to 75.02 mph with the penultimate lap timed at 84.41 mph. The true potential of the higher-performance Tiger 100 was inhibited by a puncture on the 10th lap which dropped the average to below that of the Speed Twin at only 70.12 mph but by the conclusion of the six hours the average had soared to 78.56 mph with the penultimate lap timed at 88.46 mph. A truly remarkable performance.

Virtually nothing untoward had occurred throughout the whole trip. During the public road mileage the Tiger 100 punctured near Fort William as it did later at Brooklands. With the Speed Twin the oil pipe to the tank-top oil pressure gauge fractured but the pipe was sealed by flattening the end with a hammer. The Speed Twin also needed one new sparking plug on lap 133. A new steering damper friction disc was fitted to the Tiger 100 and new tyres were fitted to both models prior to the start of the speed test.

The public road mileage had totalled 1,912 at an average speed of 42.3 mph. The overall mileage including the six hours at Brooklands and the 106 mile return trip to Coventry from Brooklands amounted to 2,362 for the Speed Twin and 2,383 for the Tiger 100. The test had gone like clockwork. It was a great credit to Triumph and they could have been excused for feeling somewhat smugly satisfied with the standard they had set.

1939 BSA Attempt

When BSA took up the challenge just one month later, they knew what they were up against so, not surprisingly, their test plan sounded more ambitious, with seven test objectives clearly defined:

Test 1. A circuit of the coast of England and Wales in anti-clockwise direction covering a distance of 2,500 miles, if possible without stopping the engine. The test to continue day and night with changes of drivers and observers every 240 miles approximately.

Test 2. To make 25 consecutive ascents and descents of Bwlch-y-Groes.

Test 3. To cover a section of the route with the gears locked in top gear position for one hour.

Test 4. To cover 100 miles at high speed on the outer circuit of Brooklands track after 2,500 miles on the road.

Test 5. To be driven at maximum speed over the quarter mile at Brooklands.

Test 6. To make 100 consecutive ascents and descents of Brooklands test hill.

Test 7. After conclusion of the above the engine to be stripped for examination and report by the ACU.

Two models were to be used for the test. A solo M23 500cc Silver Star and the old faithful 600cc s.v. M21, both of which were to be purchased at random from dealers' stocks. The former was purchased from Faulkner's of Oxford and the M21 from Percy Kiln of Southsea. Both models were then taken by the ACU to Rex Judd of Harrow where the M21 was married up with a sidecar.

With all the preliminaries done and the models ready for the off, the test got underway at 10:15 am on Tuesday 14th March from the headquarters of the ACU at Pall Mall. Jack Amott, G. Carter, Roy Evans and W. Goudling would be taking it in turn to ride the Silver Star, with the three riders sharing the sidecar driving being R. Harris, W. Johnson and the legendary Harold Tozer. They completed the coastal route of England and Wales in six days, including undertaking the 25 consecutive climbs of Bwlch-y-Groes in Wales which were done in darkness, the hill having been reached at 11:15 pm on the third night out from London. Both machines hit trouble on the Bwlch. The Silver Star solo stopped on the second climb with a choked jet. The sidecar was plagued with clutch slip and after having great difficulty in completing the third climb, both machines were stopped for a period of twenty minutes whilst the primary chaincase of the M21 was removed to tension the clutch springs. This cured the problem and the remaining climbs were accomplished without further trouble.

The M21 had been in trouble long before then however, for it had got no further than Brentwood, after leaving the start point in London, when it had come to a halt with a choked petrol tap. Near Boston the gear lever had dropped off in the road and further north in Lincolnshire, the engine had seized when nearing Brigg. The piston was freed after coasting with the clutch out then dropping it sharply. But it did the same thing again later when the speedometer total read 725 miles.

After the clutch trouble at the Bwlch, the M21 was as good as gold. But the Silver Star displayed a few tantrums, firstly by mis-firing whilst in Wales; to cure this problem a new spark plug was fitted, contact breaker points were adjusted, and a bit later, a new petrol pipe fitted. Then later, when heading for Land's End, the dynamo stopped charging and by the time Land's End was reached the battery was flat. A new fully-charged battery was fitted but with the dynamo still out of action, the new battery was flat by the time Bournemouth was reached. Then the mis-fire re-appeared. A new spark plug and a set of new contact breaker points rectified this, but they were still faced with the battery problem. During the hours of darkness on the final run into London, the battery was changed with the one from the M21, which was able to put a bit of charge into the flat battery. A subsequent check revealed that the armature shaft of the Silver Star's Lucas magneto-dynamo had sheared.

At Victoria, London, the gear lever on both machines were fixed in top gear and the final leg of the journey to Weybridge was completed in top gear, arriving at their destination at 1:30 am. At Weybridge the target mileage of 2,500 had not quite been reached, so a trip round the local Surrey roads soon totted up the balance of 64 miles required.

At Brooklands the following day, the programme did not adhere to the stated objectives, for instead of attempting both items 4 and 6, they increased the target mileage of item 4 to 150 miles and deleted item 6. This distance was completed without trouble with the Silver Star averaging just over 73.5 mph and the M21 combination averaging a little over 48.5 mph. The flying quarter speeds were 78.95 mph and 53.57 mph respectively.

There remained but the final engine strip for examination. Everything seemed in good order, although not surprisingly, there was clear evidence of piston seizure on the M21 and of excessive heat around the cylinder head and exhaust valve. (One should add that the last observation relating to a side-valve engine is somewhat fatuous – they all do it.) It was now up to the ACU and their judgement would not be made until the following September, and as the BSA test came to an end they learned that it was to be at least a three-cornered contest. Phelon & Moore had entered the fray.

1939 Phelon and Moore attempt

Their test of a 600cc Model 100 Redwing Panther solo started at 6:00 am on the morning of March 20th, the day following the conclusion of the BSA test. P & M had last won the Maudes Trophy in 1934, and they clearly believed they were capable of doing so again despite the powerful broadsides from the big boys in the business. After all, they had been the very first to take up the challenge of an ACU-observed test way back in 1911, so it seemed only fitting, in retrospect, they should provide the final act in that pre-war saga of official tests.

The test objective in 1939 was quite simple. To drive from London to Leeds and back until a distance of 10,000 miles had been completed. It was also unique in so far that the test would be officially observed by the riders recruited to do the test and furthermore, recruited by the ACU. A novel idea indeed. Three racing men were coerced for the joint responsibility – Ken Bills, H.C. Lamacraft and K.G. Bilbe with S.F. Board named as a fourth rider in reserve. North Mymms was the start and control point. The test started on the 20th March and the target mileage was completed at 14:37 on the 30th March. The weather during that period included three days of snow and three days of fog. The lights were used for 42% of the time. The average time for the round trip was 8 hours, 58 minutes with an average of 15 minutes for change of riders and turn-around at North Mymms. The total mileage was 10,017 with an average speed working out at 40.29 mph. However, with the change of driver and turn-around time subtracted, the actual running time was 209 hours, 49 minutes – an average speed of 49 mph. Petrol consumption worked out at 56.87 mpg and oil consumption at 2,671 mpg.

By pre-war standards the A1 was a good fast road – and I am assuming the A1 was used by the Panther team – but in no way did it come up to present day standards, and that meant that on average the round trip took nearly nine hours with at least one trip taking almost twelve hours. That was a long time for any one person to be in the saddle. They indeed had hearts of oak. Unfortunately, the heart of the Panther engine had proved less robust. When stripped for examination the big-end assembly was in poor shape. There was a slackness of 0.007" between the rollers and the outer race. Both crankpin and outer race showed signs of wear and most of the rollers were badly chipped on their ends. There was evidence of heat and the con-rod had worn a groove on the inner faces of each fly wheel. The ACU Engineer considered this resulted from an assembly fault.

There were no further tests in 1939 and in the autumn the ACU awarded the Maudes Trophy to the Triumph boys at Coventry. The award was justly deserved and merited. The performance of the Speed Twin and the Tiger 100 in the test held during the previous February had been exemplary and was a portent of things to come when they went on to become probably the most famous four-stroke vertical twins of all.

By the time the Maudes Trophy was presented in 1939, the world was at war. During the 16 years history of this prestigious silver trophy, it had been awarded fourteen times – four times to Norton and three times each to Ariel and Triumph, twice to Dunelt, and once each to Panther and BSA.   It was to be thirteen long years before once again the trophy would be dusted down and handed over in recognition of an outstanding achievement.

1940 – 1951 Not Awarded

1952 BSA, Austrian ISDT and Norwegian Speed Trial, Maudes Trophy Winner

Described in detail in this book .

1953 Triumph Terrier Attempt

It was just twelve months after the BSA success that the Triumph Engineering Company of Meriden lodged their test with the ACU. Producers of larger-capacity twin-cylinder machines only during the post-war years, they had decided to re-enter the smaller-capacity machine market with a 150cc single-cylinder model which they named the Terrier. To promote this new model for the 1954 selling season, they decided to subject three of the models on a 'test of general reliability and economy' over a distance of approximately 1,000 miles from Lands End to John O'Groats. The test was timed to start on the 6th October 1953, and this alone indicates that the main purpose of the observed test was publicity, without any ambitions of winning the Maudes Trophy. If the latter is the main objective then October is not the best time of year.

With the new model to be launched at the forthcoming Earls Court Show, the timing was important, and to achieve maximum publicity it was boldly announced that the Terriers would be ridden by the Managing Director himself, Edward Turner, the General Works Manager, Bob Fearon, and Service Manager, Alec St.J. Masters. To have the Chief Executive himself riding one of his products over that sort of distance was wonderful publicity, and in striking contrast to events of later years when the then Chief Executive of the BSA Motorcycle Group (which included Triumph) not only could not ride a motorcycle himself, but made it known that he disapproved of senior executives of the company riding motorcycles, and to be seen riding them. Such was the 'progress' the company made over the intervening years.

So on the 5ᵗʰ October our friend John McNulty, again detailed to conduct the official observation, went to the Meriden factory to examine the three Terriers produced for his inspection. The models were not selected by him, but he had no reason to believe that they were other than standard catalogue models. With all the usual parts duly sealed with special paint, the bikes were then ridden from Meriden to Exeter where they were filled with Esso Extra (the Esso company again sponsoring the project, as they had the BSA test) ready for the start the next day. From Exeter the bikes were taken the 71 miles to Roche in Cornwall by van.

Next morning, the 6ᵗʰ October, the three Terriers set out from Roche on the 1,000 mile, five-day jaunt in fine weather which was to bless the trip for most of the way. It was probably this, more than anything else, which enabled these rather senior gentlemen, no longer used to coping with the caprices of the elements from the saddle of a motorcycle, to endure the miles which lay ahead. This is rather borne out by the spot of bother experienced by Bob Fearon in the later stages when the weather went against them for the first time.

Having gone down to Lands End and turned round for the trip up-country, the first night was Exeter with a first-day mileage of 122. Not too taxing by any standard. Next day with a mileage of 163, which took them to Leamington Spa for the overnight stop, could not be described as over-taxing either. But the third day was rather more impressive, by reaching Carlisle with a day's mileage of 263. By then the weather had turned dull and windy and the next day, for the final leg to John O'Groats and the end of the test at Wick when the mileage was to be 162, it was wet and in places misty, giving rise to poor visibility. It was this condition which caused Bob Fearon to overshoot a bend and run off the road, jumping a ditch in the process.

Soon after that slight mishap, a bad misfire set-in on Bob's Terrier and a subsequent check diagnosed a flat battery. Thereafter, until the conclusion of the test at Wick, the Terrier ran on the emergency ignition position. Back at the factory, the flat battery was found to have been caused by the screw on terminal 13 on the multi-terminal switch having worked loose and the exposed end of the wire coming adrift and shorting. This may have been caused when Bob Fearon had aviated over the ditch in Scotland which, fortunately, he survived without coming off the bike. Prior to that the throttle cable on his bike had frayed and broken, but they repaired that at the roadside.

During the early stages of the test, they had been plagued with dirt in the petrol, and as a result the carburettors had been stripped for cleaning. The ignition timing on Edward Turner's model had been retarded in the belief that it was over-advanced. When it was realised that it was contaminated fuel causing a lean mixture, the ignition timing was again advanced and the points adjusted. Apart from the following ACU observer losing the riders in difficult traffic conditions in Leicester when they were thus not in view for a period of 27 minutes, no other problems were experienced. They had completed 1,008 miles in a total running time of 17 hours, 29 minutes. This brought an average speed of 36.68 mph, with an overall petrol consumption average of 108.7 mpg.

The three models were returned to the factory by van and duly examined and found to be in excellent condition. It was a good introduction of the new Terrier, made more so by the practical involvement of senior executives. Now in retrospect, that performance was merely indicative of the true potential of that little model when it was allowed to grow-up into the highly successful 200cc Tiger Cub. No doubt Triumph themselves were the least surprised of all when the test was not considered Maudes Trophy material.

1953 Ariel, Eight Countries in Seven Days Attempt

Having won the Maudes Trophy no less than three times previously; in 1927, 1928 and 1931, it was no surprise to see Ariel Motors of Selly Oak and their dynamic Sales Director Tom Davies, jump into the arena to take on the challenge when they mounted their effort just one month after that of their associated company Triumph. Both companies must have been planning their respective tests more-or-less simultaneously, for on 6th November Ariel handed over to the official ACU observer, once again John McNulty, a 650cc FH Huntsmaster twin with sidecar. The stated objective was to visit eight European countries in seven days. The first rider was to be George Buck, a rider with an excellent sidecar competition track record to his credit including trials, grass track racing and International Six Day Events, and always Ariel mounted. The second rider was to be C.M. 'Bob' Ray, the company's post-war star solo rider who had rocketed to fame when he won the first post-war British Experts trial of 1946. He was a superb and dashing rider on a solo, but his capabilities with a combination might be described as an unknown quantity.

The party set out from Moon's Garage, Davis Street, London on the 7th November, heading for Lympne in Kent where they boarded a plane for Le Touquet and then headed south to Paris and beyond to that day's destination, Avallon. That represented a total of 352 miles for the day which had entailed 9 hours, 12 minutes of driving. The weather had been good during daylight, but as darkness fell, it became very frosty with misty patches.

The severe frost and cold persisted next morning when they set out and headed for Geneva, and as ice formed on the rider's goggles they had to be discarded. In turn, ice formed on the rider's eyelids and this forced them to stop for relief. Nonetheless, they reached Geneva in good time, but there they were delayed when repairs were carried out on a crack which had developed in the neck of the right hand side silencer. This had been damaged accidentally in a parking manoeuvre earlier in the test. Vesoul was the destination that day with a mileage of 355, which had taken ten minutes short of nine hours to complete.

The third day was a case of full-steam ahead northwards for Antwerp in Belgium. A total distance of 357 miles, first through Luxembourg then Brussels, with fine weather to assist; with no problems of any nature, it was covered in 8 hours, 36 minutes. It was a similar uneventful pattern for the next two days when firstly they covered 314 miles in fine weather to the night stop at Bremen, Germany, and then a further 294 miles to reach Nyborg in Denmark. Although mostly fine weather, rain set in for the last four hours preceding Nyborg.

Next morning with the Danish city of Copenhagen as the day's target, they crossed to the main Danish island of Sjælland on the same ferry from Nyborg to Korsør which we had used previously on the BSA trip. It must have looked familiar to John McNulty!

There remained but 70 miles to reach their destination at Copenhagen, and in showery rain, they made very slow progress into the city despite enjoying a police escort. Although the observed trip was planned to finish in London from where it had started, the mileage of 1,722 clocked up on reaching Copenhagen was the final mileage recorded for the observed test.

Once again using Esso petrol, but this time Mobil oil, they had experienced a trouble-free run, other than the repair to the silencer. The distance was completed in a running time of 49 hours. This gave an average speed of 40.6 mph with a petrol consumption of 44.95 mpg. If Bob Ray and George Buck had split the driving equally, each had done no more than 861 miles.

It could not, in my view, be described as a very ambitious effort – if ambitious at all. In conception, it did not compare well with the ingenious tests that Ariel had mounted so successfully before the war. The most that could be said was that at least Ariel were being seen to support the rekindled interest in ACU-observed tests. That in itself was good, but clearly the ACU did not regard the test as worthy of recognition. The Maudes trophy was not awarded.

1954 Feridax, 'Round the Coast of Britain' Attempt with C.E. 'Titch' Allen

John McNulty had but six months respite before once again being summoned to volunteer for further observer duties. This time, rather unexpectedly, it was not one of the motorcycle manufacturers but the small accessory manufacturing and factoring firm Feridax Limited of Birmingham whose principal, Jim Fereday, was a great motorcycling enthusiast. In May of 1954 he submitted a 650cc Ariel Huntmaster with Nicholson 'Swaledale' sidecar, to be fitted with Feridax Spring Luxury Dualseat, PVC legshields, Locking Twist Grip, Twist Grip Headlamp Dipper, Touring Windshield and a Grand Alpino Pannier Set. All the accessories named were specialist Feridax lines being marketed by them.

The nature and make-up of the test was two-fold. Firstly a sidecar outfit was to be driven round the coast of Great Britain, a distance of around 3,500 miles. Then secondly, with that completed, the sidecar was to be removed and the Huntmaster as a solo, taken to Silverstone where 500 miles would be covered in 500 minutes. That looked quite ambitious. And when it was pointed out that just one man was scheduled to do all the driving round Great Britain, it looked distinctly interesting. That one man was none other than C.E. 'Titch' Allen, founder of the Vintage Motor Cycle Club, freelance journalist, and enthusiast extraordinaire.

The suitability of such equipment on a fast touring motorcycle and their robustness for the task was the main purpose of the demonstration. The role of the Ariel Huntmaster and Nicholson sidecar was, strictly speaking, secondary - at least it would be in the eyes of Jim Fereday. But nonetheless, the equipment could not be tested without a motorcycle: thus as far as the ACU was concerned, the motorcycle was as much a part of the test as the Feridax equipment. John McNulty therefore logged the performance of the sidecar outfit as on all other observed tests.

A significant difference from other tests to date was that the ACU observer was to be carried in the sidecar of the outfit under observation. There was to be no back-up vehicle. This meant that the luggage of two had to be stowed aboard the outfit, and with John McNulty being no lightweight, there is no doubt at all that the combination was heavily loaded from the outset. It was a one-man crusade, almost, and in retrospect it does seem that the dice were loaded against success from the start.

Once again using Esso fuel, the test got underway on Monday 3rd May, with a short run of 92 miles to Liverpool as the first leg of the clockwise circumnavigation of England, Scotland and Wales. Setting out from Liverpool on the Tuesday morning, Titch Allen proceeded to press on with an obvious gutsy determination, for during the next four days he had reached John O'Groats, turned round and was as far south as North Berwick, a distance of 1,156 miles since Birmingham. By the end of the next day, the sixth since the start, he had covered more miles than the Ariel team during their ACU test the previous November. And Titch had driven the over-loaded outfit all the way. The weather had been wet and showery the whole time with hail and sleet in the higher reaches of Scotland. It was on the fifth day he had his first involuntary stop when the connecting link of the rear chain broke. It took 43 minutes to effect repairs.

Next day, Saturday, saw him travel all the way down from North Berwick where they had stopped for the night, through Redcar, Hull, over the Humber by ferry to New Holland, through Cleethorpes and down through the wolds of Lincolnshire to Holbeach on the edge of the Fens, where they stayed until Monday morning. That day had been the first fine day. The daily mileage target was 350, but on the fourth day it had been as high as 365 miles – so far so good.

Sunday, termed a rest day, was no such thing for Titch who spent most of the day doing maintenance and adjustments. Engine oil was obviously changed, and the rear chain was removed for cleaning and soaking in fresh oil before refitting. A new rear tyre was fitted and the first of the broken spokes were replaced in the rear wheel. This was a problem which was to plague them throughout the test. From then on, evidence tends to suggest that the task was too great, for during the second week which commenced on the Monday morning, there were only two days free of involuntary stops. During the second week they travelled to Dover via Ipswich, Southend, Tilbury and Canterbury. Along the south coast they went, through Southampton, Weymouth, Exeter to Torquay and Thurlestone and on to Lands End via Falmouth and Lizard point, before turning north for Ilfracombe in North Devon and on to Bridgwater and Weston-super-Mare. But on the way, Titch

Allen had been working hard to keep the outfit roadworthy.

Right at the outset on the Monday after leaving Holbeach, they experienced a rear wheel problem which was a direct result of the work done on the previous day when the wheel distance piece had been incorrectly refitted. To put matters right, the oil seal retaining nut had to be refitted, bearing greased, distance piece refitted correctly and the wheel alignment checked. Tuesday brought more broken spoke troubles. This time, when two spokes broke in the sidecar wheel, the spoke heads jammed the brake drum. The broken spokes and the spoke heads had to be removed to free the wheel, but the spokes were not replaced. The rear chain was, by then, very dry and rusty and required lubricating. A choked jet had to be cleared on the Wednesday, with Thursday bringing more broken spokes when three were replaced.

By then they were heading for Aberdovey, having travelled to Gloucester in order to cross the River Severn and then to head west along South Wales, through Neath and Swansea. Before reaching Aberdovey, however, they were in trouble with the sidecar when the eye of the bottom link of the damper unit sheared. They had no alternative but to dispense with the damper unit and jury-rig the sidecar with a piece of wood and fencing wire. This had shades of the pioneering days of motorcycling! From then on, it is fair to assume the personal comfort of the ACU observer was not of the standard to which he had become accustomed.

Their ordeal was, however, nearly over. Friday, the last day of the round-the-coast trip, in showery weather, passed without a hitch as they travelled up Wales to Pwllheli, along the northern coastline to Prestatyn and back into England for Birkenhead and Liverpool. Before leaving Liverpool for their original start point, a replacement sidecar damper unit was obtained and fitted. Back in Birmingham the outfit, still under ACU observation, was put under lock and key until the following Monday morning when the sidecar was to be removed prior to the Huntmaster being ridden to the Ariel factory at Selly Oak for examination.

The first part of the test had been completed. In a total of eleven days, Titch Allen had driven the outfit over a distance of 3,625 miles, coping with all the problems and breakages. Involuntary stops had cost 4 hours, 4 minutes. The average speed worked out at 29.15 mph and fuel consumption at 51.49 mpg.

In my view that part of the endeavour is one of the great classics in the long series of ACU-observed tests. No fancy gimmicks, no stunts, and no back-up. It was a typical British 'back-to-the-wall' display of grim determination in the best traditions of motorcycling.

As for John McNulty carrying out his official duties and acting as sidecar ballast at the same time, he deserved a special award all his own. The sidecar passenger of the year, to be sure!

For the sponsors of the test, things were not looking so good however. When the engine was stripped at the Ariel factory on the Monday, the engine timing-side plain-metal bearing needed replacement. New tyres were also fitted to both wheels whilst at the same time two spokes were replaced in the front wheel and two in the rear wheel. The engine sprocket was changed for a larger solo sprocket and the handlebars changed for standard solo-type bars. All work was completed during the day, and the Huntmaster was ready for an early start to Silverstone next morning when it would be ridden there under observation.

At Silverstone, Titch was joined by three other riders who would be sharing the riding when the objective was to be 500 miles in 500 minutes. The additional riders were H. German, H. Williams, and J. Terry, all better known for their sprinting activities. After four practice laps, the test got underway at 10:26 am with Titch riding the first stint. After 21 laps H. German took over and went on to cover 41 laps before pulling-in for H. Williams to take over. Williams covered 44 laps and then made way for J. Terry who completed a further 35 laps. The final 31 laps of the 172 laps target were then ridden by H. German again in the saddle. They had easily achieved the target in a total time of 8 hours, 5 seconds which gave an average speed of 62.5 mph with fuel consumption of 39.85 mpg. During the 172 laps there had been two involuntary stops. A choked jet had to be cleared on lap 128, and on lap 140 the spark plugs needed to be replaced and at the same time a missing oil tank filler cap was replaced. At the conclusion of the test the replacement tank cap was also missing. During the final examination it was found that the dynamo was not charging and inspection revealed the drive chain to be broken with several fractured rollers. Of the accessories, the only faults were cracks round the top mounting holes on both legshield blades.

In October of that year, the ACU had three observed test to consider. The Triumph Terrier test of the previous October; the Ariel factory test of November and the Titch Allen test just described. To my mind, this rather suggests that the timing of a test is important. Where a test is undertaken early in any test year it can establish a standard for the later contestants to aim at and beat. For example, the Titch Allen project put the earlier Ariel factory effort in the shade. But for mechanical problems which plagued his progress, Titch could well have won the Maudes Trophy.

It is of interest to record that at the conclusion of the test at Silverstone the speedometer showed a total mileage of 6,770. With 4,125 miles covered throughout the test it shows that there had already been 2,654 miles recorded at the start of the test.

I have dealt with the Feridax-Titch Allen observed test at some length, despite its failure to win the Maudes Trophy, because as history now reveals, it was the last British motorcycle to undergo an official ACU-observed test. The last of a long line of British endeavours dating right back to 1911 when P & M had set the ball rolling with test number one.

If personal achievement and the will to win were taken into account, this surely had been one of the best. Like Dunkirk, it was victory in defeat.

1955 NSU Quickly, Lands End to John O'Groats Attempt

After the initial spurt of observed tests which followed the BSA example of 1952, interest seemed to diminish thereafter. Only one test was undertaken in1955 and again only one in 1956. There was not one at all in 1957 and only one in 1958. The total of observed tests undertaken during the 1950s was therefore seven.

The last three of these seven tests were all demonstrations of small capacity lightweight machines normally used for local commuting. Clearly the makers of these lightweights submitted for the test wished to show that despite their small size, they were quite capable of doing a serious job. The first manufacturer in this bracket was NSU Distributors (GB) Limited. They submitted one 49cc NSU Quickly (described as an 'autocycle' in the official ACU test report) to undertake the ever-popular Lands End to John O'Groats run, starting on the 16th April 1955. Also to be observed by the ubiquitous John McNulty – this time from the comforts of a following car. He deserved it.

With T. Wood riding and with Shell two-stroke mix in the tank, they set out from Sennen Cove, a mere 1.25 miles from Lands End, heading-up country. With 265 miles completed on that first day, they halted for the night at Worcester. Next day they peeled off another 271 miles, staying at Crawford for the night. It was a more modest 203 miles next day to reach Inverness, and on the final day's run to John O'Groats a gentle 141 miles were completed. The end-to-end trip had taken a riding time of 37 hours, 20 minutes. This gave an average speed of 23.61 mph and a petroil consumption of 139.64 mpg. In the main the weather had been kind, with a period of one hour of rain on the second day, and also with a few patches of mist. There had been no involuntary stops; no adjustments or repairs. All fuel used had been supplied from sealed cans in the custody of the ACU observer. The final total recorded for the test was 881 miles.

It could only be described as a highly successful run – if somewhat unspectacular. The main hazard for the rider must have been one of boredom, a run which I would not have relished on such a lightweight. If the world had not been aware of the remarkable durability of those small 49cc machines before the test started, it was very clear by the time it finished. It is also evidence showing that good reliable lightweights were available long before the Japanese products reached the British market. All the same, the Maudes Trophy was not awarded.

1956 Douglas Vespa at Goodwood Attempt

Nearly eighteen months slipped by before the next test appeared, this time with Douglas (Kingswood) Limited deciding to put two of their 125cc Vespa scooters through their paces with a 24-hour, non-stop test at the Goodwood racing circuit in Sussex. Once again the timing of the test looks curious, with a full twelve months to go before any test results would be finalised by the ACU.

The test objective was stated to be a 24-hour, non-stop run without stopping the engine. This objective was defined much too specifically, for no matter how well the scooters performed, the moment either engine stopped inadvertently - which in fact they did - they had failed the test.

The test was scheduled to start at 1:00 pm on Friday 19th October, with two teams of four riders lined up to share the hours in the saddle. It was a novel idea to include a lady rider in each team, with Miss J. Manson down to share Vespa registration number RLK 724 with R. Perry, M. Pole and J. Seale. The other Vespa, registration SXV 702, was shared by Miss B. Harley, J Saxton, V. Perry and B. Lewis. Once again John McNulty was in charge of observation, but he had assistance because each scooter would be followed continuously throughout the 24 hours. Once underway, riders and observers were changed at intervals whilst the machines were kept in motion; and refuelling was also carried out without stopping – petroilers being mounted on the tailboard of a lorry.

Keeping the engines running at all times proved the difficulty. The motor of SXV 702 stopped twice before midnight on the Friday - the first occasion as a result of petrol shortage and the second time when the rider stalled it accidentally. Before the test was concluded at 1:00 pm on the Saturday, the engine of this scooter had stopped a further four times, but on each occasion except the last, the scooter was kept in motion. A spark plug change brought it to a standstill on the final occasion. This scooter completed 324 laps in the 24 hours, a distance of 778.8 miles.

Scooter RLK 724 completed 321 laps, a distance of 770.8 miles, and like its counterpart, the engine stopped several times. Twice during the night the engine stopped and the machine came to a standstill, once at 1:53 am when being refuelled and again at 3:00 am with a spark plug problem. At 3:41 am the motor stopped yet again when being refuelled, but they managed to keep the scooter in motion. Before the 24 hours were completed, one further stop was caused by plug troubles.

The weather had been kind, though frequent showers during the night had kept the track surface wet. Both scooters finished in excellent condition although during the subsequent inspection only the cylinder barrels and pistons had been removed. So, during the 24 hour test the eight riders and two scooters between them had logged 1,548 miles. That was an average of 193.5 miles per rider. As good as the test had been, it wasn't really up to the standard set during the 1950s, when a number of top-rate, publicity-attracting demonstrations had been staged by Vespa's dealer in Northampton, Frenchman André Baldet, who had put the Vespa firmly on the map in his area.

The Douglas Company were capable of greater things. Undoubtedly the Vespa scooter was too. When October 1957 came around, it seems that the ACU came to a similar conclusion and the Vespa test went unrewarded.

1957 Not Awarded

1958 Raleigh Moped at Goodwood Attempt

After the Douglas effort, nothing happened for two whole years. Then Raleigh Industries of Nottingham, the bicycle-producing conglomerate who themselves had been motorcycle producers until the early 1930s, decided to put their 49cc moped to the test. It was a case of emulating the Vespa test with a 24-hour non-stop run at Goodwood. The test objective, stated as a trial of general reliability, would embrace three models which would be ridden by a team of nine riders - three per moped.

Moped registration 568 CTO would be ridden by P.M. Hall, M.E. Pennington and E. Sulley. Machine number 565 CTO would be ridden by J.M. Larcombe, F.A. Adcock and S.J. Simpson, and the third machine, 567 CTO, by H. Pickersgill, R.G. Bettesworth and R.H. Harris. A point of interest is that one of the riders in the first team, Eric Sulley, was in later years to join Honda and become their U.K. Sales Director.

With our old friend John McNulty in charge yet again, the test was scheduled to start at 2:00 pm on Wednesday, 29th October. The weather conditions were dry. The whole test was completed without a single hitch, but a certain amount of servicing was carried out in accordance with the service book instructions. For example, on two machines the exhaust pipe and silencer needed to be cleaned, and the rear chain and freewheel oiled on all three models. The headlamp contact required cleaning on machine 568 CTO together with a headlamp bulb replacement. This latter moped covered 642.3 miles with an average fuel consumption of 174 mpg. Moped 565 CTO did not cover the ground quite so quickly completing only 623.1 miles, but it used less fuel with a consumption of 183 mpg. The third machine was slower still with 623.1 miles covered and with the heaviest fuel consumption of 163 mpg.

ACU Engineer, Mr. L.M. Barnes, examined all three mopeds and declared them as in excellent condition. There is no doubt that all three machines had done everything asked of them, but the nature of the test lacked appeal. It seemed fairly mundane and had been done before. Furthermore, by then, it was generally known that small, 49cc two-stroke engines were very robust and more than capable of circulating a flat, undemanding, smooth-surfaced track without undue exertion. The ACU committee probably came to a similar conclusion and thus the Maudes Trophy continued to grace the BSA showroom at Small Heath.

1960 BSA/Triumph Scooter, John O'Groats to Lands End Attempt

The Raleigh moped test was to be the last one officially observed by the ACU in the 1950s, for not one test was submitted throughout 1959, and it was nearly two years later, in September 1960, that the services of an ACU observer were required, when once again BSA took up the challenge. But this time not with motorcycles – with scooters instead. Although the Triumph Engineering Company had been taken over by BSA in 1950, they had nevertheless since then pursued independent engineering and marketing policies as previously. However, during the late 1950s, Edward Turner had developed a new scooter at the Meriden factory which employed a 250cc o.h.v. twin-cylinder, four-stroke power unit. As Managing Director of what was then termed the BSA Automotive Division, Turner elected to produce the scooter at the more spacious BSA plant in Birmingham, and to apply what is termed 'badge engineering'. Machines would be produced for both brands, one using the BSA name and the other badged as a Triumph, in order to satisfy the differing dealer networks. The former was endowed with the aristocratic name of Sunbeam, the latter with the rather feline name of Tigress.

Although the scooter had been launched at Earls Court two years earlier, it was considered that an ACU-observed test would have beneficial results, so a combined test was planned involving one Sunbeam and one Tigress to tackle the ever popular Lands End to John O'Groats favourite - but in reverse order. It was a modest target and the Management had no illusions about it, and not for one moment did they consider the test as potential Maudes Trophy material. Nonetheless, they felt that it would be good publicity and help to promote both scooters.

Brian Martin, by then Competitions Manager at BSA and responsible for arranging and planning this latest effort, decided on a team of four riders - himself and John Harris to ride the Sunbeam with Derek Handy and Henry Vale riding the Tigress. The first three riders were all employed at Small Heath – John Harris in the Competitions Department and Derek Handy a production road tester – with Henry Vale from Meriden being Triumph's Competitions Manager.

Sunday 18th September was the start date, with the new name of Mr. H. Clenshaw officiating as the ACU observer. With the hope of engendering additional publicity right from the start of something which it was admitted would not attract headlines thereafter, Geoff Duke and John Surtees had been arranged to ride the Sunbeam and Tigress respectively for the first few miles before handing over to the team. Neither scooter, incidentally, had been selected at random from stock by the observer. Both were presented to Mr. Clenshaw as ready to go.

Once underway and having dispensed with the publicity aids of Geoff Duke and John Surtees, they made short work of the trip, completing the 320 miles to Edinburgh by that Sunday evening. John O'Groats was reached during Monday with another 307 miles ticked-off. Tuesday saw them return down Scotland and back to Edinburgh for the night. By Wednesday evening they had reached Kidderminster with a mileage of 311 for the day, and on Thursday they made Penzance with a further 274 miles recorded. The job was completed on Friday when they made the short hop to Lands End where they turned round and rode back to Meriden – a day's mileage of 318.

The total distance of 1837 miles had been covered in a running time of 52 hours, 20 minutes. Petrol consumption on both models had been virtually identical; 102.06 mpg on the Sunbeam; 101.18 mpg on the Tigress. There had been no involuntary stops, neither scooter had been touched with a spanner, no adjustments of any sort had been made, tyre pressures had not been touched - and neither scooter had even been cleaned. At the lunch stop on the first day however, an electrical short on the horn wire of the Sunbeam had to be rectified.

ACU Engineer, Mr. R.H. Player, examined both scooters at the conclusion of the run, and whilst neither power unit was removed from the frame, each engine was stripped. The offside cylinder on the Sunbeam had been slightly scored vertically, almost certainly caused by a fragment of carbon from the piston crown according to Mr. Player. There was slight scoring on the nearside big-end lower shell bearing on the Tigress which Mr. Player considered had occurred during assembly.

As expected, the test did not really attract any headlines. It had all been too easy. Clearly both scooters had been capable of a great deal more, their true potential barely tapped.

The end-to-end run could have been used as a warm-up for a more strenuous second phase such as, for example, 100 consecutive climbs of Bwlch-y-Groes in Wales, and in so doing have been the first scooter to be matched against that infamous mountain road which had proved so irresistible in pre-war days. But it was not to be. Once again, no Trophy was awarded.

1961–1962 Not Awarded

1963 Honda at Glorious Goodwood, Maudes Trophy Winner

The year 1961 came and went without a single manufacturer undertaking an ACU test. The Maudes Trophy, in all its silver glory, still languished at Small Heath where it had been allowed to stay beyond the time BSA were officially custodians by virtue of having won it in 1952. Was it going out of fashion? Had BSA set too high a standard after all? Were motivation and inspiration lacking?

Certainly Harry Louis, Editor of *The Motor Cycle* was conscious of the lack of activity and in an endeavour to rekindle interest he published on his leader page of the 13th July 1961 issue a picture of Fred Rist, Brian Martin and myself taken during the BSA test of 1952. This picture appeared at the top of the page, and at the foot of the same page appeared a picture of the Triumph Tiger 100 and Triumph Speed Twin taken at Brooklands during the Triumph test in 1939. These two pictures were used to illustrate the leader in which Harry Louis wrote as follows:-

> Does my picture remind you of anything in particular? Here are a few clues. It was taken in Austria in 1952. The riders are Brian Martin, Norman Vanhouse and Fred Rist. 'International Six Days Trial' you might say. You would be right. But the shot might also remind you of something else. Of the Maudes Trophy. Those three runners on random-selected 497cc BSA twins won it for a 5000-mile ACU-observed trip. They went to Austria by way of Holland, Belgium, France and Switzerland, gained gold medals for clean runs in the trial and returned through Germany, Denmark, Sweden and Norway. Then, at Oslo aerodrome, all three machines were timed at means speeds of over 80 mph.

That was a first-class show. One of the most enterprising, in my opinion, of efforts to win the Maudes Trophy since it was first presented in 1923. Competing for this trophy, which is awarded for the best performance each year in an ACU-certified test, was a regular thing in pre-war years. Not so since. No one has had a crack since 1952. Why not? Enthusiasts like to see the machines they can buy put through their paces. The kudos for the manufacturer concerned is immense. True, it is difficult, these days, to think up tests which are arduous enough yet sensible. But it is not impossible.

Thus wrote Harry Louis, and other than the error concerning lack of attempts since 1952, all very true. The sentiments he expressed prompted me to write an article for his magazine which he published in the 28th September issue of that year. Whether the reminders both Harry Louis and I had made ever helped can never be determined. Certainly there was no apparent initial response – not until October 1962, just ten years since the BSA success – when the mighty Japanese company of Honda laid claim to the trophy.

Having established their British subsidiary, they set out to market their lightweight machines in the United Kingdom in the vigorous and determined manner typical of their new top executive, Jim Harrison, who had left a senior position at Raleigh Industries of Nottingham to tackle this new challenge. Today we are familiar with the fact that Honda always do things in a big way, so maybe now, it would be no surprise if they announced they would be putting some of their little scooters into orbit. For when they boldly announced in October 1962 that they would be running three of their little 49cc machines around the Goodwood race circuit, non-stop, not for 24 hours, but for a whole week, it sounded almost suicidal. We knew little 49 cc two-stroke engines were very robust by then and quite capable of withstanding abuse. But a small o.h.v. four-stroke unit? That was quite different. Think of all the small parts which go to make up a four-stroke engine, those tiny valves and that small-capacity oil sump. For a whole week! They must fly apart!

Honda did not think so. And they proposed to prove it, with official ACU observation. The stage was then set for October. In this instance, the October timing was vital for the test would support the launch of the new models at the Earls Court Motorcycle Show in November.

Once again with John McNulty in charge of the party of official observers, everybody involved assembled at Goodwood for a noon start on Wednesday 24th October. The three models to be used had not been selected by the ACU, but assembled and prepared by Honda themselves and conveyed to Goodwood, at which point they came under the jurisdiction of the ACU. Three teams of riders had been recruited, including several familiar names associated with road racing and motorcycle journalism, plus Olga Kevelos, the lady rider who had retired on the second day of the ISDT in Austria in 1952 as noted earlier in this story. The riders and the Honda models they would use were as follows:-

C110D (Reg. EXO 777)	C102 (Reg. EXO 778)	C100 (reg. EXO 773)
W.D. Ivy	P.R. Alexander	T.F. Burtonwood
E.J. Swain	J.V. Hatcher	R. Nunn
B.J. Swain	F. Harvey	R.G. Butchers
S.B. Benn	G.V. Clarke	P. Braithwaite
C.E. Deane	O. Kevelos	B.C. Allen
D. Degens	G. Gulder	R.A. Prior
J. Martin		

Throughout the test, each machine would be followed by an observer all the time. The course measured 2.363 miles per circuit. At 12:00 noon, in ideal weather conditions, they got away on what was to be another landmark in the long history of ACU-observed tests.

Every twelve hours each machine was pulled into the pits for examination and maintenance. Oil level was checked and topped-up when necessary and each machine had one complete oil change during the test. Chains were lubricated and adjusted, front forks greased, tyre pressures checked and corrected where necessary. Batteries were topped-up as needed, and tappets also checked and adjusted. During the last three days of the test, weather conditions deteriorated and ice formed in places on the track and also there was some ice formation in the carburettors. As a result of this, lagging was applied to the carburettors and manifolds.

During the first day, not one of the three machines required any attention other than the routine one hour service. But on the second day various minor items needed attention over and above the routine service. The 49cc C110D machine being particularly troublesome – the front headlamp bulb, reflector and lens plus rear light bulb had to be changed. By the third day the rear tyre tread was showing serious signs of wear, so the whole wheel assembly was changed. Next day, the speedometer bulb required replacement. Then by the fifth day, the machine caused greater worries with the engine showing signs of losing performance. First they had to remove a flapping portion of the rear number plate which had fractured, then, suspecting that the flywheel generator had worked loose, the side plate was removed for examination but found to be in order. Three hours later at 2:00 in the morning, it was decided to remove the cylinder head and barrel in order to examine the piston and valves. According to the report, nothing was changed and 43 minutes later the bike was back on the track circulating.

There was still something affecting this machine's performance and shortly before 4:00 am the carburettor was removed and the jets cleaned. Two hours later the spark plug was then changed. On the sixth day another headlamp bulb was required, and mid-morning the original rear wheel, now carrying a new tyre, was fitted. For the last day this machine went without a hitch.

The C102 model (EXO 778), the Scooterette with self-starter, like the C110D motorcycle, had a faultless opening day but by day two, things were happening. Firstly, early in the morning the spark plug had to be changed. Then mid-morning it came to a standstill shortly after leaving the pits and was pushed back the reverse way along the course. The carburettor float chamber screws had worked loose. On the next day the complete carburettor was changed. At the same time, the spark plug was changed and the ignition timing adjusted. During the night the headlamp bulb had to be replaced, and at 6:30 am the machine again failed around the course and was towed back to pits, where it was found that the battery was dry. This was re-filled, the rear light and stoplight bulbs replaced and the bike sent on its way. But once again on the following day, it had to be pushed back to the pits where a blown fuse was replaced. On the fifth day a new headlamp bulb was needed, and on the sixth day a new rear tyre was fitted. On the last day the performance faded. Firstly the spark plug was thought to be at fault. Then the contact breaker points were adjusted, which still did not resolve the problem. The carburettor complete was removed for cleaning and the contact-breaker assembly replaced, and another spark plug fitted. Thereafter it gave a trouble-free ride for the remainder of the last day.

The C100 (EXO 773), the basic and cheapest Scooterette, and following regular updates a model still manufactured today in 2015 over 87 million sales later, gave the most remarkable performance. It completed no less than four consecutive days without a single snag. On the fifth day the rear light bulb required changing, then the spark plug. Then at the rather curious time of 8:30 in the morning, it stopped halfway round the course with ice in the carburettor. When this was removed, the model restarted quite happily and after fitting a new rear wheel and tyre assembly complete, away it went. From then on until the conclusion of the test, all that this model needed was another headlamp bulb and the spark plug gap adjusted.

This basic C100 had completed a distance of 5,023 miles during the week at an average speed of 29.90 mph and a fuel consumption of 124.30 mpg. The electric-start C102 completed 4935 miles with a remarkable consumption of 140.52 mpg. The rather higher performance C110D motorcycle covered 5,897 miles at an average speed of 35.10 mph and a consumption of 124.30 mpg.

Although a routine inspection with adjustments where necessary had been conducted every 12 hours on all three machine, translated into mileage means an average of every 377 miles, it had proved to be a most convincing demonstration of reliability. When Mr. Barnes, the ACU Engineer, examined the machines he found them in virtually perfect condition, praising in particular the clean and oil-tight exterior of each unit. Whereas the maximum bore wear on both the Scooterettes was a mere 0.0005", wear on the C110D motorcycle proved to be 0.0025". Mr. Barnes also recorded that there was evidence on the cylinder bore of the piston having picked-up, probably during the running-in period. He also considered that the condition was not so satisfactory as the other two machines; that the engine had been run at its maximum. That view seemed consistent with the fact that Bill Ivy had completed a lap at 51.43 mph at the conclusion of the test. The C102 did a lap at 41.86 mph and the standard C100 at 38.25 mph.

No other ACU tests took place throughout this 1962-63 period, so with a test as convincing as this one, presentation of the Maudes Trophy to Honda seemed assured. When the presentation was announced twelve months later, it was a mere formality. So the Maudes Trophy, at long last, left the confines of a British factory at Birmingham and was handed over to its new Japanese custodians. Clearly the shape of things to come.

The award was fully justified. The test had been a rigorous and demanding one for the machines, if less so for the riders. But the basic principle is to be a test of reliability and performance of the motorcycle or scooter – not the rider. However there needs to be more to it than this, otherwise elaborate routines involving teams of riders could be dispensed with and replaced with a simple test rig on which a machine could be run to destruction – as with development work. That sort of thing cannot be measured in human terms, so we need familiar situations to which the man in the street can relate and recognise.

So it is not enough to prove the mechanical reliability of the machine. We need a human element provided by the rider and, in addition, we need an environmental element. The latter can be provided by genuine surroundings and conditions or by synthetic means – such as a closed circuit. If these three elements are accepted in principle, then the Honda test would score ten out of ten for technical ability – for want of a better definition – average marks for human content, and average marks for environmental content.

Riding round a 2.3-mile closed circuit on any power driven vehicle, whilst boring in the extreme, could not be classed as taxing. And if the 755 miles covered every 24 hours had been covered on a continuous and natural road with varying gradients and surfaces, it would have been that much more convincing and exciting. That is not a criticism. I have analysed it thus to make it easier to assess the merits of the tests which were to follow.

1964 not Awarded

1965 Suzuki, Welsh and Manx Three Days Trials Attempt

Despite the fine example set by Honda in October 1962, there was another gap, this time of over two and a half years, before anyone else saw fit to take up the challenge [1]. Now it was Suzuki who decided that what their deadly Japanese rival could do, they could do also. Thus they committed three of their standard 79cc K10 motorcycles to six days of enduro-type competition activity, by entering them into the Welsh Three Days Trial and then the Manx Three Days Trial which followed soon afterwards.

On the 16th May, John McNulty went along to the Suzuki warehouse at Whalebone Lane, Dagenham and selected one crate of standard K10 models, three machines in all. This crate was then transported to Llandrindod Wells, which was to be the base for the Welsh Three Days Trial due on the 19th, 20th and 21st of May. The bikes were placed under lock and key by the ACU observer, ready for assembly from the crate next day, again under observation.

With each machine assembled and made roadworthy, complete with registration plates, they were taken on a 50-mile trip for running-in purposes, again under observation, and then taken to a nearby steep hill to determine gear ratio suitability. After this assessment the gearbox sprocket was changed for a smaller one with twelve teeth (the standard sprocket having thirteen teeth). In addition a few other jobs were carried out to adapt them more for the task ahead, including replacing the standard Japanese tyres with Dunlops, 2.50 x 17 K70s. On Tuesday evening, 18th May, the three models were weighed-in and thus came under the jurisdiction of the event officials until it finished on the following Friday.

---

1   In November 1964, a private individual, Mr.D. Noys, had the speed performance of his tuned 198cc Lambretta scooter officially observed. It achieved 78.763 mph.

The three men to ride the bikes would include John Harris who, it will be recalled, was one of the team of riders involved with the BSA-Triumph scooter observed test back in 1960. Also John Stone, a trials rider from Birmingham of some ability whose father Bill Stone had been the last works manager at the Bracebridge Street Norton factory before Associated Motor Cycles transferred Norton production to Plumstead. The third rider was an ex-TT rider of considerable experience, Stan Miller, who had first ridden in the TT, where he finished tenth in the Lightweight race, in 1938. His highest placing in the post-war TTs was ninth in the 1948 Junior race.

Next morning the three riders, with John Harris riding number 10, Stan Miller on number 12 and John Stone on number 15, all got away to a good start and headed for the rigours of the Welsh mountain tracks. But it didn't stay that way for very long! John Harris was brought to a standstill with ignition failure. It was either a coil or a condenser problem. Whatever the fault, John was unable to restart the machine and was excluded from the trial when the time allowance was exceeded. To make matters worse, both Stan Miller and John Stone lost marks on time as a result of stopping to assist their team-mate, all to no avail. Miller lost six marks on time and John Stone lost one mark. During the second and third days, the latter lost a further 37 marks on time as a result of dealing with a series of punctures.

It was a big disappointment for John Harris. Exclusion from the event also meant exclusion from the ACU-observed test. But Stan Miller went on to make the best performance in the 100cc class, with John Stone collecting a bronze medal. Other than broken front mudguard stays and some loose spokes, the two machines were in pretty good shape.

It is somewhat ironical to record that the outright winner of the Welsh Three Day Trial that year was Don Barrett – riding a 79cc K10 Suzuki, the smallest capacity machine ever to win that event.

After the trial, the remaining two machines were locked-up in Llandrindod Wells by John McNulty, pending the 29th May when they were due to be collected and transported by pick-up to Liverpool for shipment to the Isle of Man. This was completed under observation, with neither bike having been touched from the conclusion of the Welsh Three Days event until Monday 31st May in Douglas, when the day was devoted to maintenance and adjustments. The broken front mudguard stays were replaced and new Dunlop K70 tyres were fitted.

The trial got underway at 7:00 am on Tuesday morning from the TT grandstand, but neither John Stone nor Stan Miller were really able to excel. Although the former did complete the course, he was excluded from the results for having missed one part of the special check. With a loss of 30 marks, Stan Miller won the 100cc class cup plus a bronze medal. When John Stone finished, his nearside footrest was missing and the silencer was dropping off. Stan Miller's model had lost its silencer completely.

Obviously the outcome of the test had proved disappointing for both Suzuki and the riders. Despite the success of Don Barrett on one of these little 79cc machines in the Welsh trial, it did seem that the Welsh mountains and the glens of the Isle of Man had been rather too much for them, but it does reflect much credit to Suzuki for having the courage to commit them to such rough treatment. With only two of the three bikes finishing the test, a negative response concerning the Maudes Trophy from the ACU was inevitable.

1966–1972 Not Awarded

1973 BMW in the Isle of Man, Maudes Trophy Winner

Sadly the Suzuki test was the last ACU-observed test for no less than eight years. In searching for a plausible explanation, one is forced to the conclusion that the answer must be an economic one. There had been a great deal of contraction within the British motorcycle industry and from the record peak sales of 331,806 machines in 1959 (mopeds, scooters and motorcycles), decline had set in during the 1960s reaching a record low in 1969 of only 85,414 sales. By the 1970s, however, things were again looking up and by 1973, unit sales had reached 193,612. Even so, the British industry was that much leaner; indeed by 1973 there were only Triumph and Norton machines being produced. All the smaller independent makers had fallen by the wayside and even the mighty BSA manufacturing complex at Small Heath had closed down.

To a certain extent, the ACU-observed tests, the Maudes Trophy and the British motorcycle industry were as synonymous as Lord Wakefield, Castrol oil and land speed record breaking in those distant days before the Second World War. As the British industry faded, so did interest and activity in such ACU tests. With the decline of the British, it now seemed left to the foreign manufacturers to fill the vacuum. It is true, as we have recorded, that German-made NSU mopeds had made an attempt as long ago as 1955 with the Italian-made Vespa only twelve months behind. Then there was the sensational Honda success of 1962. But all those tests featured lightweight machines which lacked the glamour of putting full-blooded, large capacity motorcycles through their paces.

When BMW then came along in May 1973 and submitted details of a marathon test involving two of their large 750cc twins, the news must have been welcomed in all quarters. It sounded like old times. It had been almost twenty years since the ACU had observed a test involving a large-capacity motorcycle. That was the courageous effort of Titch Allen with the Ariel Huntmaster sidecar outfit.

The BMW plot was quite simple: to circulate two R75/5 twins round the TT course in the Isle of Man for seven days and seven nights of 'continuous running'. Those two words were stated in the test objectives, and it is important to remember them (even if the definition of 'continuous running' is debatable). A small army of fourteen riders in all were gathered to share the riding under the control of team manager Ken Heanes – himself a brilliant rider with an enviable string of successes in the International Six Days Trial. He was assisted by Alec Smith, at the time an Inspector in the Traffic Division of the Metropolitan Police, another expert and talented motorcyclist. Both Ken and Alec were to complete a certain amount of relief riding in the test.

Most of the fourteen riders involved were well-known names in the world of motorcycles, being a mixture of experts like Tony Jefferies, Allen Killip and Dave Minskip – the latter another Metropolitan policeman with a great deal of two-wheel competition behind him – and noted journalists such as Charlie Deane, John McDermott and John Nutting. The complete register of riders being:-

D. Davies	C. Deane	M. Hemmings
T. Jefferies	P. Kelly	D. Kewley
A. Killip	J.McDermott	D. Minskip
M. Nicks	J. Nutting	B. Preston
A. Robinson	D. Woods	

John McNulty was once again the ACU official in charge, assisted by Dr. W. Pycraft, Mr. H.M. Rowell and Mr. P. Ryall.

The two R75/5 models to be used in the test had been selected at the Munich factory in Germany by Herr Hans Richter, an official of the O.M.K, the West German Motorcycle Federation, and after running-in the cylinder heads and barrels (to quote the official report), they were packed in sealed cases and despatched to the Isle of Man where they were un-crated in the presence of Dr. Pycraft. Thereafter, work carried out included changing all wheels, fitting crash bars, auxiliary headlamps and registration plates. For ready reference during the week, the machine with registration RLE 58L was designated 'Machine A', and RLE 59L was to be 'Machine B'.

With the whole operation controlled from the TT grandstand, it was formally flagged off jointly by the mayor of Douglas and local resident Geoff Duke, at 12:00 noon on Thursday, 3rd May. Just prior to the start a short test run of five miles had been undertaken, under official observation, and following that the speedometer on Machine A recorded 1632 Kms (1,020 miles) and that on Machine B showed 2243 Kms (1,401 miles)[2].

The weather throughout the test proved almost continuously wet and cold, with fog on the mountain section at night. At times visibility was nil all the way from the Guthrie memorial to Creg-ny-Baa. At one time there was a river of water running across the road at Signpost Corner. After 100 laps had been completed, each machine underwent a normal 4000-miles service, but in addition to that, Machine A had the carburettors re-tuned, a loose horn wire re-attached and a missing push-on plastic cover to the swinging-arm axle replaced. Both motorcycles had engine oil and filters changed, and tappets, front brake and control wires all adjusted.

Everything progressed smoothly and according to plan during the first four days and nights, with the riders each normally completing four laps in daylight and two laps in darkness. Then, quite suddenly after this period of trouble-free regularity, shortly after 4:00 am on Monday, 7th May – the fifth day of the test – disaster struck in a large way. The rider of Machine B ran out of road at Brandish Corner, destroying the front-end of the motorcycle. No other vehicle was involved and the rider was unhurt. The severely damaged machine was collected by trailer and returned to the grandstand for repairs. The accident occurred whilst the bike was on lap 119.

Working as quickly as possible, it took nearly five hours to repair the damage. The work involved fitting new front forks, new front wheel and mudguard, new handlebars and control levers, headlamp and switch assembly, new exhaust pipes and off-side silencer, front and rear indicators, nearside petrol tap, one rear-view mirror and the offside rocker-box cover. The centre stand was also no longer serviceable, but was not replaced. It was a tidy old prang which must have given rise to a great deal of concern, because the test objective of 'continuous running' had now disappeared.

---

2   This contradicts the official report that after Herr Richter selected the machines in the German factory, 'the cylinder heads and barrels were run-in'. The mileage suggest rather more than nominal 'running-in'.

The repair team had no sooner relaxed from their hectic labours getting Machine B back on the road (despite it having failed the test objective) when it happened all over again. This time it was Machine A, at 1:30 pm on lap 131, whilst travelling along the Quarter Bridge Road. A lorry pulled across the path of the approaching rider whilst making a right-turn. Under severe braking on the wet road, combined with attempted avoiding action, the bike skidded and went along the road on its side before hitting the front-offside of the lorry. It was a repeat of the accident to Machine B – the rider was unhurt but the front of the machine was written-off. It was collected by trailer and returned to the grandstand area for repairs. This time the repair work took just under three hours and items replaced being virtually identical to those fitted to Machine B earlier – new front forks, front wheel and mudguard, headlamp and switch assembly and indicators, handlebars, control levers, clutch and brake cables, petrol tank and battery.

It was a disappointment for all concerned for the test objective had now been completely negated, and they must have wondered if it was worth continuing. However, Machine A restarted lap 131 after the repairs had been completed, but all was not right. At the end of the lap it pulled into the pits where the nearside exhaust pushrod was replaced. A few laps later, it came in yet again and this time the nearside cylinder head was unsealed and removed in order to replace the exhaust valve. The cylinder head was refitted and resealed. The ACU observer recorded that these repairs to the engine could be fairly attributed to the effects of the accident.

On lap 140, Machine B was back in the pits having its battery replaced. Then Machine A suffered another ignominious trip back to the pits on the trailer when its clutch burnt-out on lap 203 at Cronk-y-Voddy. This further repair to machine took just two minutes short of three hours to complete.

Jointly throughout the week, the two machines had consumed six rear tyres and one front tyre. Three bulbs were also replaced during the week.

At 12:00 noon on the 10th May, the test came to an end. At that point both bikes were together at a point 28 miles round the course, having set-out on the last lap together. At the end of that lap they thus crossed the line at the grandstand together.

Machine A completed 216 laps plus the 28 miles of lap 217, which gave a total mileage of 8,178.54 with an average speed of 48.68 mph.

Machine B covered marginally further with 224 laps plus the 28 miles, giving a total of 8,480.39 miles with an average speed of 50.47 mph.

Although a well-planned operation with the support group proving very efficient and capable with the volume of work it was called upon to perform, they must have been disappointed with the overall results, knowing that the test objective had not been achieved.

We can guess that a great deal of deliberation took place behind the closed doors of the ACU the following October when the merits of the test were considered. With several grey areas to influence a decision, one factor could well have weighed in favour of BMW. There had been another long gap of ten years since the Maudes Trophy had been presented. There was a need to stimulate renewed interest in this historical trophy, and it may well be that the ACU leaned over backwards in their deliberations for this reason. So in October they duly found in favour of BMW, and once more the coveted Maudes Trophy came out of mothballs.

BMW must have been delighted. They had won the trophy at their second attempt which probably atoned for their first abortive attempt. In 1936, on 5th May, Jock West aboard an R5 model had set-off round Brooklands track to cover 750 miles in 12 hours. But less than halfway, with just 281.5 miles completed, on lap 103 the engine had failed and the test had been abandoned.

With the announcement of the award to BMW, eyebrows were raised in various quarters and old records were retrieved to show that a similar, and Maudes Trophy-winning test, had been undertaken by Dunelt no less than 43 years before in 1930 (see p141). On that occasion, a 500cc o.h.v. Dunelt with rigid frame and girder forks had covered no less than 350 laps of the TT course – a distance of 13,199 miles. It should also be remembered that in those days the road conditions were much inferior and the weather was atrocious with deep snow drifts on the mountain.

It is a coincidence that the Dunelt, like the BMW 43 years later, was also involved in an accident when it collided with a car at Ballaugh Bridge. The rider was unhurt but the machine 'sustained considerable damage' and unlike the BMW, the damaged Dunelt was repaired on the spot at the roadside.

1974 Suzuki, Round Britain Three Times, Maudes Trophy Winner

When Suzuki undertook their previous test in May 1965, 51% of the shares of the UK distribution company were owned by Associated Motor Cycles Limited, manufacturers of Matchless, AJS, Norton, James and Francis Barnett machines. When this company was taken over by the official receiver in 1966, for a time the company which continued to distribute Suzuki motorcycles in the UK market was wholly controlled by the industrial bankers who then owned all the share capital.

In due course, this company was taken over by Peter Agg who, in the 1950s, had demonstrated his marketing talents with the Lambretta scooter to such an extent that whereas in all other European markets Vespa had enjoyed the dominant scooter market share, in the UK market the Lambretta brand had reigned supreme.

From the moment he took over the marketing of Suzuki, Agg and his company made their presence felt with positive and aggressive marketing, so it was no surprise when they announced details of an ACU-observed test planned to take place in November 1974, almost 18 months after the successful BMW project. They decided on three circuits of the coastline of Great Britain which ran to 2,846 miles per circuit. It did look as though in planning their effort, they had used the BMW success as their yardstick. If they could achieve roughly the same as BMW, but with three machines instead of two, then success must surely be theirs. And they would go one better by travelling round the coastline rather than using the TT course. The environmental merit, as I term it, would be far greater for it would involve 2,846 miles of unfamiliar and constantly changing roads - a much more daunting prospect than the relatively cosy 37.73 miles used by the BMW team in the Isle of Man or the nursery-like 2.36 synthetic strip of the Goodwood circuit used by Honda in 1962. Three times round would be pretty convincing.

So the ball was kicked into play when John McNulty went along to the Suzuki warehouse to select the three models it had been decided to use. These were the 750cc water-cooled, two-stroke triple GT750; the GT550 three-cylinder counterpart, and the air-cooled GT 380 triple. The GT 380 came from a batch of eight crates of this model, the GT 550 from a selection of fifteen crates, and the big GT 750 was chosen from eleven crates. This took place on the 10th and 11th of October and after the machines had been assembled, John McNulty sealed the cylinder heads, barrels and crankcases. Thereafter, the three bikes remained in the care of Suzuki until the start of the test at Brighton on the 23rd November, from which moment until the conclusion of the test on 7th December they were under the observation of the team of ACU observers.

At 12:30 pm on Saturday, 23rd November, the convoy got underway from the official start point of Beamish Motors Limited at Portslade in Sussex, with observation of the three motorcycles maintained from a Range Rover which either followed or preceded them as best fitted to the traffic and weather conditions. The observers and the squad of riders were divided into four teams. As a team they completed a section of around 300 miles, then being followed by the other teams for three further such sections before taking their turn again, and so on. Travel between finishing and re-starting another section often involved a very long journey made in caravanettes. Sleeping on the move was theoretically possible but did not work out well in practice. It was usually possible to park somewhere to permit a short period of rest but conditions were, by any standard, arduous.

The officiating observers consisted of J. Ashworth, C.C. Cann, R.G. Owen and F.E.G. Vigers. Together with Suzuki's Technical manager, Graham Malyan, John McNulty controlled the observation room set-up in the premises of Sports Motorcycles Limited of Liverpool Road, Manchester, and from there they had radio-telephone communication with the Range Rover, and also by telephone to the various change-over points. A 24-hour watch was maintained. It was probably the most elaborately organised ACU test yet.

A squad of no less than seventeen riders were recruited for the task, consisting of:-

G. Ascott	T. Fagon	R. Marshall	A. Robinson
G. Bailey	G. Hatcher	K. Newman	B. Sprawson
G. Bazley	I. Henning	J. Nutting	M. Wilmore
J. Bedson	P. Mansfield	C. Parr	S. Woods
R. Benson			

Of these riders both Allan Robinson and John Nutting had participated in the BMW test on the Isle of Man the previous year. Some of the riders were also members of the Suzuki Owners Club.

The weather conditions throughout the test were described as truly appalling, with rain and high winds, or alternatively fog, and at times, snow. On one occasion a wait of one hour resulted from dense fog. On another occasion a delay of fourteen hours was experienced when one section of road was impassable due to snow. This happened on a single-track road in the Highlands of Scotland. The chosen route followed the coast as far as was practicable but did avoid unduly intricate paths or those which necessitated the use of ferries. The distance as measured by the Royal Automobile Club was 2,845 miles for one circuit. Therefore the three lap objective would be a total of 8,535 miles in total.

All three machines were given a normal 2,000 mile service at the conclusion of the first and second laps, including a change of spark plugs and cleaning of contact-breaker points. New rear tyres were fitted after two laps.

Nothing untoward happened until 6:00 am on Thursday, 28th November, when the rider of the GT 750 came off on wet roads near Liskeard in Cornwall. As a result of this spill, the timing cover and clutch lever were damaged and subsequently replaced at Truro. On the following Wednesday, 4th December, the GT 750 was involved in two further accidents. The first of these two spills occurred very early in the morning, just before 4:00 am, when the rider came off near Kilmarnock in Scotland. This caused a fair amount of damage to the windscreen, headlamp, electronic box cover, mirror, handlebars and crashbars. As a result, a new headlamp unit was fitted along with a new condenser and contact breaker points set (although it is difficult to relate the last two items with accident damage).

Less than four hours later at 7:40 am, the GT 380 was dropped rather heavily near Dumbarton damaging the front forks, headlamp, handlebars and gear lever, as well as denting the fuel tank. New front forks were fitted along with new handlebars, with the other damaged items being straightened out as much as possible. For good measure, so to speak, both the GT 380 and the GT 750 were dropped again that evening at 7:45 pm, when near Braemore Junction, as a result of the heavy snow. This time neither machine was damaged.

During the course of the three coastal circuits, the GT 750 had two new rear chains fitted together with one new final-drive sprocket. Both of the smaller machines had one new rear chain and one final-drive sprocket each changed. In addition, the GT 550 was fitted with a new shock absorber unit. The rear wheel and tyre on the GT 380 was replaced following a puncture, and the front tyre was changed as a precaution when a cut in the tread of the original tyre was inflicted by a stone or piece of glass. Additionally, the GT 380 consumed four sets of spark plugs, one headlamp bulb and required some general attention to the lighting system.

The GT 550 needed one set of spark plugs only. The GT 750 required a cracked alternator brush to be changed and a flat battery to be recharged. The alternator on the big model came in for further attention, and it was recorded that trouble with the dipped headlamp beam was rectified - two new bulbs were fitted. It was recorded in the report that the electrically-heated clothing worn by the riders made heavy demands on the electrical systems.

Just after 10:00 am on Saturday, 7th December, the test was concluded at the point from which it had set-out from, at Portslade, 13 days, 21 hours and 34 minutes earlier. The total running time had been 9 days, 22 hours and 13 minutes. The balance of 3 days, 23 hours and 21 minutes had been the time taken to make rider changes plus time lost with the delays caused by fog and snow, and the involuntary stops when the two models had been dropped five times in total. The machines had been under continuous observation except for a period of twenty five minutes on the 2nd December when the GT 380 and GT 750 lost contact with the observer in heavy traffic conditions whilst negotiating Southampton.

Each machine had achieved the target mileage of 8,535 in the running time recorded. This gave an average speed of 35.8 mph.

No further ACU-observed tests were undertaken throughout the balance of that 1974/75 test year. As usual, the merits of such a test were not considered by the ACU committee until the following September, and after due deliberation, it was felt that the test did not merit the presentation of the Maudes Trophy. To say that Suzuki were disappointed when the ACU Secretary General notified them of that decision is an understatement. It seemed totally unexpected and it came as a shock. Their reaction was immediate and challenging. And their reasoning was quite simple – if the BMW test of 1973 had proved meritorious enough for Maudes Trophy recognition, then the Suzuki test was good enough also. And a study of comparative facts tends to support that view.

On technical merit, the points would go in favour of Suzuki who, on balance, had fewer mechanical problems. Whilst on the one hand, Suzuki achieved a greater mileage than BMW, this was only marginal and the average speed was very much in favour of BMW. Against that, the ratio of riders per machine was less with Suzuki than BMW and thus the seventeen Suzuki riders averaged 1,506 miles each whereas the BMW team of fourteen riders averaged only 1,189 miles per head (which incidentally, is less than Fred Rist, Brian Martin and I completed in the six days of the ISDT on its own, 21 years previously). But then the BMW boys had completed their mileage in only seven days, thus their daily mileage was greater than that of Suzuki. But it was the environmental merit which was heavily in favour of Suzuki which made all the difference. There is obviously far greater merit in facing the hazards of a 2,845 mile route than circulating a familiar 37.73 miles loop which should easily be memorised.

Suzuki requested the ACU committee to reconsider the facts and their first verdict. This they did, and after further deliberation, the committee reversed their former decision and as a result it was with pleasure that the ACU Secretary General notified Suzuki of the award of the Maudes Trophy after all. Great credit is attached to the ACU committee for having the courage to do that, and it does seem that their first decision was based purely on the merits of the test and the results obtained. The second decision was clearly reached after comparison to the BMW test.

It was rider performance which did not impress with the Suzuki test, and it would seem the ACU committee took this into account when reaching their initial decision. Assuming all seventeen riders undertook an equal share of the daily riding, it amounted to no more than 152 miles each per day. Even T. Wood on the NSU moped back in 1955 was covering approximately 220 miles per day during his Lands

End to John O'Groats run, with one day's total actually 275 miles. The Suzuki riders' daily mileage of 152 amounted to little more than four hours in the saddle.

What of other yardsticks for comparison other than BMW which had such a profound effect on the second decision? Let's look at the Panther test of 1939, a test which failed to win the Maudes Trophy. On that occasion 10,000 miles were completed in ten days including all stops, with a running time average speed of 49 mph - with but three riders plus one reserve. They must have been made of sterner stuff in those days.

1974 - 1993 Not Awarded

1994 Yamaha, Isle of Man TT, Maudes Trophy Winner

Nineteen years after Suzuki's successful Maudes Trophy test, their keen adversary Yamaha decided the award had been with Suzuki for long enough. In March 1994 the New Zealand Auto-Cycle Union in conjunction with Mitsui (the Yamaha UK importer) issued a press release announcing that a team of ten Kiwi riders, organised by New Zealand's road race commission director John Strand, would compete in that year's Isle of Man Supersport 600cc TT and in so doing would attempt to win the Maudes Trophy. The leading rider of the team, Robert Holden was already a successful TT competitor, however the remaining nine riders were all new to the TT, and so also new to its formidable racing demands and unique challenges. The stated test objective was to race ten, brand new, Yamaha production machines in the Supersport 600 TT achieving a 100% finish rate. The motorcycle in question being Yamaha's newly launched FZR 600R 4-cylinder, 16 valve, 98 bhp machine.

Throughout historical Maudes Trophy tests we have seen that straight forward and concise objectives have always made interpretation of a successful test easier. Written in words the Yamaha test objective was indeed straight forward and concise. However the enormity of such a challenge, Isle of Man TT racing, must have been very daunting to those involved. The ten New Zealand riders were :-

Robert Holden	Nathan Spargo	Blair Degerholm
Jason McEwen	Anthony Young	Douglas Bell
Chris Haldane	Paul Williams	Russell Josiah
Hugh Reynolds		

The press release also stated that throughout the 'two week ordeal' the team would be assisted in preparation and TT course learning by three of New Zealand's road racing legends, Rod Coleman, Hugh Anderson, and Graeme Crosby.

The ACU appointed Mr Ernie Woods to be their Technical Official in charge of the test, and on 10th May he randomly chose ten crated FZR 600R machines from the Yamaha UK warehouse. The crates were sealed and marked by Ernie Woods, and then despatched to the Isle of Man. Twelve days later each rider was allocated a crated machine by Woods, and under ACU scrutiny, the bikes were unpacked and assembled. Engines, frames, gearboxes, carburettors, silencers, brake assemblies and clutches were all marked and the machines then stored under lock and key. The riders were next permitted to start familiarising themselves with the demanding 37.73 mile TT circuit whilst running-in the machines, during which time 1,278 miles were completed by each, with a combined average fuel consumption of 47.98 mpg.

Prior to official TT practice the machines were fitted with steering dampers, new tyres, lights were removed, race number plates added, and the first service completed. An unfortunate practice crash caused extensive damage to one machine, particularly to the engine and crankshaft. Happily the rider was fine and, since this event in no way resulted from a mechanical failure, it was agreed another similar machine that was on loan to the ACU from Yamaha for transportation purposes in the Isle of Man could be substituted. This machine had already accumulated 1,500 road miles.

The four lap (150.9 miles) Supersport 600 TT was scheduled for Monday 6th June but, as is sometimes the case on Mona's Isle, significant rain caused the race to be postponed until the following day. For Tuesday's race there were 80 starters and 68 of these finished. Importantly, all ten of the Yamaha FZR 600Rs completed the race. The stated Maudes Trophy test objective had thus been achieved. The ten machines completed the race with an aggregate average race speed of 104.78 mph! The icing on the cake for Yamaha was the winner, Iain Duffus, who was also FZR600R mounted but was not part of the ACU Test. Throughout the whole Maudes test the team completed 15,363.8 miles, with 1,584.9 miles recorded during the Supersport TT itself, recording an average fuel consumption of 19.259 mpg during the race. This fuel consumption alone indicates the strenuous demands of a TT race. The ACU technical report recorded that other than routine maintenance there were no adjustments, replacements, or mechanical faults encountered throughout the test.

This was indeed a bold and challenging Maudes Trophy test, and very much in the full public eye. Firstly, ten machines were included in the test, statistically very significant and much increasing the probability of encountering a mechanical problem. Secondly, as seen earlier in Maudes Trophy history, circulating the arduous

TT circuit was not a new idea for such a test - but competing in the TT itself under racing conditions certainly was, and to achieve 100 mph plus race speeds was indeed impressive! And finally, nine of the riders were new to the TT – a course renowned to take several years to master. Their achievement alone was immense.

The ACU Technical Committee subsequently met on the 28th June, and they were clearly impressed with the Yamaha test. It is true there had been little interest in the Maudes Trophy since the Suzuki test of 1974, and also the likelihood of a further test before the end of September of that year was small. However, the ACU chose to break with tradition. The Technical Committee's unanimous conclusion was '...an attempt as bold, imaginative and demonstrably successful as this should be rewarded without delay...'. The ACU did not wait until the end of September to confirm the award as procedure had dictated since 1923. The Maudes Trophy was awarded to Yamaha and the New Zealand riders with immediate effect.

This was clearly a meritorious performance of man and machine under extreme environmental conditions – demonstrating the true spirit and traditions of the Maudes Trophy since its inception by Mr George Pettyt of Maudes Motor Mart in 1923.

Appendix 1
Results of the 1952 ISDT

Trophy Contest Results
For riders using machines made in their home country

Country	Marks lost
Czechoslovakia	5
Austria	600
Great Britain	700
Sweden	950
West Germany	1,407
Italy	2,080

Vase Contest Results
For riders using machines not made in their home country

Country	Marks lost
Czechoslovakia B team	12
West Germany	60
Holland B team	62
Czechoslovakia A team	182
Holland A team	338
Great Britain B team	501
Sweden	571
Great Britain A team	624
Italy A team	708
Italy B team	829
Austria A team	905
Austria B team	1042

Manufacturers' Team Results

Manufacturer	Marks lost
Jawa A team	9
CZ A team	12
BMW	60
BSA (Dutch)	67
BSA (GB)	94
CZ B team	169
Jawa B team	181
Alpino	309
AJS / Matchless	500
Norton	500
Triumph	500
Royal Enfield	525
Puch A team	600
Aermacchi	721
Ariel	732
Puch B team	900
Rumi	934
Parilla	1537
Guazzoni	1775

Club Team Results

Club	Marks lost
ADAC Gau Wurttemberg (West Germany)	0
ADAC Gau Sudbayern (West Germany) Team 1	0
ADAC Gau Sudbayern (West Germany) Team 2	0
SAMS Strangnas (Sweden)	0
Birmingham MCC (Great Britain)	0
Motorclub de Hoeksewaard (Holland)	6
Moto-Club (Switzerland) Team 1	11
ADAC Gau Nordrhein (West Germany) Team 1	14
STAMK Puch-Motorsportsektion (Austria)	31
STAMK (Austria)	72
ADAC Gau Nordrhein (West Germany) Team 2	93
Worcester Auto Club (Great Britain)	148
ADAC Gau Nordbayern (West Germany)	305
SMK Stockholm (Sweden)	404
Moto-Club (Switzerland) Team 2	449
British Army Team 2 (Great Britain)	492
British Army Team 1 (Great Britain)	500
ADAC Munchen (West Germany)	500
Motor Cycle Club of Wales (Great Britain)	506

Gotha M.S. Enkoping (Sweden)	574
DMV III (West Germany)	605
DMV II (West Germany)	660
Moto-Club (Switzerland) Team 3	708
Real Moto Club de Cataluña (Spain)	845
Moto-Club (Switzerland) Team 5	877
Sunbeam Motor Cycle Club (Great Britain)	900
KNMV (Holland)	902
Wolverhampton MCC & CC (Great Britain)	915
DMV I (West Germany)	1100
Moto-Club (Switzerland) Team 4	1130
Nottingham Tornedo MC (Great Britain)	1155

British Gold Medal Winners

Rider	Machine
C M Ray	500 Ariel
D M Murdoch	
F M Rist	500 BSA
H L Williams	500 Norton
B W Martin	500 BSA
J E Breffitt	500 Norton
N E Vanhouse	500 BSA
E Usher	500 AJS
F E Lines	
W E Dow	500 BSA
B H M Viney	500 AJS
R A Rhodes	500 BSA
S E Cunningham	500 AJS
T U Ellis	500 BSA
D S Tye	500 BSA
D G Miles	500 BSA
W J Stocker	700 Royal Enfield

British Silver Medal Winners

Rider	Machine
J W Morris	
D C Osmond	500 BSA
J Giles	500 Triumph
G Barker	
E Wilson	
D J Redmore	

British Bronze Medal Winners

A Shutt

H Neild   500 BSA

J R Hebden

D G Rowthorn   500 BSA

Other British Finishers

M G Shephard   123 BSA

A W Glassbrook

Mrs M A Briggs   500 Triumph

Results by Nationality

Nationality	Entries	Gold	Silver	Bronze	None	Retired
West Germany	63	31	3	5	2	22
Great Britain	55	17	6	4	3	25
Italy	31	2	1	3	7	18
Austria	29	10	1	5	1	12
Holland	23	8	5	2	4	4
Sweden	20	8	3	0	3	6
Switzerland	17	4	2	3	0	8
Czechoslovakia	12	4	4	2	1	1
Spain	7	0	1	1	0	5
Belgium	1	0	0	0	0	1
Denmark	1	0	1	0	0	0
Ireland	1	0	0	1	0	0
Totals	**260**	**84**	**27**	**26**	**21**	**102**

Appendix 2
Official Programme

27th International Six Days Trial 18-23 September 1952, Bad Aussee. Official Programme. (Reproduced by courtesy of the OEAMTC)

Austria and the International

"Six Days"

For the first time in the history of the "Six Days", a history of nearly fourty years, the honour of organizing this greatest and most difficult test run which is singular in international motorcycling has been bestowed upon Austria.

The Österreichische Automobil- Motorrad- und Touring Club as the representative national association of Austria accepted this task from the Federation Internationale Motorcycliste in full recognition of the responsibilities derived from the great tradition of this classical competition.

We can be proud of the fact that more than 260 competitors of twelve nations have resoundet our call and have come to Bad Aussee to start in this run and to pass the hard trial of reliability on Austrian soil. To all of them we present a sportsmanlike welcome together with sincere wishes that the "Six Days"' 1952 may be for them a sporting event ever to remember.

The course prescribed to the competitors asks for an extraordinary performance of riders and their machines which is in full accordance with the aim and purpose of this competition, namely, to put to the proof the sporting qualities of those partaking as well as the reliability of the construction. As the most difficult criterion of its kind the "Six Days"' has in its 26 reiterations accomplished a scientific mission what regards the technical development of motorcycling which, also for this year's competition, will be the recurring motif in the roaring of motors. Again and again knowledge shall be gained from its results fertilizing to-day's production of motorcycles.

In this way the motto of FIM: "Pro virtute et scientia" is to be interpreted. Let us translate it like this: "For Sport and Science".

Österreichischer Automobil- Motorrad- und Touring Club, Vienna.

Introduction to the Official Programme (Coutesy of OEAMTC)

Internationale Trophy-Teams:

	ÖSTERREICH (A)				ČECHOSLOVAKEI (ČS)	
69	E. Beranek, Wien	Puch 171 ccm		51	Č. Kohlíček,	CZ 150 ccm
83	J. Kramer, Graz	Puch 171 ccm			Strakonice	
89	S. Cmyral, Graz	Puch 171 ccm		78	J. Pudil,	CZ 150 ccm
122	H. Weingart-	Puch 248 ccm			Strakonice	
	mann, Graz			148	R. Dusíl, Prag	Jawa 248 ccm
130	Ing. H. Rauh,	Puch 248 ccm		169	J. Kubeí, Prag	Jawa 248 ccm
	Graz			177	J. Novotný, Prag	Jawa 248 ccm

	DEUTSCHLAND (D)				GROSSBRITANNIEN (GB)	
4	O. Kollmar	NSU-Fox 98 ccm		183	C. M. Ray, Esq.,	Ariel 498 ccm,
17	G. Reinhardt	NSU-Fox 98 ccm		213	S. B. Manns,	Matchless 498 ccm
23	R. Dollmann	NSU-Fox 98 ccm		233	B. H. M. Viney,	AJS 498 ccm
65	U. Pohl	Maico 173 ccm		242	P. H. Alves,	Triumph 649 ccm
101	H. Danger	Maico 173 ccm		251	W. J. Stocker,	Royal Enf. 692 ccm

	ITALIEN (I)				SCHWEDEN (S)	
3	L. Albertazzi,			18	C. Nehlin,	
	Bologna	Motob. Alp. 73 ccm			Uppsala	N V 123 ccm
34	D. Cavalli,			118	S. Lindvall,	
	Bergamo	Rumi 124 ccm			Uppsala	N V 244 ccm
59	N. Grieco,			143	F. Larsson,	
	Milano	Parilla 150 ccm			Stockholm	N V 244 ccm
88	G. Premoli,			165	G. Lidström,	
	Varese	Aermacchi 125 ccm			Uppsala	N V 244 ccm
102	D. Serafini,			181	E. Forsberg,	
	Bergamo	Guazzoni 175 ccm			Uppsala	N V 244 ccm

Silbervasen-Teams:

	ÖSTERREICH (A)				ČECHOSLOVAKEI (ČS)	
	Vase a)				Vase a)	
76	F. Gnaser, Raaba	Puch 171 ccm		194	K. Rykr, Praha	Jawa 350 ccm
137	H. Csakol, Wien	Puch 248 ccm		212	J. Praisler, Praha	Jawa 350 ccm
248	W. Denzel, Wien	BMW 600 ccm		214	W.Šedina, Brodce	Jawa 350 ccm

	Vase b)				Vase b)	
25	H. Zezula jun.,			58	F. Bláha,	
	Wr.-Neustadt	Puch 123 ccm			Katowice	CZ 150 ccm
32	E. Platzer,			62	V. Kolář,	
	Wr.-Neustadt	Puch 125 ccm			Strakonice	CZ 150 ccm
96	K. Devoty, Graz	Puch 171 ccm		74	B. Kabát,	
					Vodnany	CZ 150 ccm

	GROSSBRITANNIEN (GB)					
	Vase a)				Vase b)	
206	D. S. Evans,			215	J. V. Brittain,	
	Willenhall	Royal Enf. 496 ccm			Walsall	Royal Enf. 496 ccm
219	E. Usher,			226	P. F. Hammond,	
	Doddington	AJS 498 ccm			Leckhampton	Triumph 498 ccm
229	R. Clayton,			259	D. S. Tye,	
	Orrell	Matchless 498 ccm			Birmingham	BSA 499 ccm

	DEUTSCHLAND (D)				SCHWEDEN (S)	
239	H. Roth	BMW 590 ccm		196	A. Strandberg,	Triumph 498 ccm
244	W. Zeller	BMW 590 ccm		201	H. Ring,	BMW 490 ccm
260	G. Meier	BMW 590 ccm		216	B. R. Nyström,	Royal Enf. 497 ccm

*Teams in the 1952 ISDT at Bad Aussee, Austria.
The 'Maudes' team of Rist, Martin and Vanhouse is
under the Birmingham MCC banner at the bottom!
(coutesy of OEAMTC)*

	ITALIEN (I)				NIEDERLANDE (NL)	
	Vase a)				Vase a)	
26	B. Romano, Ca-	Rumi 125 ccm		131	H. Veer, Borculo	Jawa 250 ccm
	sale Monferrato			139	C. van Rijssel,	Jawa 250 ccm
29	M. Riva, Lecco	Rumi 125 ccm			Den Haag	
40	G. Strada,	Rumi 125 ccm		156	Ph. J. T. Haaker,	Jawa 250 ccm
	Mailand				Badhoevedorp	

	Vase b)				Vase b)	
66	M. Fornasari,	M. V. 150 ccm		207	P. Knijnenburg,	BSA 500 ccm
	Cascina Costa				Wassenaar	
70	G. Benzoni,	M. V. 150 ccm		231	J. L. Flinterman,	BSA 500 ccm
	Cascina Costa				Den Haag	
68	M. Ventura	M. V. 150 ccm		235	M. Rozenberg,	BSA 500 ccm
	Cascina Costa				Kerkrade	

Fabrik-(Marken)Teams:

	ÖSTERREICH (A)			
	PUCH I			PUCH II
83	J. Kramer		69	E. Beranek
89	S. Cmyral		76	F. Gnaser
122	H. Weingartmann		137	H. Csakol

	TSCHECHOSLOWAKEI (ČS)			
	JAWA I		JAWA II	
148	R. Dusíl	177	J. Nowotný	
169	J. Kubeš	194	K. Rykr	
212	J. Praisler	214	W. Šedina	

	C. Z. I			C. Z. II
51	Č. Kohlíček		62	V. Kolář
58	F. Bláha		67	J. Paštíka
78	J. Pudil		74	B. Kabát

	DEUTSCHLAND (D)			NIEDERLANDE (NL)	
	BMW			B. S. A.	
239	H. Roth		207	P. Knijnenburg	
244	W. Zeller		231	J. L. Flinterman	
260	G. Meier		235	M. Rozenberg	

	GROSSBRITANNIEN (GB)			
	ARIEL		ASSOCIATED MOTORCYCLES	B. S. A.
183	C. M. Ray	213	S. B. Manns	252 G. Brouwer
221	G. Parsons	219	E. Usher	(Holland)
236	P. J. Mellers	233	P. A. M. Viney	258 T. U. Ellis
				259 D. S. Tye

	NORTON		ROYAL ENFIELD	TRIUMPH
185	N. S. Holmes	206	D. S. Evans	226 P. F. Hammond
195	J. V. Smith	215	J. V. Brittain	238 J. Giles
208	I. E. Breffitt	251	W. J. Stocker	242 P. H. Alves

				ITALIEN (I)	
	AERMACCHI		ALPINO		GUAZZONI
84	U. Premoli	1	S. Camporese	79	G. Passera
88	G. Premoli	3	L. Alber:tazzi	98	B. Santiani
91	M. Pasolini	5	G. Borri	102	D. Serafini

	PARILLA		RUMI	
59	N. Grieco	34	D. Cavalli	
61	A. Menani	37	P. Carissoni	
64	C. L. Cuzzolin	42	V. Massano	

Club-Teams:

ÖSTERREICH (A)

STAMK-Puch-Motor-			STAMK:	
sportsektion				
6	W. Kramer		19	K. Zöhrer
21	M. Platzer		54	H. Waska
155	H. Volzwinkler		162	E. Bilek

SCHWEIZ (CH)

Moto Klub FMS I		Moto Klub FMS II		Moto Klub FMS III
167	S. Mazzola	14	K. Meier	117 E. Haller
174	M. Müller	16	H. Stärkle	241 M. Müller
250	F. Bracher	237	W. Hurni	246 W. Flückiger

Moto Club FMS IV		Moto Club FMS V	
140	G. Sauteur	81	E. Sager
179	W. Grubenmann	151	D. Bongard
225	E. Studer	228	E. Hurni

DEUTSCHLAND (D)

DMV I		DMV II		DMV III
82	O. Krebs	13	M. Kraus	8 G. Dotterweich
184	H. Oele:ich	28	P. Schulteis	10 R. Ebert
188	D. Louis	205	W. Pfeiffer	138 G. Goppert

ADAC München		ADAC Gau Südbayern I		ADAC Gau Südbayern II
111	H. Ernst	105	M. Klankermeier	12 H. Kirchberg
113	G. Weiß	107	W. Kraus	15 F. Ischinger
115	G. Keitel	223	H. Meier	180 O. Sensburg

ADAC Gau Württemberg		ADAC Gau Nordrhein I		ADAC Gau Nordrhein II
71	K. L. Westphal	73	R. Hellmann	152 K. Krämer
77	W. Haas	90	K. Keck	159 U. Krämer
80	G. Ilgenstein	119	R. Poensgen	164 W. Vogel

ADAC Gau Nordbayern	
87	K. Bauer
92	H. Best
146	R. Grenz

SPANIEN (E)

Real Moto Club de		Real Moto Club de	
Cataluna I		Cataluna II	
45	E. Vidal	39	V. Giro
50	J. Vidal	43	A. Vidal
52	J. Romeu	47	J. Humet

GROSSBRITANNIEN (GB)

M. C. C. of Wales		Sunbeam M. C.		Worcester A. C.
30	F. A. G. Allen	112	R. W. Wagger	125 I. W. Morris
255	E. Wilson	189	D. M. Murdoch	200 H. L. Williams
262	D. I. Redmore	257	P. G. K. Baldwin	224 I. R. Hebden

Nottingham Tornedo M. C.		Birmingham M. C. C.		Wolverhampton M. C. & C. C.
104	G. L. Buck	193	F. M. Rist	22 E. W. Smith
108	F. H. Whittle	202	B. W. Martin	123 A. Shutt
197	M. A. Briggs	209	N. G. Vanhouse	154 E. B. Herbert